THE POLITICAL UNIVERSITY

ROBERT M. ROSENZWEIG

THE POLITICAL UNIVERSITY

Policy, Politics, and Presidential Leadership
in the American Research University

The Johns Hopkins University Press
BALTIMORE & LONDON

Printed in the United States of America on acid-free recycled paper
07 06 05 04 03 02 01 00 99 98   5 4 3 2 1

The Johns Hopkins University Press
2715 North Charles Street
Baltimore, Maryland 21218-4319
The Johns Hopkins Press Ltd., London

Library of Congress Cataloging-in-Publication Data will be found at
the end of this book.

A catalog record for this book is available from the British Library.

ISBN 0-8018-5721-x

For the next few years Newman, unaided and ignored, struggled desperately, like a man in a bog, with the overmastering difficulties of his task. His mind, whose native haunt was among the far aerial boundaries of fancy and philosophy, was now clamped down under the fetters of petty detail, and fed upon a diet of compromise and routine. He had to force himself to scrape together money, to write articles for the students' Gazette, to make plans for medical laboratories, and to be ingratiating with the City Council; he was obliged to spend months travelling through remote regions of Ireland in the company of extraordinary ecclesiastics and barbarous squireens. He was a thoroughbred harnessed to a four-wheeled cab; and he knew it.

Lytton Strachey, *The Eminent Victorians,*
describing the life of John (later Cardinal) Newman, as he labored
to start a college in Ireland

Gentlemen of the Legislature, I now leave you; I shall never set foot in this capital again. You have insultingly refused, as you have generally refused, to grant the university a dollar. I wait for a better time, which I distinctly foresee, a time when better men than you will occupy the seats which you now hold—better men who are now my boys at the university.

Dr. Henry Phillip Tappan,
president of the University of Michigan, 1852–1863

Contents

Acknowledgments

I have been fortunate throughout my career to work with talented and supportive people. During the twenty-one years I spent at Stanford, I was educated by such extraordinary teachers as Albert Bowker, Richard Lyman, Donald Kennedy, James Siena, John Schwartz, Larry Horton, William Miller, Herbert Packer, William Clebsch, and many others. I was lucky to arrive at Stanford as it was becoming a great university. Witnessing that process, and participating in it, was the best education in the dynamics of a modern university available anywhere.

I was no less fortunate in my colleagues at the Association of American Universities. Carol Scheman, Jack Crowley, John Vaughn, Newton Cattell, Joan Kindred, to mention only those who were there at the start, were wiser in the ways of Washington than I, and their knowledge, wisdom, and warm friendship eased what could have been a difficult transition. Not all of our plots succeeded, but most were worthwhile, and all were fun in the doing.

In the preparation of this book, I am indebted first of all to the past and present university presidents who were so generous in their time, their candor, and their confidence in me. I hope I have not betrayed that confidence in these pages. Familiarity may sometimes breed contempt, but that was not my experience with the many university presidents with whom I worked at the AAU. Without exception, we became colleagues, and in many cases friends, as well.

A special word of appreciation is due to David Hamburg and Barbara Finberg of the Carnegie Corporation of New York. In addition to being old friends with a shared love of Stanford, they were the most patient and forebearing of patrons.

Barbara Kaye Wolfinger advised me on how to conduct an interview; those whom I interviewed should not blame her for the results. She also read and commented on parts of the manuscript, as did Raymond Wolfinger, Barbara Shapiro, Paul Sniderman, and Donald Kennedy. They were unfailingly helpful, but they categorically are not responsible for such errors of commission and omission as have found their way into print. Andrew Blauner, a good bookman, was cheerful and optimistic at times when I was not and was an effective advocate, in the bargain. Jacqueline Wehmueller's editorial ability produced clarity at many points.

Nothing I have done in the last forty years could have been done as well—and in some cases, done at all—without the help and support of my wife, Adelle. She is a woman of great sensitivity, courage, and creativity, and more than once she has pointed me in a direction I could not have found on my own.

This book is for young people. The generation of my daughter, Kathryn, and son, David, has already benefited from the great universities that were waiting for them when they came of age. As they move into responsible positions in American life, decisions made by them and others of their age will determine whether their children and grandchildren will have the same good fortune. There is every reason to believe that they will meet the test.

Finally, and most of all, this book is for Leah and Sarah. Their future is what matters. The quality of their lives in the years ahead is being shaped in important ways by the institutions that are the subject of this book. They are too young to know that now, but when they are old enough to understand, I hope that they will have good cause to think well of our efforts.

Introduction

On a long bus ride across Brussels in the summer of 1991, Joseph Duffey, who was at the time president of the American University, and I fell to talking about a subject close to the hearts of most university presidents: the fate of other university presidents. It occurred to us that something unusual had happened in the last several years that was worth noting and perhaps worth taking advantage of: an unusually large number of very visible presidents of very visible universities had left office around the end of the decade after having served during most or all of the 1980s. Several of them would undoubtedly write books drawing on their experiences in office, but it seemed to us that their collective experiences as leaders of major institutions during a pivotal decade in the history of American universities were a unique resource if one wanted to understand what actually happened during those years and where those institutions were now heading.

By the time our bus ride ended, we had agreed that we would try to capture that resource by interviewing each member of the group we had identified and then bringing them together in a symposium for a general discussion of the issues that emerged from the separate interviews.

Alas, by the time the idea was reduced to practice, Joe Duffey had become director of the United States Information Agency and a statistic in the calculation of annual presidential turnover. However, the study went forward with the generous support of the Andrew W. Carnegie Corporation of New York. Twelve former presidents were interviewed at length: Derek Bok (Harvard), John Brademas (New York University), David Gardner (University of California), Hanna Gray (University of Chicago), Paul Gray (MIT), Sheldon Hackney (University of Pennsylvania), I. Michael Heyman (University of California at Berkeley), Donald Kennedy (Stanford), Steven Muller (Johns Hopkins), Benno Schmidt (Yale), Michael Sovern (Columbia), and John Toll (University of Maryland).

On April 26, 1995, eight of the twelve presidents whom I had interviewed came together in Washington, D.C., for a day-long symposium called "The American Research University: Continuity and Change."[1] They were joined by eight incumbent university presidents and several other knowledgeable observers for a day of discussion in which strongly held opinions were vigorously articulated.[2]

In all the interviews and in the symposium, the participants were promised anonymity. My purpose in doing so was, obviously, to encourage full and open discussion. That is always a difficult trade-off, but in this case I believe it was justified. All the conversations were candid and the more valuable for being so.

Books, once begun, have a way of charting their own course, and this one is no exception. What started as an effort to understand the recent past as it was experienced by important participants in it became somewhat more personal. In the end, what follows draws on three main sources: the interviews, the symposium, and my own experience, first at Stanford University and then as president of the Association of American Universities from 1983 to 1992.[3] The AAU, with its office in Washington, D.C., represents the common interests of the major public and private research universities in America. It is viewed as the principal voice for universities on matters of national policy on research and doctoral education, and it was an active participant in every significant policy debate on those issues during the 1980s. The member universities are represented by their presidents, and so the AAU provided an unusually good vantage point from which to view research universities nationally, their presidents, individually and as a group, and the issues that dominated the period. Those issues, and the capacity of universities to deal with them, form the core of the book. I had the good fortune to be both participant and observer in the substance and the process of both the politics and the policy making of the times, and much of what appears here is inevitably refracted through the lens of my own experiences and the conclusions I drew from them.

Two additional points will help make clear what this book is about and what it is not about. The need for the first was brought home to me

1. The eight were John Brademas, Paul Gray, Sheldon Hackney, Michael Heyman, Donald Kennedy, Benno Schmidt, Michael Sovern, and John Toll.

2. Presidents attending the meeting were Judith Albino (University of Colorado), Miles Brand (Indiana University), William Greiner (State University of New York at Buffalo), Stanley Ikenberry (University of Illinois), Eamon Kelly (Tulane University), J. Robert S. Prichard (University of Toronto), Steven Sample (University of Southern California), and Charles Young (University of California at Los Angeles).

3. Over a twenty-one-year period, I served in a variety of positions at Stanford, covering a range of academic and other administrative responsibilities. Starting as associate dean of the Graduate Division, I moved on to associate provost, vice provost, and, finally, vice president for public affairs.

by an early reader of this manuscript, Professor Barbara Shapiro, distinguished historian, a good friend, and an experienced and perceptive veteran of the university world. "You write about the research university that I know about through my past involvement with the Center for Studies in Higher Education," she said, "not the one I have lived and worked in for over twenty years. You tell the story of the science university. That's the story from the point of view of Washington—at least most of the time—and from the presidents' perspective, at least a good deal of the time. You are probably correct in focusing on the sciences and the way they have propelled the university from one era to the next, but it is as if the humanities and much of the social sciences do not exist. One gets the impression that if the humanities and the social sciences were sloughed off from the research university, little would be changed."

That observation captures a real dilemma. There are many ways of looking at the complex whole that constitutes every research university. Many recent critics have chosen to view the university through developments in humanistic scholarship and teaching, and they have, in my view, produced a distorted image. Others have seen the university through the lens of social policy—affirmative action, or investments in South Africa, or some other cause for which they see the university as an instrument of (generally malign) outside forces. Both of those approaches, and others as well, have some merit, and something can be learned from them, as long as they are not mistaken for the whole. The primary lens through which the university is viewed here is the lens of public policy—science policy, tax policy, financial aid policy, regulatory policy—those and many more have shaped the modern university in profound ways. Research universities are unique among all elements of education in the extent to which they are sensitive to policies of the national government. Understanding what shapes those policies and how they affect universities is an indispensable means for understanding how those institutions have developed. Public policy is not the whole story of the modern university, but there is no denying that it is an important, if not the most important, part of it.

Nowhere is that more apparent than in the workday of the modern university president. It is hardly an exaggeration to say that, before World War II, the president of a major university could arrive at the office in the morning, leave it in the evening, and in between not think of the federal government once. There may be some days on which that is true of today's president, but they are rare, indeed. Research policy and funding, student aid, personnel policies, workplace safety, environmental hazards, animal safety, protection of human subjects—the list goes on and on, and each item on it is a product of the last half of the twentieth century.

The second necessary clarification is that this is not a book about all of American higher education. One of the reasons that much of the recent popular writing about higher education is so unsatisfactory is that it fails to take account of the extraordinary variety of our colleges and universities and consequently the difficulty of generalizing about them. There is a world of difference between the purposes and methods of the eighteen-hundred-odd community colleges and those of four-year liberal arts colleges. Both are different from those institutions that call themselves universities; and within that last group, only a minority can be classified as genuine research universities—institutions in which research and undergraduate and graduate education are done in the same place by the same faculty. All are important. But it is that last group—the research universities, perhaps one hundred in all—that are the focus of this book.

Although that may seem a small number—indeed, is a small number, in comparison with the total of thirty-five hundred postsecondary institutions—it is a group whose influence and importance far exceed its percentage of the total. Not only do these universities conduct most of the nation's basic research; they also educate the vast majority of future college teachers and research scientists of all types as well as leaders of the learned professions. They are the most visible of all educational institutions, and, for better or for worse, they are the models that many others in this country and abroad strive to emulate. What happens in them and to them matters, and that is why they are singled out from among all the others as the subject of this book.

Whatever lens one chooses to use, it will be clear that the second half of the twentieth century was a remarkable period for America's universities. They rose from the shadow of the great English and continental universities of the nineteenth and early twentieth centuries, to which the best American students aspired for their graduate education, to a position of unchallenged world leadership, to which students the world over aspire for their graduate education. That transition was not made without difficulties along the way, and I discuss here instances in which institutions failed to foresee or failed to confront issues that accompanied their evolution. The problem of research fraud and the related problem of conflict of interest are two such. Nor have all the changes involved in the transformation been for the better. The balance between undergraduate education and research, heavily skewed toward the former in earlier years, toppled to the other side of the scale as the money and recognition that went with research grew—for faculty and their universities alike. It is worth repeating, then, that at the center of the story is the federal government and its policies. There is no understanding the modern university, its recent past, its present, or its future, without understanding the profound effect of government policies and the ways in which universities have tried, with mixed results, to shape them to their own ends.

The point of understanding the past, though, is to understand the present better in the hope of shaping the future. The 1980s were an important decade for the research university. They left their legacy for the years to follow. One part of that legacy raises serious questions about the kind of institutions research universities will become. Growing relations with industry and the urgent need for new sources of revenue have exacerbated an already evident fracturing of interests and loyalties within the university that raises profound questions about the future shape of what academics are pleased to call a "community of learning." Just so, the prospect of a long period of little or no growth, indeed, even of contraction, is likely to strain intrinsically shaky governance arrangements and put heavy new demands on traditions of collegiality and on institutional leadership. Those are matters internal to every university. All institutions exist in and are affected by national and international trends, but the response to those trends is worked out on each campus in the light of local circumstances, traditions, and leadership.

There is much in this book about both presidents and faculty, not all of it wholly admiring. It may seem to some that I am especially harsh on the behavior of faculty. But there is no avoiding the plain fact that what happens in any university is often led by, and always limited by, the willingness of faculty to accept change. The faculty of America's major universities have extraordinary privileges. Tenure is one of them, but perhaps not the most important. Few other professionals are able, with generous support, to do what they love best, and to do it in ways and on terms largely of their own making. Privilege of that kind calls for corresponding responsibility, and the bonds that reinforce responsibility have frayed over the years. William H. Danforth, for more than twenty-five years chancellor of Washington University, St. Louis, and a true educational statesman, put the matter neatly:

> The duty of presidents, chancellors and deans to promote the well-being of their institutions is clear, but in recent decades, many faculty, especially scientists, have given their primary loyalty to disciplines and to national and international groups. This tendency is not new, but it has been magnified by the focus on outside resources and on an international reputation as a criterion for tenure.
>
> If it was ever true that faculty members' pursuit of individual interests automatically created a great university, it is certainly not so now. Rather, the loosening of institutional ties has become a major risk, for today's successful university requires effective internal operations aimed at

agreed-upon goals. Because faculty do the essential work of teaching and research, their participation and leadership are key.[4]

The analytical focus of this book is on the substance and the politics of public policy toward universities. That requires consideration of the role of presidents and faculty and the capacity of institutional governance systems to deal with new kinds of stresses. But it requires, too, concern for questions of value and values. Therefore, I also address the question of what we want to save and why. These are enormously expensive institutions. At times, they have seemed to some to be almost more trouble than they are worth. Students can be taught at less cost, and research of substantial value can be done more efficiently than is possible in these rather messy institutions. Why bother? Or, to take another aspect of the same question, why, as many ask, can't universities be directed in such a way as to be of more immediate value to society in the solution of pressing economic and social problems? Universities and their leaders increasingly are being challenged to address those issues as the competition for public favor and public patronage, in which for so long they competed so well, becomes a harder fight for a share of a smaller pie.

I confess to having a life-long love affair with universities. It began when I was an undergraduate at the University of Michigan, deepened as a graduate student at Yale, and has continued throughout my professional career. As with all long-term relationships, this one has had its lows, its periods of disappointment, even disenchantment, as well as its highs. Thus, while no one will mistake this book as another contribution to the literature of university bashing, neither is it an apologia. I am not an uncritical observer of America's universities. I have spent too much time in and around them to have failed to notice that the people in them have their full share of human defects: rigidity, obtuseness, insensitivity, arrogance, self-righteousness, venality, to mention only a few in a list that could easily be extended. And I have seen too many instances in which self-interest was represented as inevitability and principle was seen as an obstacle to be overcome rather than a light by which to steer. I do not believe that the right choices have always been made among available alternatives or that our universities are as good as they could or should be.

But neither do I believe that they are the cesspools of moral cowardice and anti-intellectualism described by their critics on both the right and the left. The truth is more complicated and more important. America's universities comprise the most extraordinary collection of intellectual talent in history. They are remarkably creative places in which the future of

4. William H. Danforth, "We Must Understand, Universities Are Our Responsibility," *Science* 269 (September 22, 1995): 1651.

us all, to a very significant degree, will be shaped. They are also, in a society badly in need of living examples, the only institutions whose highest aspirations include the promotion of civil discourse, commitment to seeking truth, respect for honest error, and a belief in reason over unreason. Those are precious commodities in any time; in a time of such awesome and widely shared destructive power, they are essential for survival. Only a fool would seek to damage so much potential for good, and only a demagogue would stand to lose by the achievement of such aspirations.

As universities confront the problems that lie ahead, those who are responsible for the way they do so—faculty, administrators, trustees, legislators, patrons—will, in addition to their own intellectual and moral resources, need the loving and critical support of the rest of us who must depend on the wisdom of their decisions. They do not need, and will not be helped by, the shrill anger and the transparent ideological and political agendas that mark the overheated assaults of the last decade. Criticism is healthy, challenges to prevailing practices are necessary, some kinds of change are not only needed, they are inevitable. But the overarching truth is that our universities are near the top of the list of our society's greatest achievements. Part of what we are as a nation derives from them and is expressed in them—overwhelmingly, but not entirely, for the good. But more to the point, part of what we will be is, even now, being formed in them. They must be held to high standards of performance; they must be helped in their efforts to meet them.

The Political University

Chapter One

AFTER THE WAR

U NIVERSITIES ARE OFTEN portrayed as the most conservative of institutions, and there are important respects in which that is true. The Oxford and Cambridge of today, though very different from their medieval forebears, are still recognizable as the descendants of those early universities. And American higher education, though incomparably larger, more varied, and more complex than the Harvard and William and Mary of three hundred years ago, can still see some of those first institutions in its modern self. That continuity looks, indeed is, profoundly conservative, but it can also be misleading. As one former president put it, "We generally think in terms of structures. And when one makes the observation about universities being very persistent and resilient and conservative, it is generally the structures that we're talking about. But what I think we frequently miss is that the real changes are occurring within the structures. . . . New disciplines, new fields of study, are being created, but [. . .] within the existing structures of the university, so the whole content of what universities do has changed dramatically, radically, since the 1950s. Yet, the structures still look pretty much the same."

Both institutional continuity and institutional change are grounded in the proposition that institutions whose primary purposes are to transmit to the young what is known and thought about the world and to add to the sum of what is known and thought will not change in their basic processes much more rapidly than the methods of accruing and transmitting knowledge change. And the fact is that for most of human history, those methods changed very slowly, indeed.

So strong are the elements of continuity, they may serve to mask a more profound truth, or at least a truth that is more relevant to American universities: universities are very much creatures of their surroundings, and like their surroundings, they are always in motion. Their processes are less autonomous than the stereotype would suggest, and changes in their external environment will bear in on them in ways that they may not be able to or wish to resist.

Many examples could serve to make that point. By the middle of the nineteenth century, dissatisfaction with the inability or unwillingness of the existing state and private universities to serve the needs of the rising agricultural and industrial society and the middle class it was spawning led to the creation of the "land grant" college system. Equally profound, however, that development forced the existing public universities to become more open and responsive, lest they lose their constituencies and their bases of support. Some of the established public universities became land grant institutions and changed in the process, while others, over time, necessarily became more open and populist in response to new competition.

Nearly one hundred years later, a world war and its aftermath led to the most sweeping changes ever in American higher education. Among them was the elevation of research to a place of primacy in the university, producing for the first time a group of institutions that could realistically be called "research universities." American universities before the war had available to them from all sources $31 million for scientific research. A quarter of a century later, that figure had multiplied twenty-five times in constant dollars. Virtually all of the increase was the consequence of policies of the federal government that stressed the importance of research as a central university function, a sharp departure from earlier years. The response of universities to that change belies any notion of universities as rigid, unchanging, and unchangeable institutions. Nor was money the only measure of the capacity of universities to change in a changing environment. In the period after World War II, American universities led the scientific revolution, opened their doors to a degree previously unthinkable, grew enormously, and became agents of or lightning rods for virtually every important social change to sweep the American landscape.

Much has been written about the post–World War II period in higher education; indeed, much of the period lies within the professional experience of senior faculty and administrators still active in universities. But it is still worth taking the time at the outset to review the ebb and flow of those decades as prelude to the 1980s and 1990s.

The "founding myths" of institutions and societies, especially successful ones, tend to present their histories as seamless wholes, moving with the force of inevitability from auspicious beginnings to mature success, overcoming obstacles by shrewd maneuvers and bold stratagems. That may occasionally be the case, not very often one imagines, but it is not a picture that captures the development of the research university in the second half of the twentieth century. In graphic terms, that development requires two curves: One would chart growth in resources, students, degrees granted, research activity, honors won, international esteem, and other indexes of success. The second would chart doubts, misgivings, errors of judgment, miscalculations, flawed policies, and other failings easily forgotten but better remembered. The slope of both curves would be up, and at about the same rate.

This book is about both of those curves, and though the focus is on the 1980s and 1990s, those decades make little sense standing alone. They grew out of the success and the failures of the previous decades. I have divided the period into segments that may seem to some arbitrary and are certainly subject to dispute. Not the least of the reasons to dispute them is that they are so closely connected to policies of the federal government. That is not the only way to view the development of the postwar university. Focusing in that way tends to undervalue the importance of changes in the humanities and social sciences that are very important to the conduct of undergraduate education. It does, however, have the compensating virtue of placing science and technology at the center of attention and recognizing the extent to which universities have been driven by the explosive growth of those fields. It also gives proper emphasis to the influence of government on campus as a patron of research, as a stimulus to the growth and changed composition of student bodies, as a regulator, as a critic, and as an ally. That is a phenomenon unique to this period. What happened to universities would not have happened without active involvement of the federal government, even though not everything that happened was the product of that involvement. The divisions I have chosen are arguable and the perspective perhaps too Washington-centered, but the picture that emerges is nevertheless true to life.

From the End of the War to *Sputnik:* Laying the Foundation

Between 1946 and 1957, the lessons of the war were absorbed and given institutional form. The war had demonstrated the central place of science and technology in modern warfare, and it took no great leap of imagination to see their application to other areas of modern life, as well. Moreover, it had become obvious that much of the talent for the conduct of science resided in universities. Translating even the obvious into policy is no easy matter, but with the intellectual and political force generated by Vannevar Bush, director of the wartime Office of Scientific Research and Development and a leader in postwar science policy, and his allies, American public policy moved to use the university base that already existed rather than to create new institutions devoted wholly to science and technology in the public service. The agencies of government that were the most adept at using science and technology were, of course, those that had been the primary wartime users. The basic research arms of the military became major sponsors of on-campus research, conducted by faculty and graduate students.

Without the enlightened and farsighted policies of those agencies, the course of American science would have been very different. But the dominant early role of the Defense Department was not an unmixed blessing. The wartime experience of both the military sponsors and the academic scientists had understandably emphasized the importance of secrecy. The habit of secrecy had been built into the fabric of academic engineering and some fields of science, and as a consequence most universities accepted rules of classification that controverted all previous notions of free and open communication as a key value in its own right and as a prerequisite to good science. On a number of campuses, the anti–Vietnam War movement forced an end to the practice of accepting secret research, or at least isolated it in units separate from mainline academic and research activities.

Bush and his allies saw that the responsibility for civilian science should not long be lodged in the military. New structures were required, designed specifically for that task. The battle to create a National Science Foundation charged with promoting fundamental research, research training, and science education was fought and won, although with results rather different from those intended. It had been Bush's intention to lodge virtually all government-sponsored research, military and civilian alike, in the new agency. Instead, the foundation that was created was a small one, and it remained so for years to come. It was established outside of any existing government agency as an outward sign of its independence. Its governing body, the National Science Board, was given a broad charter with respect to science policy, but its program responsibilities and its budgets were considerably narrower, and its role as the lead government agency in setting and carrying out science policy never came to pass.

Instead, a different set of arrangements arose in which most science funding was lodged in line agencies whose responsibilities required access to scientific and technological competence. The Atomic Energy Commission and its successor, the Department of Energy, were the main patrons of high-energy physics, with its large capital demands; the Department of Defense retained its research and development programs; and the National Institutes of Health began significant extramural programs in support of biomedical research and training, with university science as the principal beneficiary. They all supported basic research, but it was research whose political justification was rooted in the national need for a strong defense and cures for disease and, as time passed, in the Cold War–fueled space race, economic competitiveness, and other national goals. The National Science Foundation (NSF) eventually became a major source of funds for investigator-initiated, project-based basic science in a variety of fields, a major patron of graduate education in the sciences, and an active supporter of science education in the schools and colleges. However, the distinctive character of American science support formed in that period made science the adjunct of the practical missions of operating agencies.[1]

Also during this period, the demography of higher education shifted in an entirely new direction with the enactment of the GI Bill of Rights. A new student body emerged, consisting of large numbers of students who, before the war, would not have thought of attending college or had the resources to do so. Once started in that direction, the movement could only grow as first-time college graduates insisted that their children, too, deserved the right to an education. The step from there to the assertion of a broad entitlement to a college education was a short one. The foundation was laid during this period, and the step was taken in the next.

From 1957 to 1968: The Golden Age

Either the rise of science or the new demography of higher education alone would have markedly changed America's universities; the two together provided the basis for the universities' virtual reinvention and for a vast expansion in their number and scale and, in some respects, in their mission. A trigger was necessary, however, to generate the political momentum needed for truly dramatic change. It came in the form of a grapefruit-sized object hurled into low earth orbit by the Soviet Union. As if purposely designed to advertise itself and produce the maximum irritation to Americans, *Sputnik* contained a transmitter that emitted a beeping sound as it orbited the globe. The reaction in the United States was electric. This galling show of Russian technological superiority galvanized the political system into action, and it focused its energies on the supposed inadequacies of American education and science.

As an explanation for the Russian lead in space, this one was surely wrong; the Russians got there first not because they had better high school mathematics programs but because they made it their goal to do so and organized their resources to reach the goal. But conventional wisdom rarely pauses to consider evidence, and in this instance, the result of a bad diagnosis was a course of highly beneficial therapy. If we can speak at all of a "golden age" in the modern history of the research university, this is it. During this period, total academic R&D expenditures more than tripled. Academic research personnel in public universities grew from 13,000 to 23,000 and in private universities from 12,000 to 23,000. The federal share of research funds grew from 53 percent to 75 percent in public universities and from 66 percent to 82 percent in private universities. Total higher education enrollment grew from three million to more than seven million.

---

1. There are a number of histories of this period. An especially useful one can be found in Bruce L. R. Smith, *American Science Policy since World War II* (Washington, D.C.: Brookings Institution, 1990).

Enrollment in public doctoral universities grew from 800,000 to 1.9 million. Private doctoral university enrollment went from 440,000 to 650,000. The number of doctorates awarded in science and engineering grew from 5,800 to 14,3000.

Bruce L. R. Smith, combining the earlier period with this one, describes the view from government in this way:

> The nation celebrated the impact of science in terms resembling Priestley's view of its liberating influence on human affairs. The need for policy amounted mainly to devising the means to support basic research, to link applied research effectively to national priorities, to coordinate the jurisdictional issues that inevitably arise in the wake of scientific and technological advance, and to regulate a few obviously dangerous technologies while, of course, promoting beneficial developments.[2]

On campus, the prosperity was not limited to science and engineering. Every part of the academic enterprise prospered. The high demand for faculty raised salaries in all disciplines. The federal interest in research was accompanied by a corresponding interest in the research infrastructure. In addition to the building boom necessitated by the growing enrollments, federal programs stimulated a corresponding boom in the construction of new research facilities for science and engineering. Large fellowship programs encouraged and supported the production of ever more Ph.D.'s to man the bursting classrooms and laboratories. It is estimated that in 1965 government support of research was allocated as follows: 68 percent to project support, 10 percent to institutional programs, 16 percent to training, and 6 percent to facilities.

During this period, too, the major elements of an entitlement to higher education were put in place. California instituted its Master Plan for Higher Education, which guaranteed admission to college to any high school graduate who wanted to enroll. The Great Society also produced its entitlements, in the form of the Pell Grant program and a variety of subsidized student loans. Toward the end of the period, energies unleashed by the assassination of Dr. Martin Luther King produced the first truly broad-scale efforts to recruit black students and faculty into colleges and universities at all levels.

One other kind of entitlement was spawned during this period, in this case not legal but psychological. Faculty who began their careers in these years experienced something that previous generations hardly dared dream of—readily available funding for their own work and for their graduate

2. Ibid., 3.

students, as well. Their picture of academic life, and the picture that their students could see for themselves, was formed during what was perhaps the least representative period in the history of American higher education. However, the sense that one is entitled to what one has always had, and the consequent sense that to be denied what one has always had is a breach of faith, is hard to avoid. That is the essence of an entitlement, and those who came of age in the golden age felt about their government funding much as farmers and social security recipients feel about theirs.

Moreover, the entitlement mentality was not limited to faculty; it pervaded the system. Successful institutions always needed more and believed, naturally enough, that they deserved and were entitled to it by virtue of the high-quality work that had led to success in the first place. Those in aspiring institutions were convinced that they were as entitled to government support as those who were already benefiting from it merely because they had been in line at the beginning. Prosperity thus carried with it the seeds of bitterness and conflict that would flower in later decades. It was the period in which good regional institutions took their largest steps toward becoming national, indeed international, universities and in which state colleges became state universities and sizable numbers of existing state universities became major players in the research and Ph.D. game.

My own first university position was at Stanford in 1962. Stanford is perhaps the outstanding example of a university that built on the wartime experience of its faculty and academic leaders and used the postwar opportunities to change from a good if rather sleepy regional institution with some areas of distinction to a leading national university with strength broadly across the board. Stanford's development was led by its strength in engineering and science, but aggressive recruiting of star faculty in the humanities and social sciences soon built programs of real distinction in those areas, too. It was a model that others emulated.

I have dated the end of this period at 1968, the last year of growing financial abundance from federal research support programs. In reality, though, the end of the period was signaled earlier by Berkeley's Free Speech Movement (FSM). The FSM energized the student Left and, along with the civil rights movement, provided the lessons in organization and tactics on which the antiwar movement soon built. More fundamentally, though, the FSM was the first important sign that there was brass in the golden age and that it was beginning to tarnish. "Do not fold, spindle, or mutilate," a prominent slogan of the time, struck a responsive chord among students enrolled in universities that had grown at an unprecedented rate and in which faculty rewards increasingly went to those most active in research. It is an ironic coincidence that these first dramatic signs of discontent came from the University of California, whose president, Clark Kerr, had so clearly described the developments out of which the discontent arose in his 1963 book, *The Uses of the University*.

What started at Berkeley as a protest over a so-called free speech area escalated there and elsewhere into a challenge to the legitimacy of policies that were, or could be made to seem, contrary to student interests and that were made through processes in which students had no voice. In a democratic society, that is a powerful argument when it can be made plausible. With the Free Speech Movement, the argument gained wide currency, with consequences for the way in which universities are governed and the way in which they came to be viewed that reach to the present day.

From the Antiwar Movement to Nixon's Resignation

The Vietnam War, the campus reaction to the war, and the public and political counterreaction brought two decades of growth in federal support for universities to an abrupt halt. Federal support of university research peaked in 1968, then declined and did not return to the same level in constant dollars until 1977. During this period, funds for science facilities virtually disappeared, and federally funded fellowships for doctoral study went from a high of sixty thousand per year to a low of fewer than ten thousand. In sum, the strategy of the federal government in its support of university research shifted sharply from one of consumption supported by investment to one of consumption alone. What had been a rounded set of policies that helped build the human and material infrastructure on which the research product was based suddenly changed to a policy that bought the product and left the other matters for others to worry about. Amid the turmoil of the times, it was hardly noticed, but it was a change of policy with the profoundest consequences for the future health of research universities.

During this period, too, many campuses were in turmoil. Order and civility were early casualties of the time, and only with the winding down of the war and the ending of the draft did they reemerge. Not surprisingly, it was also an extraordinarily difficult time for university presidents. Clark Kerr and Marian Gade assert of this period, "Never before in American history had higher education gone from so high a mountain to a place so low in the valley, and so quickly. No time was ever better for university and college presidents than the late 1950s and early 1960s, and no time was ever worse than the late 1960s and early 1970s. The best of times became the worst of times in no time at all."[3] The data bear out that judgment. As

3. Clark Kerr and Marian L. Gade, *The Many Lives of Academic Presidents: Time, Place, and Character* (Washington, D.C.: Association of Governing Boards of Colleges and Universities, 1986), 82.

they report, "The fifty-one U.S. members of the Association of American Universities, the most prestigious research universities, suffered a 77 percent presidential turnover between 1968 and 1973."[4]

The Vietnam War and the Watergate scandal that followed marked a sharp decline in public confidence in many important American institutions, universities among them. Most universities had been unprepared for the challenge to their processes mounted by the student antiwar movement. Thus, their leaders were uncertain about how to respond even to challenges to civil order on campus. Politicians were angered by violence and disruption on campuses and by the use of campuses as privileged sanctuaries from which sometimes violent and often disruptive demonstrations were mounted and aimed off campus. They found ways to retaliate in lower appropriations accompanied by more onerous conditions on them. Internally, institutions were wracked by fierce challenges to the nature of their curriculum, the legitimacy of their governing structures, and practices in admitting students and recruiting faculty that produced student bodies and faculties overwhelmingly white and male.

Among the most profound shifts in the period was the retreat from the widespread belief that science was the benevolent source of progress and scientists were the white-coated wise men who were its bearers. Antiwar politics on campus focused heavily on the complicity of university scientists in prosecuting an immoral war. At Stanford, for example, the principal physical targets of student demonstrators were the president's office, the ROTC headquarters, the electronics laboratories, and the computer center. On many campuses, scientists themselves were among the most vocal opponents of the war, dividing the scientific community into two camps: those who saw the war and those who cooperated in it as immoral, and those who deeply resented the challenge to their patriotism and their freedom to do the research they chose to do.

Outside the university, an even deeper challenge to science was being mounted. Its principal focus was on the use of atomic energy as a source of electric power. The near meltdown of the Three-Mile Island reactor gave life to a movement that eventually brought the development of nuclear power in America to a halt and forced the closing of nuclear generators that had been built at enormous cost to stockholders and ratepayers. But the question raised went far beyond the future of nuclear energy; it went to the larger issue of whether, given the knowledge that scientific discoveries and their applications are often accompanied by risk, those who are responsible for the science can be trusted to be honest about the risk. For many people and their politically active organizations, the answer was no;

4. Ibid., 25.

theirs was a view that quickly found its way into the regulatory policies of government agencies and the staffs of congressional committees and onto the agenda of members of Congress.

Expectations of science remained high. The preferred solution to any problem remained the scientific or technological one, because such solutions avoided the need for messy political wrangles and, in the best of worlds, for social sacrifice. But that was no longer the only view of the matter. A social and political force had grown that was deeply suspicious of science, and those who shared this suspicion learned their political and organizational lessons well during this period. The period in which scientists could do their work with little examination and less resistance, short as it was, was over. For universities, the age of regulation lay just ahead.

President Richard Nixon's resignation in August of 1974 is a convenient marker for both symbolic and substantive reasons. By then, virtually all institutions had learned to deal with disorder on campus in ways that the outside community, at least, largely approved of. It helped, of course, that the war had ended and that the student movement had lost energy, but that does not diminish what had been accomplished in the way of stronger and more clearly stated rules of conduct and improved processes for dealing with their breach. Symbolically, Nixon's departure from the presidency is a useful marker because, with Gerald Ford's accession to office, the cold war between America's president and its universities also ended. Everyone seemed ready for recuperation and repair.

From 1974 to 1980: Steady State Revenue, Inflated Costs

The slogan of the period, reflecting the general expectation of little or no growth in resources, was "Managing the Steady State University." Relations with the federal government began to improve. Federal expenditures for university research hit their lowest point in nearly a decade in 1974 and then began to increase slowly. The largest increases were in applied research and development, but the overall trend was up. The second half of this period, during the Carter administration, saw the enactment of the Middle-Income Student Assistance Program, which produced a large increase in student aid, though most of it came in the form of loans and loan guarantees and therefore was very much a mixed blessing.

The period saw no change in federal policy with respect to funding facility or other infrastructure needs, and while several small fellowship programs were enacted in the latter part of the period, the dominant view of federal policy makers continued to be that students' decisions about whether to pursue graduate study ought to be determined by their response to the market and not by federal subsidies. That view, held strongly by the Office of Management and Budget (OMB), was described in a report issued by the National Board of Graduate Education in 1974: "The dominant view expressed by this key agency [OMB] in recent years is that graduate education is a form of investment in human capital, with the benefits primarily private, not social. Consequently . . . there is little justification for federal subsidy in the form of fellowships; instead, the student-investor should pay for his/her own education, borrowing if necessary or working as a research assistant."[5]

In the last years of the decade, a group of university presidents addressed themselves to what they described as "a relatively small but crucial part of [the relations between the needs of the nation and the responsibilities of organized education]: the places where the national interest and the consequent responsibilities of the federal government intersect with the special capabilities of the nation's major research universities."[6] This is how they saw the relationship:

> The greatest single danger before the world of education, in its relations with the government, is that it may divide against itself—public against private institutions, universities against colleges, higher education against the schools. . . .
>
> We are believers in a renewed and stronger partnership between the government and the major research universities and . . . because of the inescapable financial realities of the situation, we believe a modest increase in federal funds must be a part of that renewal.

Their belief that internal divisions within education were the greatest single danger to the relations with the government reflected the bitter battle being waged at the time over the distribution of federal student financial aid between public and private institutions. However, the fear of further division was, apparently, not strong enough to dissuade them from arguing for added funding for their own sector. Apart from that, the topics covered in the report were conventional: research, the needs of research libraries, graduate education, and strengthening international studies and research. It was a modest enough agenda and a modest enough set of demands for federal funding, as was fitting in a period of somewhat chastened institutions and lower expectations.

On campuses, the period was notable for the general relaxation of tension. The student Left had virtually disappeared, some members having gone underground, some to graduate or professional schools, and the rest

5. *Federal Policy Alternatives toward Graduate Education* (Washington, D.C.: National Academy of Sciences, 1974).

6. *Research Universities and the National Interest: A Report from Fifteen University Presidents* (New York: Ford Foundation, 1978), v.

simply having graduated. The successor student generation, while not as docile as the media sometimes made it out to be, was certainly not as intense or as overtly political as its immediate predecessors. As a result, student interests no longer dominated the university agenda. Indeed, the period is more noteworthy for what did not happen than for what did. First, many institutions did not replace outmoded facilities, build needed new ones, or adequately maintain those in use. As a result, a facilities deficit began to grow, with consequences that laid the foundation for the indirect cost battles of the next decade that so poisoned public attitudes about universities. Second, faculty salaries did not keep up with inflation or with markets for comparable talents. The strenuous efforts of the next decade to recover the lost ground helped fuel the large tuition increases that came to constitute part of the public indictment of higher education.

Several issues that came to loom much larger in later years could be seen in embryonic form during this period. Research fraud had never been wholly absent from university and scientific life, but when instances of it were discovered, they were typically dealt with quietly and out of public view. However, several highly publicized cases at prestigious universities occurred during this period, and in sharp contrast to past experience, they became matters of great interest to the media. Misconduct in science became a major theme of the 1980s, as the media and the government focused their lenses on the way in which universities were dealing with the problem. The charge that universities were not dealing promptly and effectively with scientific misconduct became an important theme in the broad attack on institutional credibility that marked the later period.

Another issue of even greater importance and durability could be seen in its early forms during this period. As much as anything else, it can be dated from the development of recombinant DNA technology in university laboratories and the birth of the biotechnology industry that directly resulted. James D. Watson and John Tooze have described the impact of the discovery by Herbert Boyer and Stanley Cohen.

> It is only the rare scientific revolution that immediately excites the public. The elucidation of the double helical structure of DNA in 1953, for example, created almost no stir outside the small band of scientists who were waiting for the discovery to be made. . . .
>
> . . . But this was not everyone's game, and the fact that the genetic code is based on a four-nucleotide (letter) alphabet had to seem to most lawyers as irrelevant to their well-being as the meaning of torts to most molecular biologists. As all busy people know, we should not waste time with abstract concepts that we shall never in our daily lives use.

In 1973, however, Herbert Boyer, Stanley Cohen and their collaborators devised simple test-tube procedures to produce "recombinant DNA molecules" derived from two different parental DNA molecules . . . and the picture changed dramatically. For with the development of recombinant DNA, genetic engineering—at least for microorganisms—was now a practical proposition. . . . Without doubt molecular geneticists now had the power to alter life on a scale never before thought possible by serious scientists.[7]

It is by no means an exaggeration to say that the discovery of recombinant DNA changed the relationship between scientists and society, and inevitably the institutions in which scientists worked, as profoundly as the revolution in physics that led to the development of atomic energy. Among the immediate consequences was fear of what might be unleashed from laboratory test tubes and the light in the eyes that accompanies the prospect of enormous economic gains. In 1980, Congress enacted the Bayh-Dole Act, which gave universities the right to patent and license inventions made by their faculty with federal research support. In the same year, the Supreme Court ruled in *Diamond v. Chakrabarty* that organisms developed in the laboratory could be patented.[8] The pieces had all fallen into place. The application for the recombinant DNA patent, made jointly by Stanford and the University of California, followed in 1981. Universities and their scientists thus became major players in real time in the birth and growth of a potentially enormous industry. Ties between universities and industry were not new, but never before had the financial stakes seemed so high for both individuals and their universities. Along with potential riches came the troubling prospect of conflict between academic and business values, as well as not-at-all-theoretical issues of conflict of interest and conflict of commitment. At early meetings at Pajaro Dunes in California and the University of Pennsylvania, attended by university presidents, deans, scientists, and business people, those issues were explored but far from resolved, and their continuing life became another major theme of the 1980s.

The period ended with a burst of inflation virtually unprecedented in the nation's history, and as inflation does, it exacerbated every other problem. It ended, too, with the election of Ronald Reagan, who, as governor of California, had made his reputation by attacking the University of Cali-

7. James D. Watson and John Tooze, *The DNA Story: A Documentary History of Gene Cloning* (New York: W. H. Freeman, 1981), 7. This is an invaluable reference for anyone wanting to recapture the genius, the hysteria, and the confusion attendant upon the dawn of a genuine revolution.

8. U. S. Supreme Court, *Diamond v. Chakrabarty*, 447 U.S. 303 (1980), 79–136.

fornia, liberal faculty, and pusillanimous administrators. All in all, the future seemed daunting.

The Reagan Years

Most of the presidents interviewed in this study took office, and all served, during the Reagan presidency. Because they all led national universities, they were necessarily concerned with the national setting in which their institutions fit. It is probably fair to say that they, like most other informed observers trying on January 20, 1981, to forecast the prospects for universities during the coming decade, found it hard to summon up much optimism. The mood of the time and the issues that preoccupied people in higher education can be seen by looking at the stories that found their way into the pages of the *Chronicle of Higher Education,* the most complete news source on matters affecting colleges and universities. The following stories appeared between September 1979 and January 1981:

> September 4, 1979: "The Decline in Enrollment Predicted for the 1980's Has Not Yet Begun"; "Are Liberal Arts Graduates Good for Anything?"; "One-fourth of Women Psychologists in Survey Report Sexual Contacts with Their Professors"; "Textbook Publishers Worry about Enrollment Slowdown."

> September 24, 1979: "What Is Good Teaching and Why Is There So Little of It?"

> October 22, 1979: New HEW auditing manual is attacked as "radical" and "unacceptable" departure from traditional federal policy toward scientific research. It represents a "general tone of distrust and suspicion toward universities."

> November 11, 1979: Medical school deans are urged to plan for realities of a steady state, says Dr. David E. Rogers, president of the Robert Wood Johnson Foundation. "Academic medical centers risk 'becoming bitter and unpleasant places, bemoaning the loss of the good old days while destroying themselves,' unless they recognize that they will have to survive on fewer resources in the 1980's"; the sad state of faculty governance; the unconscionable exploitation of the student athlete.

> January 7, 1980: From Duke University, "The existing scope of activities must be restricted"; from the University of Wisconsin, "Planning for decline is not something many universities want to think about. They are afraid of self-fulfilling prophesies."

> January 28, 1980: "Carnegie Panel Says Enrollment Decline Will Create a 'New Academic Revolution'"; "A new academic revolution is upon

us. In the 1960's the revolution consisted of many institutions trying to become research universities and mostly failing. In the 1980's and 1990's, it will take more and more the form of following the long-time example of community colleges in adjusting to the market, and often succeeding. Excellence was the theme. Now it is survival. Institutions were 'trading up'; now they are trading down."

August 25, 1980: "The Ph.D. Cabby: 'I Don't Miss It, Not Anymore' "; "For a decade, a mood of impending disaster for higher education has been building. It is premature, to say the least, and probably wholly wrong" ("Higher Education's Future: Much Brighter Than You Might Think," an opinion piece by M. M. Chambers); Professor Chambers argued that the growing tax revolt was a passing fancy and that the public would continue to pay for "indispensable public services," of which higher education was one.

November 10, 1980: "Reagan Likely to Seek Tuition Tax Credits and Curtailed Federal Role on Campus"; "The Unnecessary Burden of Federal Regulation," an opinion piece by A. Bartlett Giamatti.

One might say that the more things change, the more they are the same. One might also say that prediction is a hazardous activity, especially if it is committed in public in an age of computer databases. However, both memory and the archives agree that the dominant mood at the turn of the decade was one of worry about both the present and the future. The start of the Reagan administration seemed to confirm both. In the words of one retrospective essay, "The advent of the Reagan Administration marked a major turning point in U.S. politics. The Administration brought with it an agenda that included reducing federal spending, shrinking the role of the government in the civil sector and increasing the nation's military power."[9] At least two of those three agenda items portended trouble. It is testimony, if such were needed, to the limited human capacity for predicting even the near future that the reality turned out to be both different and more complex than the early signs indicated.

The main ingredients of public policy in the 1980s formed an odd and contradictory combination. There was an active commitment to shrink the size of the federal government that was largely unsuccessful, as both civilian and military employment rose during the period and government spending as a percentage of gross national product failed to respond to those who exhorted it to decline and remained about constant. At the same time, the effort to limit the power of the government to levy taxes was

9. Albert H. Teich and Kathleen M. Gramp, *R&D in the 1980s: A Special Report* (Washington, D.C.: American Association for the Advancement of Science, 1988), 3.

largely successful. The apparent paradox between success in the latter and failure in the former is explained by an unprecedented willingness to engage in deficit financing to bridge the gap between goals that required spending and policies that limited taxing.

The stance of the Reagan administration toward universities was also at odds with itself. As Teich and Gramp point out, domestic research and development (R&D) policy, like most other domestic policy, was driven largely by budget considerations, not by any well-developed set of views about the role of the government in the support of research. There were some major exceptions, however. In its first budget, the administration made deep cuts in social science research and in energy R&D, especially the demonstration projects favored by the Carter administration. However, there were no restraints, ideological or fiscal, limiting the use of research in support of a massive military buildup. The Reagan revision of the outgoing Carter administration's fiscal year (FY) 1982 budget proposed reductions in the R&D lines of every domestic agency, ranging from a low of 1.4 percent in Agriculture to a high of 42 percent in Education. Defense R&D, in contrast, was marked for a 7.2 percent increase. That pattern continued through the eighties, modified by increases in the budgets for the National Institutes of Health (NIH) (largely granted by the Congress) and the NSF. Between FY 1980 and FY 1988, R&D appropriations for the Department of Defense (DOD) grew by 84 percent in constant dollars. Most of that was dedicated to weapons development, but the programs in which universities participated also grew, though at a slower rate. On the whole, then, the government research programs on which universities most depended grew during this period, in spite of early fears to the contrary.

That was the good news. On other fronts, the news was less encouraging. The promised assault on student aid programs actually did occur, producing a major decline in grant funds. Private institutions were especially hard hit. In order to sustain the recruitment of low-income and minority students, a larger fraction of rapidly rising tuition was devoted to financial aid. Federal civil rights policies turned in a different direction. Opposition to affirmative action and to race-based scholarships became national policy, and enforcement of race- and gender-equity programs slowed materially. The lessening of the national commitment to civil rights seemed to produce greater racial and ethnic tensions on campus as minorities seeking to preserve and extend hard-earned gains met resistance from other student groups, encouraged by the prevailing national climate.

The appointment of William Bennett as secretary of education and the appointment of Lynn Cheney to succeed him as chair of the National Endowment for the Humanities triggered an indictment of higher education and all its works that became a major preoccupation of the decade as well as a major source of income for conservative critics and their publishers. The bill of particulars included charges of bloated tuition, defaulting students, neglect of undergraduate education, excessive preoccupation with trivial research, failure to defend Western civilization from the depredations of the multiculturalists, weak and grasping administrations, faculty who cheat in their research and administrations unwilling to prevent or punish those who do, and abuse of federal rules for the reimbursement of research costs. It is doubtful that there has been a time in our history when the criticism of colleges and universities was so strident and ranged over so broad a terrain. It should be said, too, that it was a difficult bill of particulars to deal with. That was, in part, because of its very breadth but in part also because the elements of it were sometimes true, sometimes partly true but oversimplified or exaggerated, and sometimes just false. An aggressive attack of that kind overwhelms defenses, at least in the short run.

The 1980s was, indeed, a strange decade, because in the midst of the turmoil and criticism, most universities were prospering. For universities that depend heavily on private gifts and federal appropriations—that is to say, virtually all of them—sustained economic growth is the single most important element in their financial picture. In the short run, the fact that in this period growth was built on borrowed money was irrelevant, and only a few lonely voices raised alarms about the long run. Thus, the demand for new and renovated facilities, which had been stifled for more than a decade, exploded in a burst of new building. Private universities borrowed heavily in the expectation that their debt for research facilities could be repaid by increases in their indirect cost rates. Public universities, especially those in the Sun Belt states, found their legislatures and electorates willing to take on new debt in the expectation that their improved universities would promote economic development. In the climate of the times, the idea that what goes up might one day come down was rarely spoken aloud.

It is not uncommon for one set of public policies to confound another, and so it was in this instance. First, the Tax Reform Act of 1986 set a limit of $100 million on the amount of tax-free debt that a private institution could incur, an amount lower than the debt already outstanding for many major private universities. Still later in the decade, indirect costs came under heavy attack, and the pressure to lower the highest rates, typically found in private universities, sent chills through financial offices throughout the country.

Tax policy brought another reminder of the hazards of prediction. The Tax Reform Act significantly lowered the marginal rates on personal incomes. Earlier research had appeared to demonstrate that lower rates, because they lessened the tax advantage of the charitable deduction, would decrease private charitable giving. In the event, philanthropy prospered, at least in the short run. Major fund-raising campaigns were mounted by public and private institutions alike, and they were almost uniformly successful. The billion-dollar campaign became, if not commonplace, at least no longer unthinkable, and not very newsworthy.

Finally, it was in this decade that "economic competitiveness" became the latest moral equivalent of war. The National Science Foundation was the first government agency to justify larger appropriations on the grounds that research is an essential part of economic development and promoting economic development is a responsibility of the national government. This argument went on to say that the old practice of supporting undirected, investigator-initiated research would not do the job. What universities needed to do was to create new kinds of centers and institutes that would link university scientists and engineers with industry in programs of research that had potential economic payoff. Thus, a new step was taken in the joining of industry and academia. Applications in the biotechnology industry had grown quickly from the development of recombinant DNA work in universities. It now became de facto national policy to support lines of inquiry that showed promise of having a similar result and to do so in a format that consciously rejected the traditional disciplinary basis of university organization by creating new organizational instruments on campus. There was no shortage of applicants.

The presumed role of universities in promoting economic growth also justified the vast increase in the use of targeted or earmarked congressional appropriations for specific university facility or research projects. The practice divided the university community in bitter, sometimes quite personal ways, even as it produced conflict within the Congress between authorizing and appropriating committees, between so-called have and have-not states, and between those who supported the traditional allocation methods of peer or merit review and those more concerned about product than process.

In short, it was an unusually complex decade. Changing and often conflicting currents of policy made educational leadership extraordinarily difficult. In some respects the surface looked good, others showed heavy weather. And beneath the surface, the debt-purchased prosperity of the decade held the same hazards for universities as it did for the rest of the nation. Heading a university in those years was rather like a trip through an amusement park fun house: the next turn was bound to disclose something unexpected, curved mirrors showed misleading self-images, and traps lay hidden for the unwary. Yet, overall the trip was exhilarating.

Operating in Washington during the 1980s was, for me, more like heading off on a long journey without a road map: it was an adventure and an education, but there were potholes and detours aplenty, and as is always the case, learning gained through experience can be a good deal more painful than education in a classroom. It is to Washington that I turn first.

Chapter Two

WASHINGTON, 1983

The National Agenda

IN 1983, THE REAGAN RECESSION had not yet run its course, "Morning in America" still lay ahead, Republicans controlled the Senate, and Democrats retained their hold on the House of Representatives. I came to Washington in that year to head the Association of American Universities (AAU), a group consisting of fifty (forty-eight American and two Canadian) major research-intensive universities. Since its founding in 1900, the AAU had been a grouping of the elite in the American university world. Membership was tightly controlled and highly prized. New presidents of nonmember universities often listed gaining admission to the AAU as a goal of their administration. During my time at the AAU, one newly admitted university asked if we would withhold the announcement of their admission until the governor of the state could arrange to be at the press conference. Another admission won the new member a congratulatory editorial in the *New York Times*. I mention these things not to boast of the organization's eminence but because they are indicators of both the strengths and weaknesses of the AAU as a political entity: it is an organization of the elite in a society that both admires and resents its elites.

For most of its history the AAU, which was formed by the fourteen universities that offered the Ph.D. in 1900, served as a meeting ground for graduate deans and a club for presidents. Twice a year, member presidents would come together, discuss educational matters (occasionally issuing a pronouncement), compare notes on the problems of their jobs, and then return home to tend to the real business of higher education, which took place on their separate campuses. Not only were the doings of the national government not a preoccupation of their meetings, they were rarely on the agenda.

The focus of the organization began to change at the end of World War II, as universities became more deeply enmeshed in national policy, but change came surprisingly slowly. At midcentury, the organization's longtime executive secretary could boast that he had never ventured onto Capitol Hill on business. His successor was much more acutely attuned to policy issues, especially science policy, but his was never much more than a watching brief; influencing policy was not one of the organization's goals, and it was rarely attempted.

In the late 1970s, a group of member presidents concluded that the universities most closely involved with the federal government could no longer afford to be without a voice and an active presence in the councils of government when policy affecting their interests was being made. As they saw it, the AAU was the logical organization to perform that function, but if the dominant opinion of the group was against such a change of mission, then a new group needed to be formed to assume the new, more active role.

In the end, the members voted to make the change. They decided to raise their dues, enlarge the staff, and recruit a president for the organization. The title of the office, by the way, was no small matter. In a city so exquisitely attuned to nuances of status, the word *president* conveyed weight that the title of *executive director*—thick on the ground in a town full of trade associations—could not. The goal of the changes was to increase the group's visibility among policy makers, organize and focus the activities of its members, and provide a voice for the research universities on matters of national policy as they arose in the Congress and in executive agencies.

The new order began in 1978 with the appointment of Thomas Bartlett, president of Colgate University, as the first president of the AAU. Bartlett recruited an excellent staff organized to reflect the major areas of federal policy: the hard sciences, whose funding came largely from the National Science Foundation and the Department of Defense; the biomedical sciences, emphasized primarily in the National Institutes of Health; the humanities and the arts, centered on the two national endowments; and graduate education, whose much diminished support was spread through a number of agencies. Notably absent from that array, and not by accident, was the issue of undergraduate student aid. That was, at the time, the main arena of conflict between public and private institutions. To oversimplify somewhat, the publics argued that the main goal of federal student aid should be to guarantee widespread access to a college education with the largest number of grants, even if that meant lower stipends. The privates argued for awards that provided a realistic choice of colleges with grants large enough to help pay the higher tuition in the private sector, even at the cost of a smaller number of awards. The AAU membership was divided evenly between public and private universities, and so it wanted no part of that argument. The decision was made to concentrate on issues that members had in common and to leave the divisive issue of student aid to be fought out in other forums.

When I arrived as the second president, the group had just been through a bruising battle over the rules that determine how indirect costs would be assigned to research grants and contracts. It was an issue that had bedeviled relations between the government and universities from the very start of significant government support of research and would continue to do so into the future. No agreement ever seemed to settle the matter. Indeed, it became, toward the end of my tenure, a virtually all-consuming issue, the one that best illustrated the serious problems in the government-university connection as well as the divisions within the university community. I examine it at some length later; for present purposes, its importance is that this edition of the dispute showed both the value of the new AAU and its acceptance as what is called in Washington a "player" in the game.

It became clear, as I took on my new responsibilities, that the AAU was no ordinary political interest group. It was that, to be sure, but it had little in common with others of the genre. It represented no constituency that could deliver or withhold votes, and it was forbidden by law to use campaign contributions, the main currency of political interest groups. It had no political action committee (PAC) and wanted none; indeed, my own view, contrary to the practice among some other educational organizations, was that my staff and I should make contributions only to candidates in whom we had a personal interest and not to the many who solicited us on the grounds that they had been or could be helpful. In short, whether to make a political contribution or not should be a personal, not a business, decision. It was not moral squeamishness that led me to this view but a simple calculation that life would be easier for us all if we had a policy that enabled us to avoid having to choose among the many supplicants without having it seem a rejection by the association. Our policy upset some members of Congress, but it was generally accepted and understood.

The campaign money game was never for us in any event. Any influence we might be able to exert was due largely to the general perception that universities were different from other kinds of organizations because they were committed to the public welfare. They were usually not seen by politicians as self-regarding. What they asked of the government was generally thought to be for the public good, and although that perception had suffered serious blows in the 1960s, the blows were not fatal. By the 1980s, early signs of further erosion were visible but not yet alarming.

Bolstered by this general goodwill, the main basis for optimism that universities could influence public policy was the fact that they had naturally what others fought for or bought: access. Universities were important entities in their communities, and their presidents were visible, respected, and usually noncontroversial citizens. Members of Congress recognized that. When a president called, the call was taken or promptly returned; when he or she asked for an appointment, it was always granted. Once the door was open, the case could be made. It might not always be accepted, but it was always treated respectfully and taken seriously.

I believed then, and still do, that public service groups cannot ask for more than that in Washington. The rub is that, once in the door, how seriously you are taken is likely to depend on that basic belief that you really are different from others, that public service and not self-service is your business, and that your representations can be taken at their face value and do not serve some hidden interest. As time went on, all of those preconditions were eroded, with terribly damaging effects to the cause of higher education and research.

All of that lay ahead, though not as far as I might have hoped. The immediate agenda, however, was of a different character. I am struck, as I look back at the issues that occupied my attention in the first months after my arrival, at how undramatic, how ordinary, they now seem compared with those that quickly came to dominate the agenda. I was concerned, for example, with issues of graduate education. The National Commission on Financial Aid to Students was doing its work at the time, and we were deeply engaged with its subcommittee on graduate education, chaired by John Brademas, a former congressman and the recently installed president of New York University.

Our testimony before that group was our first attempt to uncouple graduate fellowship policy from the often dubious and always unreliable predictions about the future demand for Ph.D.s that had always dominated decisions about the government's role in graduate education. We followed that with a larger policy statement on the support of graduate students in which we argued that the proper role of the government was not to try to outguess the labor market—almost certainly wrongly—but to make sure only that a sufficient number of the very brightest college graduates each year were able to attend graduate school in order to provide a core of high-quality teachers and scholars for the future. If larger numbers of the best college graduates were attracted to careers in law and business because the training time was shorter and the rewards larger and more immediate than in an academic career, then so be it. It was a legitimate function of government, however, to make sure that those highly talented students who really wanted to pursue a scholarly career were not prevented from doing so because the cost of attending graduate school was beyond their means.

Our model was not the huge National Defense Education Act (NDEA) program of the 1960s but the relatively small National Science Foundation Graduate Fellowship Program. The NDEA program, which at its height awarded tens of thousands of fellowships a year, was driven by the need to expand doctoral programs in order to produce teachers for rapidly expanding college enrollments. In the latter, awards were given after a stiff national competition, and the winners could take their awards to any university that would have them. In practice this meant that a large number of NSF fellows wound up at a small number of top universities, laying the program open to charges of elitism. That was a fair charge, but it never seemed to me a bad one, except in political terms. Scholarship is, by definition, an elite activity in which the best is far more valuable than the second best. There was, it seemed to me, an important public interest to be served by assuring that the calling of scholarship got a reasonable share of the best.

Unfortunately, the only argument that has ever carried any weight with national policy makers is alarm over some predicted shortage that will cripple universities and industry. Those predictions are usually wrong, or at least ill-timed, and therefore they are usually discounted at the outset. When they are believed and then are not borne out, the result is increased cynicism about the motives of those who make the predictions and makes it less likely that a real shortage will be detected in time to do anything about it. For example, at the end of the 1980s when several confident, authoritative, and highly publicized predictions of drastic shortages of Ph.D.s fell victim to the recession, the tightening of research funds, and the end of mandatory retirement for faculty, the result was a congressional investigation of the National Science Foundation, the source of one of the mistaken predictions, and a general decrease in confidence in the ability of the higher education sector to diagnose its own problems. The boy crying wolf is a familiar figure in Washington.

I wish I could say that my own record was better, but in truth, we did not succeed in our effort to provide a sounder basis for formulating federal policy. Indeed, when the chips were down and there seemed to be a real possibility of having a new program enacted, we joined with others in making the same old discredited, but still useful, arguments in its behalf. In a letter containing supplemental questions following my testimony before the Senate Budget Committee, Senator James Sasser asked me this question:

> Dr. Rosenzweig, as we look to the future of science in our country I believe that one of the most fundamental questions is how we will train and recruit our next generation of scientists and engineers. It seems that every time I pick up a paper or magazine there is a story about how industry is in desperate need of technically trained personnel.
>
> Clearly, something must be done. But if I understand you correctly, you are sounding a note of caution. You have stated that government

involvement in adjusting the normal market forces for scientists and engineers probably will do more harm than good.

In this ever increasing high-tech age, can we really have too many scientists and engineers? In your opinion, what should be the government role in the supply of technically trained personnel? [1]

If ever a witness were tossed a softball by a friendly senator, that was it. As I now read my letter in reply, however, it is embarrassingly clear that I gulped hard and swung and missed. I started by agreeing that "there is serious concern about the future supply of scientists and engineers," and I went on to cite the conventional wisdom: in the mid-1990s, increased faculty vacancies will coincide with increased college enrollments; industry and government will need more Ph.D.s to meet mounting economic competition and national defense needs and to develop major new initiatives such as the supercolliding superconducting accelerator (aborted shortly thereafter). Moreover, the demand was increasing as the supply was diminishing. An analysis done by Richard Atkinson, chancellor, at the time, of the University of California at San Diego and president of the American Association for the Advancement of Science, had demonstrated that present trends would produce an annual shortfall of seventy-five hundred science and engineering Ph.D.s early in the next century.

Perhaps to salve a bruised conscience, I added the following: "Manpower predictions are notoriously difficult to make with precision. Moreover, past experience has shown that aiming a federal manpower response at an elusive target is not likely to provide an optimal solution." My optimal solution, which I then described, was to increase every existing federal program in support of graduate students and start some new ones. In the real world, good analysis does not always carry the day, and good intentions frequently must yield to more practical considerations.

Good intentions came acropper in yet another way. Early 1983 was a time of renewed focus on the plight of elementary and secondary education. "A Nation at Risk," the report of a commission appointed by Secretary of Education Terrell Bell and chaired by David Gardner, president of the University of California, appeared in April 1983 and struck a responsive chord with the public. Washington was awash in talk of what was to be done. It was in this setting that I wrote my first letter to the member AAU presidents:

It has become clearer in recent weeks that political leaders at all levels of government have seized on the notion that there is a connection between education, technology, science, economic growth, and, consequently, jobs.

1. Senate Budget Committee, 101st Cong., 1st sess., March 9, 1989.

In putting the matter that way, I have imposed about as much order on it as one can find in most public discussions. The main point, though, is that the political convergence on this subject makes it likely that new programs will be started and new money made available for education. . . . There is good reason to believe that we will be able to influence what happens, and so our responsibility to think clearly about the needs of our institutions and the ways in which our institutions are connected to others is a very heavy one. . . .

It strikes me that our case will be easier to make if we can be creative in respect to a cluster of issues. . . . Much attention will be devoted to ways to improve science and mathematics teaching (and perhaps teaching in other fields, too) in secondary schools. If we can suggest ways to reestablish the connections between the schools and the intellectual resources of our faculties—connections that were quite fruitful in the '50s and '60s—I think that we will be widely seen as seriously addressing a national problem rather than simply seizing an opportunity to promote our particular interests.

That summer, the presidents of Harvard, Stanford, Michigan, California (Berkeley), and Columbia attended a small meeting with their education deans to discuss ways in which universities could become involved in school reform. Subsequently, the subject was discussed in a session of the semiannual AAU meeting, and it was encouraging to learn that more than a few universities were engaged in programs with their neighboring school districts aimed at improving curriculum and instruction. Several were, indeed, very impressive efforts. However, it was clear, then as now, that there is nothing like an organized, national push to find ways to join the resources of the nation's universities in the cause of school improvement. In most universities, K–12 education was the job of the schools of education, which was another way of saying that the regular faculty was not interested.

Nor, as it turned out, was the AAU. The initiative died a quiet death, for a reason that was honorable, even if wrong in principle and politically unwise. It was not clear what an organization like the AAU could do to affect so massive a problem as the deplorable condition of the nation's schools. At most, it might have served as a forum for the exchange of ideas and information and as a device for publicizing promising initiatives. Weighed against that limited role was the diversion of energy and resources required to do even that. In the end the members decided that the AAU should do the work that it could do best and that all the members wanted to have done, namely, the job of representing universities in Washington. In organizational terms, it was probably the right decision. It was also probably the result of many such "right" decisions that led one of the presidents interviewed to make this judgment:

> I think the universities really have done a very, very poor job of thinking through what their responsibilities are for K–12 education. It's really remarkable that we could have ten years of putting public education close to the top of the national agenda, and when you look back you have to ask, what is the contribution of higher education? I think most people in the United States would identify universities and schools of education more readily with the problems than with the solution.

It is hard to argue with that judgment.

The Industry Connection

I brought with me to Washington one issue that was just beginning to surface on the national scene but would become much more prominent as the decade wore on. The issues and the stakes involved in the relationships between universities and industry deserve the more extended treatment they will be given later, but the early rumblings are of interest, too.

Universities and industry are not natural collaborators. Their time horizons are very different, as are their forms of organization, and their practices with respect to communication among researchers about work in progress and research results are sharply divergent. In one respect, their interests coincide. Universities educate future managers and train highly qualified scientists and engineers, and industry needs those people. But apart from that important common interest, which is often expressed on industry's part by philanthropy, relations between the two sets of institutions might best be described as a search for specific areas in which different motives and styles of work can be reconciled in the name of mutual advantage. Success in that search differs among different fields of study; chemistry, for example, has long had closer relations with industry than has physics, because of a large chemical industry that employs many university-trained chemists, a natural bridge that joins the two sides solidly. And it varies over time as circumstances change. University-based scientists needed industry less as government funding became plentiful, and as a result relations grew more remote.

In an earlier period, the circumstances were reversed, but the result was the same. Herbert Hoover had a remarkably modern appreciation of the value of the university. He was closely associated with Stanford, to which his most visible legacy is the Hoover Institution for War, Revolution, and World Peace. But he was also the key figure in the creation of the School of Earth Sciences, the Food Research Institute, and the Graduate School of Business. His understanding of universities took him well beyond service to Stanford, his alma mater. In 1925–26, as secretary of commerce, he set out to move American industry beyond its acknowledged genius at tinkering and improvising onto the more solid footing of generating developments from an assured and sustained flow of basic research. To do that, he organized a campaign under the auspices of the National Academy of Sciences to raise $2 million a year from industry to endow basic research in universities. Hoover's words in announcing the initiative have a startlingly contemporary ring. "Not only is our nation today greatly deficient in the number of men and equipment for this patient groping for the sources of fundamental truth and natural law, but the sudden growth of industrial laboratories has in itself endangered pure science research by drafting the personnel of pure science into their ranks—depleting at the same time not only our fundamental research staff, but also our university faculties, and thus to some degree drying the stream of creative men at its source."

The *New York Times* applauded his initiative.

Secretary Hoover ... made a powerful appeal for the support of pure science. He did it on the grounds of the "dollar results"—not that he would put these first. The plea might well, as he said, be put wholly upon moral and spiritual grounds, from the unfolding of beauty to the "inculcation of the veracity of thought," in Huxley's phrase. But he asks for the larger support of research in the field of pure science upon the basis of its money returns, leaving the other reasons out of account. . . . The income of Michael Faraday did not, even in his most prosperous days, exceed $500 a year, and yet a hundred years after one of his discoveries, what he gave to the world is more valuable to the world than all the annual transactions of the institutions of commerce and finance in New York City.

When some business executives resisted the appeal on the grounds that such philanthropy was illegal for an entity devoted to making profits for its shareholders, Hoover commissioned the three most eminent lawyers of the day, Charles Evans Hughes, Elihu Root, and John W. Davis, to argue otherwise. Hoover's initiative failed. Timing is everything, and this was not the moment for the identification of a mutual interest in research by industry and universities. It would be another quarter century before resources began to flow into universities in amounts that were adequate to produce the results Hoover envisioned, and then the source was the national government, not private industry. Entering the 1980s, however, the moment had finally come for stronger connections between industry and universities.

In the summer of 1982, I helped organize a meeting at Pajaro Dunes, a Pacific Ocean beachfront development south of Santa Cruz, California.

The idea for the meeting was first advanced by Donald Kennedy, the new president of Stanford University, late in 1981. In a speech at the University of Pennsylvania, Kennedy pointed to the growing connections between universities and business, noting that some of the most important issues had to do with the proprietary influences on the conduct of science. He argued that no group other than scientists could address those matters effectively. He recalled the Asilomar Conference on the safety of recombinant DNA research and suggested that perhaps an Asilomar II, dealing with the effects of commerce on biology, might be in order. He concluded by saying, "Helping in the genesis of that sort of consideration may be the most important contribution the universities can make as institutions. But in the end, the scientists, themselves, must direct the effort, and be responsible for making the arguments stick."

Kennedy's proposal was met with what the *New York Times* described as resounding silence. Certainly, there was no visible interest in the scientific community for such an enterprise. Some months later, though, the industrialist Arnold Beckman urged Kennedy to move ahead toward a meeting at which some of the leading actors in these new relationships could discuss the array of problems associated with them. In the weeks that followed, Kennedy discussed the idea with the presidents of Harvard, MIT, Cal Tech, and the University of California, and they agreed to come together, each bringing with them their principal research officer, several faculty members knowledgeable about the issues, and two business people experienced in university relationships.

Much was later made of the composition of the group. Why only five universities? Why those five? The more conspiratorial explanations saw an attempt to create an OPEC of biological research, in order to control the market from the outset. I was never sure whether to be insulted that anyone would think we were dumb enough to try such a thing or flattered that we would be thought smart enough to pull it off. In any case, the truth, as usual, was more prosaic. The number was small because the whole point was to convene a conversation, not a parliament. The only reason those five universities were involved was that each was among the leaders in modern biology and the most aggressive in finding connections with industry, and their presidents were comfortable with one another. They met under the auspices of no organization, and they claimed to represent no one other than themselves. A wholly different set of five might have done the same thing; it just happened that these five did.

The statement produced by the participants at Pajaro Dunes was measured, thoughtful, and realistic in its recognition that they had not been elected to legislate policies for institutions entering into agreements with industry. The conferees noted that the purpose of the meeting was to contribute usefully to a more fruitful process of policy-making—but not to make policy. This responsibility rests with the individual institutions. . . . The overriding concern of the participants was to explore effective ways to satisfy the university community and the public that research agreements and other arrangements with industry [will] be so constructed as not to promote a secrecy that will harm the progress of science; impair the educational experience of students and postdoctoral fellows; diminish the role of the university as a credible and impartial resource; interfere with the choice by faculty members of the scientific questions they pursue; or divert the energies of faculty members and the resources of the university from primary educational and research missions.

The document was cast in terms of concerns and principles and was largely nonprescriptive. Inevitably, therefore, it was disappointing to some. The press was especially harsh. In our innocence, we thought it would be better to have a private meeting, and so no reporters were invited. I learned a hard but useful lesson: There is no such thing as privacy when organizations in which the public has an interest are involved. Privacy and secrecy are one and the same, and if the press are excluded, they will find ways to vent their displeasure. The *Washington Post* (April 3, 1982) was in especially high dudgeon. "Though the 'elitist' composition of the academic delegation (Stanford, Harvard, Berkeley, MIT, and Cal Tech—who else?) and the secrecy of the session itself predictably attracted much irritated attention, the meeting's actual outcome—a short, unsigned document—hardly merited all the excitement," said the *Post*, commenting on its own wounded *amour propre*.

What the five university presidents produced last weekend doesn't really get to the problems. It is largely a statement of unexceptionable general principles, combined with hortatory language on the need to preserve "basic academic values" and so forth. It winds up, disappointingly, as an "agenda of issues" not of "attempted" answers. Perhaps that was inevitable, considering the narrowness of the group. But the effort shouldn't stop here. Universities, and science as a whole, would benefit from an attempt to hammer out rules to guide the development of relationships with business that won't endanger academic science.

The questions raised in the Pajaro document, to which the *Post* was confident there were answers in the form of rules that only needed to be hammered out, have worried the world of university science ever since.

The AAU's entry into the fray was a modest one. It was obvious that many universities had already entered into various agreements with industry and that even more wished to. But, as was usual in this universe of autonomous, not to say isolated, units, there was no ready way to share experience, to compare policies, to warn of pitfalls, and to publicize solutions to difficult problems. Therefore, we set out in 1983 to organize a clearinghouse on the subject of university-industry relations. For three years, the clearinghouse collected and disseminated information on such subjects as policies governing delay in publication of research results and conflict of interest. I have no way of knowing whether it helped some universities avoid traps they might not otherwise have seen. I am confident, however, that it served a useful purpose until the level of attention given to the issues and the widespread discussion of them made a central clearinghouse less necessary.

Budgets and Appropriations

Most of the issues that turn up on the agenda of an organization of universities based in Washington, D.C., have to do with money. Money is at the heart of the relationship between universities and government, and so increasing the amount while trying to decrease the number of strings that come attached to it necessarily forms a large part of the work of a group like the Association of American Universities. In fact, the part of the job that has to do with increasing the amount of money available or, as in recent years, holding the decrease to the minimum feasible amount has become fairly routine. It starts with trying to influence the budget of the president of the United States—very difficult to do—and continues by trying to influence the congressional budget. The real work begins when the appropriations process gets under way. In general, the goals are clear and the stops along the way are well known, as are those staff people and representatives and senators who occupy them. You win some battles and lose others, in the knowledge that in either case there will be an opportunity next year to work the process again.

Throughout the 1980s, the process became progressively more complicated. The merger of appropriations with substantive lawmaking, two acts that are supposed to be kept separate, became a kind of nightmarish reality with the first Reconciliation Act in the Reagan administration. The point of reconciliation is to make the changes in underlying law required by subsequent funding decisions. It had always been a marginal step in the process, not a way to make fundamental changes in law. That changed in 1981, when a reconciliation bill reached the floors of the House and the Senate that was so large, so sweeping, and so complex that it is doubtful that any single member knew or understood its contents. It was widely reported that one staff member's jotting of his date's telephone number in the margin of the bill was enacted into law. More importantly, since a reconciliation bill cannot be amended on the floor and cannot be filibustered in the Senate, it is a powerful weapon for changing the law without having to jump all the hurdles ordinarily encountered. Every year since 1981, the reconciliation process has been a wild card in the process, requiring vigilance until the very end but with the knowledge that, if an important issue became swept up in the bill, there was little that could be done about it.

Tests of Values

However, even more of a test to an association's mettle is the part of its work that challenges the moral courage of the member institutions as they wrestle with issues in which values are on the line with a dollar sign attached. Regulatory restrictions are frequently of this character. Here, the trade-offs between money and principle are often tightly binding. A host of examples make the point, beginning with the imposition of secrecy rules by the Defense Department as a condition for much of the research it sponsored in universities. In the 1950s, loyalty oaths were attached to student loans and fellowships in the National Defense Education Act until the decision by Harvard and a few other universities to refuse to accept money on such terms eventually led to their elimination. During the 1960s, efforts were made to withhold federal funds from institutions that failed to punish disruptive students. Students were required to register for the draft in order to receive federal benefits, and institutions were made a link in the chain of enforcement of the requirement. Much more numerous than the politically inspired restrictions are regulatory provisions that attach to universities because they are engaged in research—regulation of research on human subjects and research using animals, for example—and the even larger class of regulations that apply to universities as entities doing business in a regulated economy. That last group includes, to mention only a few, occupational safety and health, pension protection, fair labor standards, national labor relations laws, and a range of environmental regulations. Many of these either did not exist before the war or were not originally applied to universities.

It is a rare and newsworthy event for a university to refuse to accept money because the conditions attached to it are too onerous. The strategy in dealing with government regulation is almost always to accept the restriction and work to mitigate its effects by loosening its terms, adding categories of exceptions, delaying its implementation, or seeking legislative relief. All of those tactics were used in dealing with the first major regulatory battle of my tenure in office: the application of the Export Control Acts to university research.

Restrictions on the export of military technology to potential military adversaries are neither novel nor unusual. However, as technology becomes more sophisticated, its applications are frequently broader, and the same technology may be equally useful in civilian or military use. A nation incapable of designing computer chips, for example, may learn something of value if it is able to buy and copy chips used in even relatively simple consumer goods such as hand-held calculators. The Reagan administration adopted an aggressive, no-risk policy with respect to exports of dual-use technology to countries in the Soviet bloc, and it constantly pressured our allies to do the same.

That was a more serious problem for American industry than for universities, because the policy often led to the loss of sales to companies in countries not so tightly bound to those particular Cold War strictures. The problem for research universities arose from the attempt to close down the flow of scientific information that might have military value. Foreign scientists were denied permission to visit university laboratories where work judged to be sensitive, even though nonclassified, was being done. Scientific meetings were declared off-limits to foreign scientists, even though the papers to be read were not classified. Demands were made for prior review of publications with the implied threat that they could be restricted even if, again, the work had been supported by a wholly nonclassified funding agency.

If there is one principle more than others that distinguishes the modern university and modern science, it is that intellectual work prospers in an atmosphere of free and open communication. Secrecy, however imposed, slows progress, protects incompetence, perpetuates error, and encourages wasteful duplication of effort. It was the judgment of the United States government in 1983 that the cost—and there was considerable skepticism in the government that it was real—was worth paying for any inconvenience or obstacle that might be imposed on the Soviet Union and its allies. So strongly held was this view that a representative of a government security agency asserted at a meeting sponsored by the National Academy of Sciences that if the only effect of restricting the distribution abroad of information in the open American literature was to force the Russians to use resources sending their agents to the library to collect that information from American journals, the restriction had served a useful purpose.

Such single-mindedness does not yield to argument or evidence, because it is grounded in doctrine that is impervious to both. The intellectual and political leader of the cause was Richard Perle, who was at the time assistant secretary of defense in charge of the administration of the Export Control Acts. Perle was a formidable figure, a dedicated Cold Warrior, smart, tough, experienced in the ways of Washington, and a highly skilled bureaucratic infighter.

From the research universities' point of view, this was a battle that was never wholly lost but never exactly won. It was a war of attrition with endless skirmishes. The main strategy was to thwart Perle and his allies by seeking our own allies higher up in the command structure of the Defense Department. The first and most effective of those was Richard DeLauer, a former executive of TRW, who became deputy secretary of defense for acquisitions—the principal technology position at DOD. DeLauer, an alumnus of Stanford University, put together with Stanford's Donald Kennedy the DOD-University Forum. The forum enabled DeLauer to bring in a group of key people from the armed services to meet regularly with a group of university presidents. The first issue they addressed was that of export controls and the flow of scientific information.

Under DeLauer's leadership, the forum also provided a line of access to Secretary of Defense Casper Weinberger. Weinberger was sympathetic to the university position, but no government official, no matter how highly placed, is ever a free agent, able to change policy on his own motion. Weinberger did, however, assign DeLauer the lead in developing a policy on the flow of scientific information, a first step in a new direction. Many drafts of that policy were advanced, each one successfully blocked by Perle. But the momentum had shifted, and serious damage to the conduct of American science was avoided.

I do not want to leave the impression that the only threat to open communication comes from the military. In fact, many agencies of government have attempted to control the dissemination of the results of work they have funded. The Departments of Education and Housing and Urban Development, and even the National Institutes of Health, have been guilty of doing so. The problem is endemic to government. The instinctive behavior of bureaucracies is to be risk-averse, to protect themselves from criticism and from information that may undermine the policies they are promoting, to avoid surprises, and to make life in general as predictable as possible. Research is, by definition, unpredictable, and so the temptation to try to make sure that it does not turn out to be awkward or embarrassing is always present. It is the job of research universities to protect themselves from that danger by being alert to it and then by refusing to accede to it. Since the faculty member involved may well think the restriction trivial, and not in any case likely to be imposed on him or her, adherence to the principle of open communication must be accepted by university administrators as an important part of their jobs. Such openness may well pit the administration against the faculty member. Fortunately, the faculty, collectively, is much more likely to be supportive of a principled position than is the individual whose funding may be threatened by a confrontation between university and sponsor.

It would equally be a mistake to leave the impression that the only threats to open communication come from the government. One of the most difficult arguments to deal with during the export control debate was the assertion that research universities were voluntarily, even eagerly, agreeing to protect proprietary information and accepting restrictions on publication of research sponsored by industry. Why, it was asked, were we unwilling to do for patriotic reasons what we were eager to do for commercial reasons?

The comparison was not entirely fair, but it was close enough to hurt. My conviction that this was so led me to write to my members in December 1983:

> We may be at some risk of doing damage to ourselves. I have in mind the possibility that closer connections between industry and academic science could have effects similar to the ones we are trying to combat when they are imposed by the government. I honestly do not know how serious this danger is. We have only the sketchiest information about the range of publication restrictions built into the various research contracts that are now in force, and we have even less information about the practices of individual scientists who may be, or may hope to be, involved with the commercial applications of their work.
>
> The new clearinghouse on industry/university relations . . . should give us a better basis than we now have for measuring the reality behind the concern; but to the extent that problems do exist, they can only be solved within individual institutions. Appropriate policies need to be articulated at every university that is involved with industry, and those policies must be combined with the willingness to say no to practices that we know to be unwise, even though they may be profitable.
>
> . . . If too many cases arise in which the prospect of gain—whether for the scientist or for the university—leads to unwise contractual restrictions on scientific communication, then we will find ourselves defenseless against those in government whose justification for such measures is an arguably more pressing concern for national security. Sorting out the differences between demands that impede the free and timely flow of information and those that merely accommodate the legitimate interests of sponsors—whether corporate or governmental—will not be easy. In my view, it will be impossible unless we hold to a very high standard of openness that will enable us to recognize when and how far we may be departing from the standard. This is a subject on which what is often represented as hard-nosed realism is, in fact, unrealistic and what is called idealistic and unreal can save us from terrible practical errors.

As it turned out, our work through the AAU clearinghouse demonstrated that most institutions had arrived at policies that allowed a relatively short interval before publication in which the sponsor could examine the manuscript in order to protect patent rights or other proprietary information. In most cases, the decision to publish was left to the investigator, not to the company or the university.

Still, there is no denying that threats to institutional values are as likely to be accepted voluntarily as to be imposed by law. It is not hard to generate resistance to overbearing government actions; the former are a good deal harder to deal with. A vivid example of that fact arose at the University of California at San Francisco, as reported initially in the *Wall Street Journal* on April 25, 1996. The headlines tell the main story: "How a Drug Firm Paid for University Study, Then Undermined It; Research on Thyroid Tablets Found Cheap Ones Were Just as Good as Sponsor's; Article Pulled at Last Minute." A major drug company had turned to a scientist at the university to do a study comparing its product with that of several competitors, no doubt confident that the study would prove the superior value of its considerably more expensive version. The contract for the study, agreed to by the scientist and signed by the appropriate university officials, contained a clause giving the company the right to prohibit publication of the results. Undoubtedly, nobody involved believed that the clause would ever be invoked. If it was noticed at the university, then no one was willing to risk the loss of the money by protesting the restriction. The study showed that the sponsor's product was indistinguishable from the competition, and the results were submitted to the *Journal of the American Medical Association* and accepted for publication. However, the sponsor had other ideas and demanded that the article be withdrawn. The university declined to challenge the sponsor's right under the contract.

Case closed, except, of course, that the results of the study were publicized in the popular press to a wider audience than would ever have seen the scientific publication, and the university was widely criticized both for originally agreeing to the restriction and for later failing to resist its application. There is no way of knowing how many such time bombs remain to be exploded in university-industry contracts. Even more worrisome, though, is the question of how many exist, will be enforced, and will never come to public attention.

Research Fraud and Research Pork

Two other issues landed on my plate while I was still learning my way around Dupont Circle. The first I inherited. In response to embarrassing public disclosures of several cases of fraudulent research, the AAU had appointed a committee to produce a policy statement on behalf of the organization. The resulting document, "A Policy on Integrity in Research," was in every way an unexceptionable document. It spoke to the responsibility of faculty to be mentors to their younger colleagues and of institutions to be alert to excessive pressures to publish. It was received politely, but I doubt that it led a single university to examine its policies and procedures in order to assure that, if a case arose on their campus, they would not be caught so embarrassingly short as were those institutions that had been recently exposed. Had more done so, some serious errors of omission and commission might have been avoided. But that lay in the future.

The last of the issues on the agenda deserves examination at length, but as in the case of university-industry relations, its origins are worth recalling here first. The practice of seeking benefits for one's constituency through earmarked appropriations is as old as the practice of constituency-based politics. Those who disapprove of the practice call it "pork barrel"; members of Congress think of it simply as doing their job for the hometown folks. In any case, it is an inherent part of our political system, and while the process of trading benefits during appropriations season in the Congress is not pretty to watch, and often produces less than optimum results, it is, like the Capitol Dome, an accepted part of the landscape.

Historically, the main items of trade have been roads, dams, post offices, military bases, federal buildings, and capital projects in general. In recent years, weapons systems and tax advantages for favored constituent groups or, indeed, individual constituents have become favored items of barter. On occasion, educational projects have been on the list, but those were viewed, in the educational community, at least, as aberrations resulting from particularly strong associations between a college and a member of Congress and not as a regular route to the federal treasury for colleges and universities. Tip O'Neill, for example, was known to have a strong fondness for Boston College, Georgetown University, and other Catholic institutions, and one or another of them would occasionally show up in appropriations bills unannounced by any prior request for funds from the executive branch or authorization from a congressional committee. Major universities, for their part, were committed to competition and merit review as the method for winning federal funds, and going around that system was, as they say in polite society, "not done."

When needs are great and money is tight, polite society becomes an expensive anachronism. By 1983, more than a decade had passed since federal funds for research facilities had been available, and a backlog of needs had accumulated. Most universities set about meeting those needs by fund raising and borrowing, but in 1983 two institutions, Columbia University and Catholic University, suddenly appeared in the Department of Energy appropriations bill when it reached the floor of the House as the designated recipients of money for a chemistry building, in the case of Columbia, and a vitreous research facility at Catholic. Both universities were members of the AAU. Had only Catholic been involved, the appropriation would no doubt have been deplored but then dismissed as another favor from the Speaker. Columbia, however, was different. Here was an Ivy League university, with great prestige and a distinguished faculty, that had judged this an acceptable way to obtain federal funds. Suddenly, the color of legitimacy had been given to what had previously been a marginal, slightly disreputable practice.

To make matters worse, Columbia, in its efforts to get the money, had retained Washington lobbyists, the firm of Schlossberg and Cassidy. The two principals in the firm had come out of liberal Democratic politics, and both had extensive congressional staff experience. They had shown their skill earlier in some work they had done for Tufts University, and they were aiming for the university market. For Schlossberg and Cassidy, Columbia was a coup in two respects. It advertised their abilities, and it made what they were selling legitimate. They quickly lined up a number of other university clients willing to pay a considerable fee in order to get an even more considerable gift from the federal government.

Two member universities had broken ranks, and the implications of this development were immediately obvious. They had engaged in a practice that posed a threat to the system of competitive merit review, hitherto a key element in decisions about what science to support with government funds. It might have been possible to avoid the issue temporarily, but it seemed better to face it head on in the hope of stopping this new gambit before it spread much further.

The AAU was in both the best and the worst position to lead this battle. On the one hand, its members had a primary interest in research policy, and compared with other educational associations they were a relatively homogeneous group. Moreover, the group expected to be, and was expected by others to be, the lead organization on issues of research policy and funding. On the other hand, the members of the AAU were, as a group, the largest beneficiaries of the system that had grown since the war and so were vulnerable to periodic charges of elitism, self-interest, market domination, and other allegedly bad practices. It was not foreseen, though perhaps it should have been, that, since two members had found a successful way to get money from the government, others would follow their example.

In October 1983, the issue of earmarked appropriations came to the floor of the fall AAU meeting, and after vigorous discussion, the members adopted a resolution affirming their support of peer review as the best way to assure scientific quality in the award of funds and calling on members of Congress and university presidents to refrain from seeking or awarding money for projects that evaded that process. There were two opposing votes and several abstentions. It is doubtful that there was a vote during my ten years in office that was so misleading as to its meaning.

In any case it was spitting into the wind. Over the next decade, the issue divided the organization as no other ever had. Year by year, more members felt obliged to take the money, and discussions of the issue became more bitter and personal. Some members were perfect colleagues and friends and never let our differences on this issue interfere with their support on other issues or with our friendship. Others, unfortunately, behaved differently. As for the onlookers, I have never in my professional career been so frequently complimented for my courage in taking on a difficult issue, always with a look of pity, a tone of voice that seemed to say, "Better thee than me," and rarely with an offer of public support.

There is much more to say about this issue, and I return to it later. Bound up in it are many of the central themes of the 1980s, some fascinating politics, and some clues about the future of research universities.

It was a rich and varied bill of fare that I found on my desk at the beginning of 1983. As tends to be the case in Washington, all of the issues that greeted me were bequeathed to my successor ten years later. And there were, of course, others. The hardy perennial of indirect cost recovery was about to return, the very difficult issue of the pending elimination of mandatory retirement for faculty simmered on a back burner, the disarray of the government's programs in international studies and student exchanges needed to be addressed, and critical issues of tax policy carried over from one Congress to the next. If, as the optimist says, every problem is an opportunity, then the road ahead was paved with opportunities.

Chapter Three

THE RULES CHANGE

I

Matters of Policy and Politics

B Y THE MIDDLE OF THE 1980s, no matter how strong the temptation to deny the evidence of one's senses, it was impossible not to see that the atmosphere in Washington surrounding university issues had changed, and for research universities the change had been very much for the worse. It could be seen in the allegations about research fraud and in the spate of books and articles critical of universities that became a reliable source of income for conservative writers. Concern over escalating tuition, combined with criticism of the research culture that had allegedly undermined undergraduate education, contributed to the change, as did a growing conviction that science, for all of the wonders it performs, also has a dark side that is not the product of out-of-control mad scientists but is inherent in the very process of scientific and technological development. Forces opposed to nuclear power had gained strength in the 1970s, and some of the same groups that had been involved in that cause joined in a campaign against experimentation with newly discovered recombinant DNA techniques. The animal rights movement grew as new and aggressive leadership, having learned the lessons of the 1960s, demonstrated once again that breaking into university laboratories, "liberating" animals and destroying research, while clearly illegal, would never be punished severely enough to outweigh the political benefits of the ensuing publicity.

Americans are fickle about their heroes and villains, so both celebrity and notoriety tend to be short-lived as their objects are succeeded by fresher models. Thus, it may be that this changed view of universities and of science was only a passing phenomenon. There is even some evidence to suggest that.[1] However, at the time that mattered little. The manifestations of the change were realities that had to be dealt with.

In this chapter and the next, we examine some of the ways in which the climate for research universities changed and the main issues that con-

---

1. See Mary Wooley, "From Rhetoric to Reality," *Science* 269 (September 15, 1995): 1495. Wooley reports on a national opinion survey that showed strong public support for science and for higher appropriations for scientific research. The survey was part of

tributed to the change and the problems that flowed from it. In this chapter we look at issues that were driven primarily by economic or political forces. In the next, we examine some matters that called into question the ability of research universities to respond to new circumstances in a manner that was consistent with the values they had always espoused.

The first political figure to ride the anti-university wave was William Bennett. Bennett had come to Washington at the beginning of the Reagan administration as chair of the National Endowment for the Humanities (NEH) from a position as director of the National Humanities Center in North Carolina. He had had a comparatively noncontroversial tenure at NEH, and most university people had few complaints with his performance. Indeed, when the post of secretary of education came open, many university people, of whom I was one, supported Bennett's appointment over that of John Silber, president of Boston University and a former employer of Bennett's, who was thought to be the leading candidate. Bennett didn't seem to have the slash-and-burn style that Silber regularly displayed.

We were wrong. In his first press conference as secretary of education, Bennett got his biggest headlines with charges that colleges and universities used federal student financial aid as a cushion that allowed them to raise tuition, that student recipients used the money they received for stereos and cars, and that in the end they defaulted on their loans. He followed these charges with assertions that left-wing faculty and weak administrations were selling out the Western cultural heritage by yielding to the curricular demands of minorities and their allies on campus. He was a strong opponent of multiculturalism and a strong advocate of a required core curriculum that would expose all students to the history, culture, and values of the Western, Judeo-Christian tradition. He lost no opportunity to make those and other points with his own forceful "take no prisoners" rhetorical style.

What was so striking about Bennett as secretary of education was not the substance of his views—they were controversial but certainly worth debating—but the way he positioned himself as the opponent of the traditional constituents of his agency. This was in sharp contrast with his predecessor, Terrell Bell, whose relations with the education community had been cordial and cooperative, a fact that made him suspect to more conservative Republicans and undoubtedly hastened his departure. From all appearances, Bennett cared not at all about the opinions of college presidents,

---

an effort to persuade the Congress to spare research funding from the deep cuts being made in the federal budget. The success of that effort, in comparison with the treatment of other social welfare spending programs, suggests that the antiscience feeling, at least, may have abated some.

school superintendents, or any other pillars of the educational establishment. He had his own audience, he spoke to them, and they listened. What Secretary of the Interior James Watt was to the environmental movement, Bill Bennett was to the education establishment, but much more successfully.

I made an early effort to establish some sort of working relationship between Bennett and the Association of American Universities by inviting him to speak to our spring membership meeting in 1984. He and I had a cordial relationship when he was at the NEH. I thought he had some things to say that university presidents ought to hear and that he would, in turn, profit from hearing their views. It was an instructive hour. By his body language, his tone of voice, and the sometimes defensive, sometimes aggressive way in which he handled the discussion, he made it clear that he viewed these people as his enemies. He took a group of people who were, in truth, disposed to accept at least part of his message and who, in any event, were constitutionally, and by the nature of their occupation, opposed to open confrontation with public figures and turned them into adversaries. And so far as I could tell, he didn't care at all.

This was a group of people unaccustomed to being treated in this way. Respect, if not deference, is far more common in their lives. What I believe we actually saw that day was early evidence that the rules were changing. That was most evident, as we saw with Bennett, in the behavior of conservative political figures, but it was by no means limited to them. Universities were becoming a regular part of the political landscape, and that meant that when there was political advantage to be gained from attacking them, then attack there would be. One of the most commonly spoken phrases in the Washington politics of higher education from the mid-1980s onward was "Universities are just like everyone else," another way of saying "You're fair game."

There were many signs of the change in the years following the Bennett appearance before the AAU, but to me the most vivid confirmation that a change had taken place, and that it was profound, occurred on March 13, 1991. That was the day on which the Subcommittee on Oversight and Investigations of the Committee on Energy and Commerce of the U.S. House of Representatives held a daylong hearing on the subject of an alleged scandal at Stanford University. The chair of the full committee, whose legislative and regulatory reach extended to virtually every aspect of the U.S. economy, and also of the subcommittee was John Dingell, a liberal Democrat from Michigan, a man widely credited with being one of the two or three most powerful members of the House and who was far and away the most widely feared.

The day had begun for me at a breakfast meeting of the University of Michigan's Washington alumni group at which the featured speaker was the same John Dingell. Since I had met him several times in the past, I went forward to pay my respects, and we chatted for a few minutes about the hearing we would both be attending immediately after breakfast. Neither of us said anything remarkable. Certainly, he gave me no reason to believe that anything that might happen that day might directly affect me.

As I came to know, congressional investigating committees operate symbiotically with the press that covers them. Reporters, especially investigative reporters, want to find scandal, and congressional investigators want to expose scandal and get the maximum possible visibility from it. Neither can fully achieve their ends without the other, so they exist in a close embrace on one side or the other of the line that marks outright collusion. It was already clear, therefore, from the months of committee leaks and "informed observer" quotes and from a television exposé that could only have been done with committee cooperation, that Dingell was out for blood. He had a successful model in the exposés of the defense industry several years earlier, and he saw Stanford as no better than those scoundrels. As he said in his statement opening the hearing:

> In 1984 and 1985, this Subcommittee conducted several investigations and hearings on the outrageous overhead charges to the government by major defense contractors—including a General Dynamics executive boarding his dog at taxpayer expense.... Defense industry overcharges resulted from a combination of the contractors gaming the system with a "catch me if you can" attitude and a lack of government oversight bordering on misfeasance and malfeasance.[2]

Dingell went on to list a series of purportedly outrageous charges the university had made to its indirect cost bills, some of which were legal under the existing rules, some of which were not, and all of which were maximally embarrassing. "What we have learned recently about Stanford," said the chairman, "has made Secretary Weinberger look frugal with his $600 toilet seat."

The chairman also made clear that anyone who might oppose his purposes risked becoming a target of the committee. "A final note," he said. "The American Association of Universities has been holding press conferences claiming that the real focus of the Subcommittee investigation should

2. House Committee on Energy and Commerce, Subcommittee on Oversight and Investigation, *Indirect Cost Recovery Practices at U.S. Universities for Federal Research Grants and Contracts,* 102d Cong., 1st sess., March 13, 1991, p. 1.

be on channeling more money to the universities—not a review of over-charging the taxpayers."[3]

Everything that looks like a fact in that sentence is incorrect, starting with the name of the organization. We had held no press conferences, had said nothing about what the focus of the investigation should be, and apart from a general predilection for higher research appropriations had urged nothing of the kind on the committee. What we had in fact done was to invite to our office several reporters who we thought might be covering the hearing, to explain to them what indirect costs were, how they were calculated, and what some of the issues were that made them controversial. Our assumption was that reporters had no reason ever to have learned anything about indirect costs, an assumption that was confirmed once again by subsequent coverage of the issue. Our real sin, however, as far as the committee was concerned, was to try to interfere, for whatever reason, in their relationship with the press. Dingell went on to say, "The AAU lobbies in Washington on behalf of the interests of 56 of the country's largest research universities. It is interesting to note that the President of the AAU is a former Vice President for Public Relations at Stanford and is provided with an adequate salary, an automobile and the use of a $1 million house on Massachusetts Avenue in Washington. We have also learned that AAU is supported by contributions from the major research universities. Not surprisingly, Stanford charged its $33,000 annual dues payment to AAU to government research"(5).

No political sophistication was required to recognize that as a shot across our bow, but to drive the point home, the committee wrote to every member university president to ask whether any part of the university's AAU dues was charged to their indirect cost rate. Nothing came of the inquiry, but the point of it had been not to solicit information but to intimidate.

The day went steadily downward. It was probably the single worst day for research universities in Washington during my time there. Stanford was represented at the hearing by its president, Donald Kennedy, and its board chair, James Gaither, a San Francisco attorney with extensive experience in Washington. Both were kept waiting throughout the day without a break for lunch while the committee heard from a carefully scripted list of witnesses called to testify about Stanford's crimes. Finally, in midafternoon, Stanford's witnesses were called to testify. Kennedy's opening statement was followed by an unremittingly hostile series of questions from Dingell and other committee members. Questions were provided to the members by the staff, but what was so striking was the common tone of contempt,

3. Ibid., 2–3.

disbelief, and derision that was directed toward the witnesses. Not since the days of the Students for a Democratic Society had I seen a university president treated in that way, and certainly never in the halls of Congress. I suppose one might have taken some comfort from the fact that the barrage was utterly nonpartisan. Republicans and Democrats alike had reached their conclusions before the evidence was even taken, and they rushed to outdo one another in putting themselves on the side of virtue by castigating the devil.

This was not a one-day story. Politics is a combination of short time horizons and long memories. The latter are aided by the existence of computerized databases readily available to the media. Every new story can be filled out by a rehash of old stories, so long as the reporter knows the right key words and punches the right buttons. As a result, for years even seemingly unrelated stories about research policy and funding would call up memories of the "Stanford scandal," editorialists constantly found in it useful cautionary tales, and politicians and public servants had a handy stick available whenever one was needed.

The rules had, indeed, changed, and they had changed in at least four ways:

First, as we have just seen, there was a change in the way in which those who came to Washington representing universities could be treated. There was less automatic deference, more wariness, and less differentiation between educators and other special interest groups pleading their case.

A second important change was brought on by universities themselves and had to do with the way in which they operated in Washington, the way in which they presented themselves to policy makers.

A third major change had to do with the kind of issues that came to dominate the agenda.

Finally, perhaps the most fundamental was a change in the view among government policy makers as to their obligation to support university funding. All of these changes are seen in the remainder of this chapter.

Universities in Washington

I had occasion around 1960 to look at the groups that were then representing higher education with offices in Washington. It was not difficult to do. It turned out that there were only about a score of them, and not all of those were involved in representing their members on public policy issues. In 1986, in preparation for a talk I was scheduled to give, I tried another count, and even after nearly four years in Washington, I was startled to find that the count was nearing 150. Clearly something very dramatic had happened in twenty-five years.

Actually, to a student of interest groups, what had happened was not surprising at all. Alexis de Tocqueville had long ago noted the propensity of Americans to form a group for every purpose, and Arthur Bentley, the first great student of political interest groups, pointed out in his pioneering book, *The Process of Government,* that whenever citizens are touched by the activities of government, their response is to form a group to protect or promote their interests. Pressure groups are older than the Republic, the first being the Knights of Cincinnatus, a group of Revolutionary War officers formed to lobby for a postwar bonus. Their numbers today include such organizations as the American Hot Dip Galvanizers Association, the Calendar Reform Political Action Group, the Chocolate Political Action Group, the Formaldehyde Institute, and the National Clearinghouse for Diet Pill Hazards, among many others.

It is not surprising, therefore, that as government became a more pervasive force in the life of colleges and universities, they responded as the Hot Dip Galvanizers did: by forming groups to represent their interests. That was a revealing process, because, as soon became apparent, higher education was far from the seamless web that its more romantic observers had thought it to be. It was a web to be sure, but with more seams than could be counted. At the institutional level, the American Association of State Colleges and Universities was formed because that growing class of institutions felt unrepresented by the National Association of State Universities and Land Grant Colleges. The National Association of Independent Colleges and Universities emerged out of conflicts over federal student aid programs in which private institutions felt they needed their own voice. A group of urban universities was formed, and historically black colleges had their group, followed by those that are predominantly Latino. Community colleges maintain a large organization, and there are several large groupings of proprietary institutions.

Faculty are no exception to the rule. The American Association of University Professors (AAUP), long the main interest group of faculty, was joined by the American Federation of Teachers and the National Education Association when unionization of faculty began to spread. And, as we have seen earlier, faculty organized themselves not as faculty but as members of their academic disciplines, and even those groups that had started with an office and a secretary on a single campus soon moved to Washington and developed a professional secretariat and a government relations arm. By the nature of their organizing principles and the fact that many members of scientific organizations are not employed as university faculty, the programs of science organizations focused on scientists as researchers. Other important parts of the faculty role were lower on the agenda and typically formed no part of the organizations' Washington activities.

As we have also seen, virtually every administrative role that exists on campus has its counterpart professional organization with offices in Washington and a staff working the government agencies to advance its members' agenda. It is not uncommon for such groups to have much more influence on national policy than their individual members have on their own campuses, the most striking example being the National Association of Student Aid Administrators. As the keepers of the technical knowledge required to navigate the unbelievably complicated federal student aid programs, their views of what constitutes sound student aid policy often carry more weight than those of the groups that represent the presidents of their institutions.

While working on tax issues, I was involved in an incident that provides a vivid example of that phenomenon. During one of the many considerations of the way the tax laws affect universities, the House Ways and Means Committee was holding hearings on the unrelated business income tax, or UBIT, as it is called. Charitable organizations, a category in the tax code that includes colleges and universities, are exempt from federal income taxes as long as their income is related to their charitable purposes. The definition of charitable purposes is necessarily imprecise; in fact, typically it has been quite broadly defined, providing the maximum exemption from taxes. However, a government strapped for revenue begins to look for revenue sources it is willing to forgo in better times, so there was much interest in narrowing the definition and increasing the yield. That more or less abstract impulse was abetted by organizations of small businesses that had long argued against what they saw as unfair competition from tax-exempt organizations. Small business in Washington ranks up there with the flag and the family as an object of uncritical veneration, and so the threat to the tax exemption was not an idle one.

Universities, of course, are no more happy about increased taxes than anyone else, and so the AAU argued against a narrowing of the definition. Unbeknownst to us, another voice in the debate was that of an organization of college bookstore operators, whose sales were among the natural targets of the tax reformers. Before we knew it, the lawyer-lobbyists who represented that group in Washington were floating proposals that would have held their clients harmless but would have imposed substantial taxation on other institutional activities.

When I heard about this group, of whose existence I had been totally unaware, I thought the time had come to try to make a point. I wrote to my members informing them of the situation and urging them to consider whether they or their bookstore operators spoke for their institutions. If the former, then perhaps they could make that clear to the latter. Fortunately, the current president of the bookstore group had just become director of the bookstore of a member institution whose president, a very blunt-talking individual, called him in and suggested that he had better decide where his loyalties lay. If they were to the university, then he should persuade his colleagues to stop making deals that could damage their institutions. Shortly thereafter, I was visited by the leadership of the bookstore group and their lawyer-lobbyists. They assured me that harming the universities or making special deals was the furthest thing from their minds, they would never dream of doing such a thing, and they could not understand how I could have gotten any other impression.

Message delivered, message received; but I have to say that this was the only occasion on which I was able to head off policies adverse to the interests of universities that were being advanced by another group purporting to speak for higher education.

The cacophony from this Babel of competing voices began to grow in the 1960s and was deafening in the 1970s and 1980s. Who, in such a situation, speaks for universities? The answer is everybody and nobody. In that setting, the process of representation is a constant struggle to keep a community of interest together among groups whose goals are not wholly congruent, to keep parts of that somewhat artificial community from straying off the reservation in pursuit of narrower interests, and, while doing that, to keep track of what one's own members might be doing on their own initiative and for their own purposes.

The last of these was no simple task, as individual universities became independent actors in Washington politics. As universities became more involved with the government, they slowly came to recognize that they needed people in their administration who were knowledgeable and experienced in the government's own peculiar ways. At first, the emphasis was on developing and sustaining contacts in the agencies that supported research, but that work really could only be done effectively by faculty whose relations with program officers grew naturally from shared scientific interests and a shared interest in higher appropriations. The role of administration typically was limited to information gathering and weak attempts at coordination.

The natural place for administrative intervention was in the Congress and at the political levels of the executive branch. In those venues, the political skills and the kind of access that university presidents command have high value. The role of the government relations specialist, therefore, typically was closely attached to the office of the president and was most often filled by a generalist who had some experience in, or at least knowledge of, the world of politics. Private universities were quicker than their public counterparts to recognize the need for such a role. Public universities had long had political specialists on their staffs, but their attention was directed to the state capitol, not Washington. In fact, most public universities were late to recognize the need to try to influence national policy. Until the 1980s, most were content to rely on their national organizations and occasional presidential visits with members of their congressional delegations.

Private universities were vulnerable to national policy in areas in which they could not fully rely on their organizations unless the universities actively worked to set the organization's agendas. It was this concern that lay behind the move to change the AAU in the late 1970s, a move that was led by the private members of the group. It was clear by then that on such issues as tax policy and indirect cost policy, the privates and the publics were differentially affected. Although the situation has changed dramatically in the 1990s, it was the private institutions that then depended so heavily on the nontaxability of charitable contributions and on liberal indirect cost rules. The publics, with a few exceptions, did not need to raise money from private donors, and their research infrastructure was typically funded by state appropriations. Indeed, in most cases, indirect costs recovered from federal research did not remain at the institution but went to the state treasury.

With the passage of time, those differences diminished. Many public universities developed aggressive fund-raising programs, and as they did, the level of their interest in the incentives to giving embedded in the tax code came to match that of the privates. By the time of the Tax Reform Act of 1986, their positions on those issues were indistinguishable, as was the urgency they felt in promoting them. They had come closer, too, on the subject of indirect costs. Significant differences still remained, but as state appropriations grew tighter, a corresponding interest grew in increasing federal grant and contract revenues.

New Alliances: Universities and Industry in Washington

In the mid-1980s another development complicated the job of representing universities. The issue of the competitiveness of American business in world markets arrived on the political agenda. It should be understood that an issue is different from a problem. A problem exists whether anyone is aware of it or not; an issue does not exist until someone successfully formulates a perceived problem in a way that catches public attention or, more accurately, the attention of opinion makers. Flag burning, for example, is an issue; it is not necessarily a problem. An issue may or may not be rooted in a real problem, though it will probably have a longer life if it is.

The issue of competitiveness did speak to some weaknesses in American business and in some government policies affecting business. What brought it into the public arena as a major theme was a report prepared by the Business–Higher Education Forum. The group had been formed at the initiative of the American Council on Education, and it consisted of equal numbers of college and university presidents and corporate CEOs. Competitiveness was the first of the topics it addressed, through a committee chaired by John Young, president of Hewlett Packard. As such things are often managed in Washington, it had been arranged that the report would be requested by the Reagan administration in order to give the exercise some official legitimacy. When the report was completed and submitted, it caught the attention of the White House, and it was received in a ceremony attended by the president himself. In a rush of enthusiasm, President Ronald Reagan agreed to accept one of the main recommendations of the report, the establishment of a presidential Council on Competitiveness to explore the matter further. John Young was appointed chair of that group.

Competitiveness was now officially an issue on the national agenda. Universities had been midwives at the birth, and they were deeply involved in the care and feeding of the child, a task requiring the formation of coalitions between universities and business groups, a new experience for all parties concerned. The first of the new alliances was called the Coalition for the Advancement of Industrial Technology, or CAIT (it is very hard to find short names for large coalitions), and it was begun in late 1984, headed by the ubiquitous John Young. Its single purpose was to lobby for the continuation of the research and development tax credit. The R&D Tax Credit was intended to be an incentive to companies to invest in research. Until it was given an extended life in the 1990s, its legislative life was like an episode of the "Perils of Pauline." It had a loyal group of supporters but never quite large enough a group to do more than eke out a year-by-year extension at the end of each congressional session. Largely because businesses could never quite count on its continued existence, the R&D Tax Credit failed to stimulate discernible new investment in research and so was constantly vulnerable to the charge that it was doing no good at all.

Universities stood to gain little from the credit, since it applied only to in-house corporate research. However, around 1984 the idea that industry would invest more heavily in university research was very much in the air, and when a high-powered business group approached a group of leading universities to make common cause, few were inclined to refuse. The AAU did not join CAIT. We believed that we needed our own separate agenda in the tax area and that the R&D Tax Credit as it then existed had little to offer and did not warrant the expenditure of our resources. However, a number of our member universities did join CAIT, and so we were well informed of its activities.

The Coalition for the Advancement of Industrial Technology was successful. In order to engage the full interests of the university partners, CAIT proposed a new Basic Research Tax Credit to stimulate industry support of research in universities. The R&D Tax Credit was extended in the Tax Reform Act of 1986, and the new credit was enacted, actions that were actually contrary to the broad thrust of the act, which was to eliminate tax loopholes or, to use the polite term, tax expenditures. In any case, it constituted the only "victory" for universities in the act.

The CAIT experience was important. It demonstrated to people in higher education that business brought a different level of influence, skill, and resources to advocacy and that where a common agenda could be identified, the combination of business and universities could accomplish together what neither could do alone. That is the classic basis for a coalition, and so it was not surprising that in 1987 a new organization, called the Council on Research and Technology (CORETECH) was created. The members were a group of high-tech companies and a group of universities (in both cases a larger number than had belonged to CAIT) and several educational and business associations, including, this time, the AAU. Most of the expenses of CORETECH were borne by the corporate members. Dues for the universities were just slightly above nominal.

The Council on Research and Technology was managed by Kenneth Kay, who had also managed CAIT. Kay was a young Washington lawyer whose good connections in the Congress stemmed from his service on the staff of Senator Max Baucus (Dem., Mont.), a senior member of the Senate Finance Committee. Stuart Eizenstat, another veteran of CAIT, was retained as CORETECH's principal lobbyist. Eizenstat was a true Washington mover and shaker. He had come to Washington from Atlanta as a principal member of President Jimmy Carter's White House staff, and like so many young people who come to Washington, he had stayed—in this case as a partner in a law firm, a leading lobbyist, and a major figure in the Democratic Party. Add to Kay and Eizenstat the Washington representatives of many of America's leading high-tech corporations, and CORETECH brought to bear on its issues more political firepower than had ever before been directed to issues in which universities were involved.

The Coalition for the Advancement of Industrial Technology had been a single-issue organization. The Council on Research and Technology was designed to address a wider range of issues. The question was, which issues? The corporations involved had no doubt about their agenda. First on that agenda for most was to gain an extension of a provision of the tax code that enabled research expenditures incurred abroad to be deductible as a business expense on their domestic tax. Large amounts of money were at stake, and the efforts devoted to it were intense. Universities, of course, had no interest in the issue, nothing to contribute to it, and no particular desire to be associated with it. Second on the agenda was the extension of the R&D Tax Credit and the Basic Research Tax Credit that had been linked to it. On those issues, there was no problem in working in harness.

The difficulty with the coalition was that while the tax issues were more than enough to insure industry interest, they would not have long sustained the interest of research universities. A university agenda had to be developed for which the industry members were willing to give their support. Endless meetings ensued, and it was finally decided that the most important item on the universities' priority list was passage of a bill creating a program to support new and renovated research facilities, to be administered by the National Science Foundation. That was an uphill battle. There was ample evidence that, in spite of the rash of building on campuses through the 1980s, the withdrawal of the federal government from its facilities programs had left a large and growing backlog of needs. Persuading the government to reenter the facilities business had long been a university goal. Moreover, the goal had been given urgency by the rise of earmarking. Many of us hoped that a regularly authorized and appropriated program in the National Science Foundation would take some of the pressure off the earmarking impulse and would, at the very least, answer the argument that earmarks were the only way to get federal money for facilities.

The proposed bill was a minefield of political obstacles. It was opposed by the Office of Management and Budget, which saw the facilities problem as so large that any federal contribution could do little to solve it and believed that programs that begin small have a way of growing very large with the passage of time. There was certainly experience to support that view, and there was little dispute about the size of the problem. In 1986, a panel of the White House Science Council chaired by David Packard had set the magnitude of the facilities deficit at $10 billion. The panel recommended that a fund be set up in the National Science Foundation in the amount of $5 billion, to be spent over ten years and matched dollar-for-dollar with nonfederal funds. Under the circumstances, it is not surprising that, to the budget watchers, every new piece of evidence in support of the need for a facilities program was cause for further alarm. The bill was also met with great skepticism by scientific groups that feared, not entirely without reason, that when budgets were so tight, every dollar spent for the construction of buildings would be one dollar not available for the conduct of research.

Notwithstanding those obstacles, the bill passed—or, I should say, a bill passed. The bill that entered the process was narrowly targeted at research facilities and would have required peer review of proposals. It was pretty much a throwback to the programs of the 1950s and 1960s. What emerged from the process was hardly recognizable. It authorized a five-year program, starting at $85 million and moving up to $250 million annually. The funds were to be used primarily for renovation of existing buildings, and they were for use at all institutions of higher education, independent research institutions, research museums, and consortia, with various assurances that the money would be spread among them. Concessions to the major research universities, whose facilities deficit had provided the impetus for the bill, were traded away incrementally at each stage of the process in order to win the support needed to pass any bill. There are two ways of describing what had happened. One is that a proposal based on a narrow interest had been broadened by the addition of a collection of other narrow interests. The second is that a good idea had been hijacked and held for ransom by others who saw an opportunity to make a profit. Both descriptions are accurate.

The outcome of the facilities legislation led to the most serious political error I made during my time in Washington. The passage of the bill required an appropriation in order to put it in operation. However, the bill that had passed contained in it very little for the AAU members, and it seemed reasonable to ask whether they wanted to support the appropriation, knowing that to do so would put them at odds with some of their own faculty, who feared that more money for buildings meant less money for their research. It seemed a reasonable question, but as I should have known and surely learned, it was the wrong question at the wrong time. The Executive Committee of the AAU responded to the question rationally and voted to support the appropriation only if the funds for the program were in addition to the 14 percent increase for the NSF that was in the president's budget, clearly an unattainable condition. But it was a question that should never have been asked. When one works with a group of allies toward an agreed-on goal, one is obligated to support the result, even if it is not an entirely favorable one. In legislation, one never gets everything one wants; that is understood at the outset. As I learned when I reported our decision to our allies in CORETECH, the only thing to do is to swallow your disappointment and take what you have been given. The anger and incredulity that greeted our decision never wholly dissipated. We lost influence within the coalition and lost momentum on other issues. In a time when cynicism about politics is so high, keeping one's word and honoring commitments is still the bedrock of the system. By asking a question that I should not have asked, I caused us to break our word, and the price was high, as it should have been.

The Council on Research and Technology continued to exist until 1993, but its condition had seriously deteriorated by the time of its demise. No single event led to the end. Rather, I believe, it became increasingly clear both to the research universities and to the businesses involved that common interests may produce temporary alliances but are not enough to make stable marriages. The search for issues on which to collaborate became increasingly artificial, and the cultural and stylistic differences between the two parties always made for an uneasy relationship. The business lobbyists who came to meetings could never understand how the university people could talk so much without coming to a conclusion. And the university people, for their part, could never bring themselves to the kind of crisp definition of goals and tactics that to the business people seemed second nature. In Washington, opportunistic alliances may work on a specific issue, but the natural and useful relationships between business and universities take place between scientists in the respective laboratories and, at a higher level of abstraction, between university presidents and corporate CEOs. Efforts to use one another in Washington may look promising but generally do not yield rich results.

I would certainly not argue that this nearly decade-long effort to create a political coalition between research universities and industry was actively harmful to the university cause. It did absorb a great deal of energy, but it also produced some useful, if marginal, results. Perhaps its most lasting effect, though, was its contribution to the erosion of a distinctive university presence in Washington. Every joint visit to a representative or senator blurred the line between the two groups and reinforced the legislators' sense that an interest is an interest and that a lobbyist is a lobbyist is a lobbyist.

The Pursuit of Private Interests: Earmarking

The task of representing universities became incomparably more difficult as the university community moved from the organized pursuit of collective interests to the unorganized pursuit of separate institutional interests, the most visible manifestation of which was the growth of earmarked appropriations. That some universities had their own individual interests to promote was certainly not new. Princeton's interest in high-temperature fusion, for example, or Stanford's in its Linear Accelerator Center, could not be dealt with within an organization of institutions that operated only on the basis of shared interests. With rare exceptions, pursuit of specialized interests did not compete with the broader goals that these institutions shared with others. Nor was there anything new in the fact that universities competed with one another. Indeed, competition for students, faculty, and research funds, while it could sometimes take unhealthy forms, was widely believed to be a source of strength for American universities. However, nothing like the forces unleashed by earmarking had appeared before. They made the job of trying to harness the energies of a group of universities that had enough natural differences in the best of times many-fold harder.

I have already described the origins of the issue and suggested the tensions and animosities it provoked between those who sought earmarks and those who believed that it was wrong to do so. But I have not yet explained why the stakes were so high and why the politics of the issue were so difficult. The most obvious measure of the stakes is the number of dollars involved. I think it is fair to say that when the first major earmarks appeared in 1983, even those of us who were alarmed at their appearance did not foresee how large a business it would become. The *Chronicle of Higher Education,* which keeps score on earmarks, reported in 1996 that earmarks had dropped from a 1993 high of $763 million to $296 million. In 1997, however, the amount rose again to $440 million, in a year marked by extreme budget stringency. Notwithstanding those pressures, the Congress was prepared to appropriate large sums of money for buildings and projects that had not been subjected to any scientific review, had not been requested by any research-supporting agency, and had not been competed for by any other interested group of scientists.

In retrospect it is clear that the earmark epidemic was a disease waiting to happen. There has always been a festering grievance hidden within the American research support system. The process of peer or merit review, in which investigators compete for funds and the competition is judged by qualified technical people (either panels of scientists or agency program officers) puts primary weight on the scientific quality of the proposer and the proposal. It rewards past success, thereby increasing the odds of future success. Moreover, in the academic world, the best way to recruit high-quality people is with the presence of other successful people. Thus, quality begets further quality and, over time, clusters in a relatively small number of institutions.

There are other considerations that tend to lead to the same result. Institution building really has local roots. A strong fund-raising base, whether residing in the state legislature or in a generous group of donors, is required in order to build the critical mass of faculty and students that will make an institution competitive for research funds. Those universities that were strong before the war obviously had a large advantage when competing for funds after the war, and they tended to be clustered in the Northeast, in the Great Lakes area, and in California. Those institutions that successfully built strong science programs after the war, institutions such as UCLA, Stanford, and the University of Washington, tended to be located in regions that had a strong economic base and educational and political leaders with the imagination to see the coming possibilities and the skill to exploit them. That is still the case. In recent years, the universities that have made the greatest gains in research support and underlying quality have been those in the newly prosperous states of the so-called Sun Belt.

There have always been more universities that felt excluded from the benefits of the system and states that felt unfairly treated and, therefore, members of Congress ready to change the system if the opportunity should arise. Thus, the pressure for greater geographic distribution of research funds has been present almost from the beginning of federal funding of research, and it has periodically produced efforts to spread the money more widely. The most ambitious of such programs is EPSCoR (Experimental Program to Stimulate Cooperative Research), a program of the National Science Foundation aimed at helping states help their universities build research capacity that will make them more competitive for grants.

It would be nice to believe that truth, in combat with error, is bound to prevail. The history of this issue makes that hard to credit. The truth is that, for all the advantages that accrue to leading research institutions and for all the clustering of funding they produce, the research support system has been remarkably open. As one would expect, indeed, as one would want in dealing with institutions like universities, rapid swings of support and quality have been infrequent, and institutional rankings have tended to be quite stable over time. Still, top universities have slipped and others have moved to higher ground. More to the point, the top universities have accounted for a diminishing share of federal research funding in every decade since the 1950s. In 1952, the ten universities that performed the most research, measured in dollar volume, took 43.2 percent of the federal research funds; by 1990, they won only 20.1 percent.[4] That is a large share for ten institutions, but the enormous growth in funding over that period meant that many universities built large research enterprises and had them funded in part with federal dollars. By the end of the 1980s, 100 universities were receiving $25 million or more in research funding from the federal government.

In politics, deprivation is not absolute, it is relative. It consists of measuring oneself against others and, if the measurement is unflattering, looking for ways to tip the scales. In research support, as in every other phenomenon that can be scaled numerically, half the population is below average and is likely to resent the other half. Among research universities,

---

4. Roger Geiger and Irwin Feller, "The Dispersion of Academic Research in the 1980s," *Journal of Higher Education* 66, no. 3 (May/June 1995): 337.

more than half felt themselves to be below average, and they knew that the reason was that the top universities had managed to rig the system so as to exclude them.

That is a powerful political impulse. It was unleashed by the belief that grew in the 1980s that having a major research university in a state was a key to economic development. It is true that wealthy states tend to have strong universities, though it is far from clear which is cause and which is effect, but the belief was enough to transform the politics of research support. The progression is clear: What had been an issue of science policy became an issue of economic benefits and, in our political system, economic benefit becomes political currency. When constituency benefits were perceived, research funds became fair game for political trading.

There was nothing terribly subtle or arcane about this, as I learned in a 1985 encounter with Senator Mark Hatfield, a Republican from Oregon, as good a friend as higher education had in the Congress until his retirement in 1997 and, at the time of this incident, chairman of the Senate Appropriations Committee. Senator Hatfield was also a good friend of the Oregon Health Sciences University, and he had helped obtain several buildings for that institution in recent years. One such had been included in the Department of Defense appropriations bill that went to the floor of the Senate in June 1985. The bill also included a number of other university earmarks. A group of senators, led by Sam Nunn (Dem., Ga.) and John Danforth (Rep., Mo.), ambushed the bill on the floor. Moved by a mixture of motives, including concern over the erosion of the research support system that the earmarks portended and the usual animosity of members of authorizing committees toward the appropriations committees because of the sometimes cavalier disregard of the former by the latter, the insurgents managed to strip the bill of the earmarks.

The debate on the Nunn-Danforth amendment was memorable for a number of reasons, not the least of which was Senator Russell Long's (Dem., La.) dismissal of peer review. "I understand there's something called a pear review system. I don't know what pear review is, but it appears that we don't have any of those pears in Louisiana."

Stripped of the earmarks, the bill went to conference with the House, and several weeks later it came back to the Senate with all of the original earmarks and a list of new ones added by the House conferees. Prepared for battle this time, the Appropriations Committee was able to defeat another attempt to remove the offending provisions.

As it happens, the AAU had not been involved at all in the decision to challenge the earmarks. That was entirely the decision of the senators involved. Once the battle had been joined, however, we pitched in with our support. When it was all over and the dust had settled, we were informed by a friend on Senator Hatfield's staff that he was less than happy with us. Powerful committee chairmen do not like to be challenged, and they like even less losing a vote in public. It was suggested that it would be a good idea for me to meet with Senator Hatfield, and a luncheon meeting was arranged.

When the day came, we met in the grand office in the Capitol reserved for the chairman of the Appropriations Committee, a room that eloquently testifies to the power and privilege of the office. We had a fine lunch, during which we spoke quietly and rationally about our mutual ties to Stanford and about the reasons for our disagreement. Neither of us persuaded the other, but since the main purpose of the meeting was atmospheric rather than substantive, that was all right. As I was leaving, the senator put his hand on my shoulder and said, "You know, Bob, you can't beat me." I replied that I was pretty sure that he was right about that, but why did he think that was so. He replied by taking from his inside coat pocket a paper with two lists of names on it. "The names on the left side," he said, "are senators to whom I have promised something. The ones on the right side are senators who want something from me. I can change them from one side to the other whenever I want. That's why you can't beat me."

It was all said in the most friendly way, and he was right, of course. He taught me that it was virtually impossible to beat an earmark once it had surfaced in the appropriations process. Opposition to specific earmarks could only antagonize the proposing member, with very little chance of winning. It was a bad bargain, as a considerably less friendly Senator Alphonse D'Amato (Rep., N.Y.) let me know when we opposed an earmark for his alma mater, Syracuse University. At the climax of a lengthy and acrimonious phone call, he told me that a member of my staff who was also a Syracuse alum "should be strung up by his balls" for opposing his own university. I assured my colleague that I was pretty sure the senator did not mean it literally.

The growing practice of earmarking brought benefits to some universities, but it threatened to strike a major blow to one of the cornerstones of American science policy, and it became a considerable political liability. The nature of the debate, at least in its more polite form, is suggested by testimony given before the Task Force on Science Policy of the House Committee on Science and Technology in June of 1985. The task force had undertaken an ambitious review of science policy, and this particular hearing was directed to the topic of science in the political process. The first witness was John R. Silber, president of Boston University. Dr. Silber was an aggressive and successful seeker of earmarks for his university and a vigorous and effective advocate of the practice. A philosopher by training, not surprisingly he grounded his position in an ancient philosophical debate over the role of experts in politics. As against the Platonic preference for a society designed and run by an expert elite, Silber chose the Aristotelian view from the *Politics* that "if the people are not utterly degraded, although individually they may be worse judges than those who have special knowledge—as a body they are as good or better."[5] He found in that view a fundamental principle of American democracy: that "in matters affecting society as a whole those whose lives are affected—the people—are likely to be better judges than any class of experts."

"In this context", he continued,

> much of the confusion that has obscured the subject of "science in the political process" disappears. Do federal investments in science involve merely technical scientific issues? Obviously not. Every thinking person knows that the massive federal support for science and technology that began during World War II and that has continued up to the present reflects America's rise to world leadership and our national need to retain military and industrial primacy in the face of the military threat posed by the Soviet Union and the economic and industrial threat posed by Japan and other nations. . . . In recent months, however, certain sectors of the scientific community, including a quintessential special interest group, the trade association for the major research universities, have engaged in much public hand-wringing. The pretext for these cries of alarm is not a revolutionary change in congressional policy towards scientific research. Instead it is claimed to arise from just fifteen congressional actions, amounting to a total appropriation of approximately $100 million, to help fifteen universities build new or improved facilities.(53)

Silber went on to reject the argument that these actions threatened the practice of peer review. He saw peer review as a practice affecting projects receiving only a small fraction of federal research funding, largely limited to the National Institutes of Health, the National Science Foundation, and the Department of Energy, and he professed not to understand how these few congressionally appropriated projects could affect those agencies. Indeed, the creation of new facilities would actually strengthen the peer review system by enlarging the number of competitors for grants.

Not satisfied with strengthening peer review, he went on to explain why in practice it is a seriously flawed method of distributing funds. "The peer review system, instead of working to realize the intent of Congress to broaden the institutional and geographic base of scientific research in this

5. Testimony of John Silber, House Committee on Science and Technology, Hearings before the Task Force on Science Policy, "Science in the Political Process," 99th Cong., 1st sess., p. 52.

country, has worked to create a tightly knit old-boy network. . . . In practice the NSF and the system of peer review have produced precisely the undue concentration of scientific research and education that the Congress has been concerned to avoid" (57).

That was a peculiar argument coming from the president of a university in Boston, the home of one of the largest concentrations of research funding in the nation, of which Boston University was a major part. Indeed, at the time of Silber's testimony, Boston University, though not an AAU member, received more federal funds than about half of the member universities. Nevertheless, he saw in the opposition to earmarking only that

> those institutions that were first to establish their excellence have shortsightedly decided that they shall restrict membership in the scientific establishment to themselves. . . . In these circumstances, it is hardly surprising that the rich get richer—or that the disadvantaged seek relief from the Congress. The Congress was created in part to prevent such exclusionary practices. For despite the intentions of Congress, federal policies towards scientific research have operated to create in effect two castes of research universities, and it is not merely appropriate but in conformity with national goals established by Congress for the "have-not" institutions to seek federal support to redress the imbalance that currently exists. (58)

I have quoted Dr. Silber's testimony at some length both because it is a strong statement of a position that deserves to be heard and because it is easy to see in it the seeds of the political problems the practice of earmarking caused. First, the argument in support of earmarking quickly becomes ad hominem, with respect to organizations and classes of universities if not to individuals. At one point, he describes the "establishment" as an OPEC-like cartel seeking to preserve a self-serving status quo. While clothed in the language of disinterested philosophical discourse, Silber's case is at bottom an argument about motives; it is essentially disrespectful of the motives of those with whom he disagrees. Second, it is an expression of the politics of grievance. It invites the Congress to treat universities and their proposals not on their merits but on the basis of an asserted injustice. It is a common argument for federal assistance, and in some areas of social policy it may carry considerable force. To introduce it into decisions about science policy, however, does a disservice to science and the public by suggesting that there is a basis other than informed judgment about the work to be done that will protect good science and at the same time protect the public's investment in it. Finally, Silber's is an explicitly divisive position. It invites the Congress to choose sides in a contest between the haves and the have-nots. It is truly difficult to see how good can come from that old war fought in this new arena.

As it happened, I followed Dr. Silber at the witness table. Not surprisingly, I cast the issue somewhat differently:

> I want to discuss with you an extremely important question of science policy, one that has taken on a new and special urgency in recent years. In its broadest and most useful form, that question is: What role should the Congress play in making decisions that affect the conduct of scientific and technological research?
>
> You will note that this is not the related question that is so frequently asked, namely: What is the proper role of experts and specialists in making policy that has significant scientific content? That question has an ancient and honorable historical lineage and has been the object of a body of literature that has grown larger as the importance of science and technology has grown larger. . . . I want to consider with you the role of the nonexpert—the member of Congress—in making policies that will profoundly affect what science is done, where it will be done, and who will do it. (120)

I went on to point out that the Congress actually played a variety of roles in scientific policy in addition to authorizing programs and appropriating money for them. The Congress was deeply involved in regulatory issues such as the use of human subjects and animals in research, the propriety of fetal tissue research, and a variety of environmental issues. It also had an important early warning and oversight role.

> The health of science in the United States is intimately connected with the wisdom of a large number and wide range of decisions made in this legislative body.
>
> It is important to understand, especially so for members of the academic and scientific communities, that the Congress is so deeply involved in science policy because so many issues of science policy touch on important values and interests of the citizenry, and because they are frequently causes of conflict. Issues of that description often find their way into the political arena in a democratic society. That is not something to apologize for; it is something to take pride in, even though the processes of resolution are often messy and in some respects perhaps less satisfactory than some hypothetical ideal.
>
> Having said that, it is also necessary to say that not all issues of that description are best dealt with through political instrumentalities, even though they could be. On occasion, political leaders, like judges, refrain from involving themselves in issues for a variety of reasons, including the judgment that other means are clearly preferable, and to preempt those means would produce less desirable results and do a disservice to the public.

The task of Congress with respect to ... science policy is to decide where to be active and where to exercise restraint; where its distinctive ways of reaching agreement will promote the public's interest in science and technology and where it will not. ... What is called for is the development of a set of expectations about Congressional behavior based on thoughtful consideration of the requirements of politics, the requirements of science and technology, and the nature of the decisions to be made. (121)

I suggested that the task force consider the classification of facilities projects recently put forward by the Committee on Science, Engineering, and Public Policy of the National Academy of Sciences. That group had outlined four kinds of projects:

1. National facilities, intended to serve a national, often international, research community—for example, the Fermi Lab

2. University-based research facilities—for example, a new or renovated chemistry building

3. Regional research facilities, often based at a university—for example, the Triangle Universities Nuclear Laboratory in Durham, North Carolina

4. Technology centers, usually located at or affiliated with universities and tied to local or regional economies—for example, the Basic Industry Research Institute at Northwestern University

I suggested that the first two project categories represented end points on a continuum, with the others standing in between. The siting of national facilities would always be heavily involved in politics, while facilities for individual universities should not be. The competition for regional facilities and technology centers would probably spill over into the Congress, but in every case, in all four categories, no decision should be made until the competitors had been evaluated by a merit review process. Even in the case of projects justified by their contribution to economic development, bad science would not produce good economics, and separating the good from the bad required more than the testimonials of the presidents of the competing institutions.

From the steady increase of earmarks it is easy to determine which side won the argument in the Congress. Still, it was important to make the case for the primacy of merit review, for the proposition that quality matters—that, as Phillip Handler once put it, "In science, the best is vastly more important than the next best" and that a system that does not attempt even to look for quality is less likely on the average to find it than one that does.

Those who purported to oppose the "old-boy" network in science had turned to the oldest old-boy network of all, the congressional pork barrel, to defeat it. In the process they made themselves indistinguishable from those who work the appropriations committees on behalf of defense contractors, dam builders, and hot dip galvanizers. It was a high price to pay, not unlike the price of the Tragedy of the Commons: No harm is done if one farmer grazes an extra cow on the common, and there is a clear advantage to him in doing so. But if every farmer does so in his own self-interest, the common will be destroyed for all.

One footnote to Dr. Silber's and my testimony: Dr. Silber had left the hearing before I testified. A month or so later, having read my testimony, he wrote me a letter. He pointed to some areas on which we agreed and took issue on some others. At the close of his letter, he made the only point in our entire exchange that angered me:

> My final comments are directed not to an individual point, but rather to the pervasive suggestion throughout your testimony that the democratic process itself is suspect. This was explicit in your discussion of the Columbia University chemistry project and of the economic development rationale for facilities funding, but was less subtle elsewhere.
>
> You complained, for example, that "national exemplar" and "national demonstration" projects "demonstrate only the political manipulation of Congressional authorizations and appropriations processes." Such a statement, implying that any project labeled "national" will win Congressional approval, imputes to the Congress a degree of gullibility that is hardly justified by the facts. In my experience of members of Congress, they are not only far shrewder, but they are far more high-minded and rational than you give them credit for. I would expect that they would be amused by the suggestion, made elsewhere in your testimony, that they need the help of AAU to defend them against the "illegitimate demands" of their constituents.

I replied as follows:

> Finally, I know of no conception of democracy, save that which is always coupled with the term "peoples," which requires agreement with any course of action chosen by any agency of government and which demands constant flattery of the wisdom of policy-makers when one genuinely believes that they may be headed in the wrong direction. If you found any suggestion in my testimony, much less a pervasive one, that I believe that the democratic process is suspect, then either you failed to read the state-

ment carefully enough or your understanding of the democratic process bears no relation to the system of government which has been practiced in this country for the last two hundred years.

Eight years later, in June 1993, the same committee, now chaired by George Brown (Dem., Calif.), an avowed foe of earmarking, held another set of hearings on the subject, and I was once again asked to testify. This time, having left the AAU, I spoke for no one but myself. "My own view," I began,

> is that science funding through primarily political processes and without regard to careful judgment of the scientific merits of the work to be done is a pernicious practice, destructive of high-quality science, wasteful of the public's money, and erosive of public confidence in the integrity of universities and the political process. Those who see the matter differently are prone to argue that they would really prefer not to seek earmarks, but they are forced to do so because there are no regularly authorized and peer-reviewed facilities programs to which needful institutions can apply. That strikes me as roughly akin to arguing that, because the bank will not lend you money for the purpose for which you want it, you are justified in robbing the bank.[6]

I saw no cause for optimism and no reason to provide false reassurance or insincere flattery.

> There, Mr. Chairman, is the root cause of earmarking: It is in the political interests of Members of Congress to help their constituencies, and it is in the institutional interests of university presidents . . . to find ways to help their Congressmen to help their constituencies. No proposal I have seen for limiting earmarking addresses the root cause, and so none seems to me to have much chance of success. Of one thing I am reasonably confident. The answer to the problem does not lie within the rules of the Congress. What has been unleashed in the last decade into the middle of science policy is one of the most powerful impulses of our entire political system, namely, that of constituency interest. The wonder is that, for so long, science seemed to be largely exempt from its operation. My speculative explanation for that fact is that it is only relatively recently that those Congressmen and Senators who created the system passed from the scene, and those who succeeded them have, understandably perhaps, a less proprietary feeling for the institutions and practices they inherited. . . . The fact remains that the Congress shows little ability or inclination to stop its

6. House Committee on Science, Space, and Technology, Hearing on Academic Earmarks, "Academic Earmarks," 103d Cong., 1st sess., June 16, 1993, p. 10.

appropriating committees from engaging in earmarking in any area. . . . Proposals to require authorizing of projects before they can be appropriated, while well-meaning, may only enlarge the number of Members who have leverage on behalf of their constituencies and would, in any case, be easy to overcome in the appropriations process. . . .

It pains me to say it, but the genie, I fear, is out of the bottle, and it is notoriously hard to put it back. (16)

Tax Policy: Universities in Gucci Gulch

The 1980s was the decade of tax reform. The Tax Reform Act of 1986 was the culmination of several decades of academic writing and political pamphleteering aimed at pressing home the argument that, so far as government finance is concerned, a tax benefit conferred on an individual or an economic entity is the equivalent of an appropriation of funds for the same purpose, with the difference that appropriations must be made every year and so reconfirmed every year, while tax benefits are given once and need never be reviewed. The ideal tax code in this formulation would be one that taxed all income, without exception, at whatever rate was required to meet the obligations of government, and those obligations would be determined through the regular legislative process.

It is an idea that combines equity and efficiency in an appealing package, and many reform movements, including the currently popular flat-tax movement, have been efforts to reach the Holy Grail of equity and efficiency. These efforts have always run afoul of the same problem, namely, it is no more likely that tax policy will be taken out of politics than it is that politics will be eliminated from appropriations decisions. Too many people seek advantages from both, and in a representative political system, elected representatives do not want to be insulated from what their constituents want. More often, as the earmarking battle showed, they prefer to give their constituents what they want.

In 1985 and 1986, though, the stars appeared to be in alignment, and a consensus appeared to exist across party lines that the tax code had become far too complicated, too encrusted with uneconomic and unfair loopholes, too large a factor in economic decisions that would be better made if tax advantages were not at stake, and too unpopular with the public, which was showing its displeasure through lower levels of compliance and a general orneriness about taxes. The time seemed right for a major assault on the tax code, whose aim would be simplification, fewer loopholes, and lower rates.

That was bad news for universities. The Congress had long ago decided that it was in the public interest to encourage philanthropy by offering individuals a considerable tax advantage for giving their money to charity rather than keeping it for private consumption or for transfer to the next generation. All private colleges and universities in the country, and a growing number of public institutions, depended for their economic well-being on the deductibility from income of charitable contributions. Assuming a hypothetical tax rate of 50 percent, a gift of a dollar to charity would cost the giver only fifty cents; the other fifty cents was, in effect, a free match to the charity from the government. Under such a system, universities and other charities clearly benefited from high marginal tax rates and unlimited deductibility. Any serious move to eliminate tax benefits and to lower rates was a potential threat to a major source of institutional funding. Since it was hardly advisable to argue against lower tax rates, it became all the more important to forestall any restrictions on giving.

Even more was at stake. In recent years, private universities in many states had become able to issue tax-exempt bonds under state authority. That had touched off a wave of building, financed by bond issues. At the same time, the whole practice of allowing tax-exempt bonding under public authority had come under attack because it was being used to enable highly profitable corporations to borrow at lower rates, presumably to stimulate economic development, with the taxpayer footing the bill for taxes forgone. That practice was clearly targeted for severe restriction, at the least, and it was not easy to explain why the higher-education benefit should be treated differently.

Finally, questions were being raised about the tax deductibility of employer-paid education benefits. Part-time degree programs, often linked to local businesses and their employees, had become a large and growing market for many colleges and universities. There was no dispute about the desirability of these educational programs; the question was whether they should be subsidized by the ordinary, nonrecipient taxpayer or by the employee, who would presumably derive economic benefit from the advanced education. In the eyes of the tax reformers, it was simply a benefit on which recipients should be taxed as they would be taxed on other employment-related compensation. In their eyes there was no more reason to subsidize this form of education through the tax code than any other form. As the issue was seen in colleges and universities that offered such programs, taxing the employee for the company-paid tuition would raise the price of the education to the student and undoubtedly lower the demand for it.

Never before had universities been forced to fight on so many tax fronts simultaneously. Equally important, the provisions at risk affected different parts of the community differentially. The threat to the charitable deduction was of much greater importance to the private sector, notwithstanding the increasingly active fund-raising programs of some public universities. The threat to tax-exempt bonding was of interest exclusively to private institutions and to only a subset of those, consisting of universities whose revenue streams would support the repayment of large bonded indebtedness. The employee tuition benefit interested the public sector more than the private, though there was some crossover on that issue. Holding together a coalition on such diverse issues was going to be no easy task.

I do not believe that any other issue produced such intense coalition building and the need for so much coalition maintenance activity. It was never possible to reach complete agreement on priorities among all of the parties involved: the Independent Sector (an umbrella coalition of charitable groups), private colleges, private universities, public universities, arts organizations, private schools, museums, and on and on. Inability to reach agreement on what we wanted most and then to speak for it with a single voice probably had a high cost. At the very end of the process, when Senator Robert Packwood (Rep., Ore.) and Representative Dan Rostenkowski (Dem., Ill.), the chairmen of the two tax-writing committees, were closeted together, it was not possible to send a unified message stating what we thought most important and what we were willing to forgo.

The result was a resounding defeat for higher education. Contributions of appreciated assets—stocks and real estate, for example—were to be deducted at their purchase price, not their appreciated value at the time of the gift, and charitable contributions were subject to the alternative minimum tax. Tax-exempt bonding was capped at $100 million per university, a total that most of the major private universities had already exceeded.

It was the worst defeat on tax issues that higher education had ever suffered, and probably the most comprehensive defeat for higher education on any issue. Always in the past, when tax policy was at stake, universities were able to deal with issues one at a time and to cast them as issues not of tax policy but of educational policy. University leaders are persuasive when talking about educational matters; they are far less so when forced to defend their preferred tax status. In the context of the omnibus tax reform bill—whose whole purpose was to drive home the point that the only thing that mattered was tax policy—universities and their charitable allies were swept up in the tide and were indistinguishable from every other interest defending its tax breaks.

The most vivid symbols of the Tax Reform Act were the corridors outside the meeting rooms of the House Ways and Means Committee, the Senate Finance Committee, and, at the final stage, the Conference Committee. They were given the generic name of Gucci Gulch, after the expensive footwear of the lobbyists who patrolled the corridors waiting to pounce on members as they came and went from their closed meetings.[7] The representatives of higher education may have been wearing Florsheims rather than Guccis, but they were right there in the corridors, and it is hard to see how members would have seen them as different from the bankers and insurance companies alongside whose lobbyists we stood and clamored.

I do not mean to suggest that there was an alternative that would have been more successful. Certainly I was unable to think of one at the time, nor have I been able to since. Circumstances had conspired to dictate a certain course of action. Unfortunately, that course, together with the lobbying for earmarks, acted to help strip from higher education its reputation as less self-interested, less self-regarding, and more public-spirited than all of the other supplicants who come before the Congress. As that difference was eroded, we lost some part of the one great advantage we had always enjoyed. Laments over lost innocence are always tedious, but that should not blind us to the fact that, even though unavoidable, the loss is real and lasting.

Indirect Costs: Who Owes What to Whom?

The last in this list of issues of the 1980s that changed the rules of the game is the driest, dullest, most arcane issue in all of higher education: the rules governing the reimbursement of the indirect costs of research. Indeed, shortly after I had arrived in Washington and found it necessary to dive into the issue, it seemed clear to me that there was no issue of principle involved at all, that it had to do solely with money, and that money issues should, in theory, be easy to solve because compromises involving money are obvious.

I think I was about half right. Government officials who repeatedly attempted to change the rules in order to limit reimbursement were largely driven to do so for budgetary reasons. They sometimes tried to justify their actions in the rhetoric of waste, fraud, and abuse—the first resort of budget cutters—but it was really money that they were after. However, I could not have been more wrong about the way the university world viewed the issue. It is not a gross exaggeration to say that the issue of indirect cost reimbursement was a grand morality play in which administrators saw the government as reneging on its promises and saw faculty as self-regarding and unconcerned about the health of their institutions, and faculty saw their administrations as taking money that they had rightfully earned by virtue of their scientific competence and diverting it from their laboratories to other university purposes.

7. The best book on the Tax Reform Act of 1986 is *Showdown at Gucci Gulch*, by Jeffrey H. Birnbaum and Alan S. Murray (New York: Random House, 1978).

There is a natural tendency to try to make issues of money into issues of principle in order to gain the moral high ground in the negotiations over money, and some of that could be seen here. But I think there was more involved; the parties really believed in their positions, and because they did, they were revealing some profound truths about the way faculty and administrators think of their institutions and about the nature of the relationship between the university and the government, the defining relationship of the modern American university. The place to start is with that relationship and specifically with how the wish to believe a metaphor has clouded reality, raised false expectations, and bred resentment.

Universities and Government: The Myth of Partnership

There is no word more cherished, and more overworked, in the literature of government-university relations than the word *partnership*. What an image it conveys. One imagines Sears and Roebuck, or Ben and Jerry, friends and colleagues working together toward mutual ends, with respect for one another and a commitment not to put personal interests ahead of mutual interests. It suggests a set of rules governing the behavior of the partners, rules that may even in some manner be enforceable.

The wish is father to the thought. The fact is that government is nobody's partner, and a democratic government least of all. Representative government is supposed to respond to the changing needs and priorities of the citizenry, and that means that any promises made are good only for so long as the needs that gave rise to them are not overridden by more pressing ones. Elections happen with predictable regularity. Congress and the presidency change hands. Today's advocates may be returned home by the voters tomorrow, to be replaced by others of very different views. New and pressing interests arise, and they must be accounted for, even by one's friends. That is all the regular stuff of governing. It does not mean that government lies or acts irresponsibly. It may do both at various times, but the more relevant truth is that government is what it is, and to expect it to be more or different is to misread its character and risk serious disappointment.

Unfortunately, the failure to understand that truth runs through the experience of universities with government policy. It was, of course, encouraged by an unusually long run of generous and growing patronage, so unusual that most people in higher education, whose predecessors had never experienced anything like it, came to believe that it was the natural course of events. In the 1970s, when some government programs ended altogether and others stopped growing, the sense of betrayal was palpable; the partner was failing to meet the obligations of partnership.

That should have been a lesson learned, but it was not. Again, in the late 1980s, when concern over the repeated enormous budget deficits began to place constraints on government spending, that same sense of betrayal returned. From scientists, one frequently heard questions about why politicians seemed unable to understand how important science is to the nation. It was a question that tended to irritate politicians, who claimed to be entirely able to understand the point and who wondered in turn why scientists could not understand the arithmetic of the budget, not to mention the calculus of pain that tight budgets imposed on everyone. In 1990, physics Nobel laureate Leon Lederman, president of the American Association for the Advancement of Science (AAAS), conducted a survey among 250 scientists. In a report called *Science: The End of the Frontier?* he told of the loss of morale among them caused by tight funding. George Brown (Dem., Calif.), chairman of the House Committee on Space, Science, and Technology, took the Lederman report as his text in a talk to an AAAS meeting that one observer described as a "political science lecture."

Brown began by pointing out that of the $1.45 trillion in the president's FY 1992 budget, only about 15 percent remained to be spent after all of the fixed obligations were accounted for. But there was good news, he said. Among all the activities of government that had to be funded from that 15 percent, science agencies had been singled out by the president for unusually large increases. Then came the bad news:

> budget cuts totaling about $10 billion for community development block grants, the National Park Service, energy conservation grants, crop insurance, senior citizens programs, low-income energy assistance, Medicare, family support programs, and veterans benefits. . . . The advocates of each of these programs will be scanning the budget for additional funding sources, for areas that seem to be getting more than their fair share. And who do you think they're going to set their hungry eyes on? . . .
>
> What worries me about [the Lederman] approach is not its validity, but its lack of uniqueness. One could easily document a similar level of despair among 250 Medicare recipients, 250 disabled veterans, 250 soldiers in Saudi Arabia, or even 250 Members of Congress. . . .
>
> I know that most of you are scientists because you love science, and not because you are crusaders for technological advance or economic growth. That is exactly as it should be.
>
> But as a politician, I must tell you that unlimited federal funding for basic research is no longer viewed as a birthright of the scientific community, and I must warn you that the generous support you enjoy today was part of the fallout of the creation of nuclear weapons, not because of the great contributions of science to a more humane society.[8]

8. George E. Brown Jr., "A Perspective on the Federal Role in Science and Technology," in *Science and Technology Policy Yearbook, 1991,* ed. Margaret O. Wilson, Stephen

What Representative Brown was suggesting, among other things, was that a sense of entitlement to federal funds had grown among scientists, and it stood in the way of communicating their case effectively. A feeling of grievance may be a spur to action, but it is not an argument on behalf of one's cause. Nor were scientists alone in this feeling. Humanists responded with exactly the same sense of entitlement when their National Endowment was threatened following the Republican victory in the 1994 elections, and social scientists were equally taken aback when Representative Robert Walker (Rep., Pa.), George Brown's Republican successor as committee chairman, was thought to have suggested that the National Science Foundation close out its social science programs.

I certainly do not mean to suggest that scientists, or, indeed, faculty, were uniquely naive in their expectations of government. Decisions made by politically sophisticated university administrators were no better, a fact that brings us back to the issue of indirect cost recovery, where comparable errors can be seen in the long and frequently acrimonious debates over the rules governing that obscure but important subject.

Indirect costs, or pooled costs, as they are sometimes called, are those costs of research that cannot easily be assigned to the projects for which research funding is awarded. They include such items as heat, light, the cost of financing and maintaining research facilities, the costs of departmental and university administration and libraries, and other institutional costs that are necessary to support the research but that cannot be metered project by project. Those costs are pooled, and the proportion that is attributable to research is determined; these figures then serve as the basis for an indirect cost rate, which is charged to each grant or contract awarded.

In reality, that description, while essentially accurate, slides over the main point of contention between research universities and the government because it suggests a kind of precision in the rate-setting process that is impossible to achieve. At the heart of the process, there is an ambiguity caused by the fact that universities produce more than one "product"; the same people whose research earns grants and contracts also teach students, some of whom participate in the research. It is far from clear where teaching ends and research begins, and the same is, of course, true for the institutional underpinnings of both activities. For example, the same building, with its attendant operational and maintenance costs, may house research and graduate teaching, undergraduate teaching, and administration; determining where one leaves off and another begins is far from an exact science. Not only, therefore, is the allocation of costs necessarily an esti-

D. Nelson, Albert H. Teich (Washington, D.C.: American Association for the Advancement of Science, 1991), 24–25.

mate, but the estimate is based on the premise, as seen from the university's point of view, that, absent federal money, the research would not be done, so the government should pay its full costs. It is a shaky premise, useful more as a starting point for negotiations than as the basis for policy.

Most universities negotiate their rates and are audited by the Department of Health and Human Services because its constituent agency, the NIH, is the largest funder of university research. A small number of universities, for reasons of history, have that relationship with the Office of Naval Research (ONR). The two agencies are different in their approaches. The ONR, coming out of the defense culture, with its emphasis on negotiated contracts and generous reimbursement, has tended to be more open to the claims of its universities. Health and Human Services, on the other hand, has tended to be more peremptory, even high-handed at times, in its rate-setting activities. Both, however, are supposed to operate under the same set of rules, given in OMB Circular A-21.

This is a cost-based system. It is, in principle, not compatible with fixed rates or arbitrary caps on specific elements of the rates. The parties are supposed to negotiate on the basis of audited costs. The goal of the university is to come as close to full reimbursement as possible. The goal of the government . . . well, there lies the problem. University people have argued that the government's promised goal is also to come as close to full cost reimbursement as possible, and it is true that, for a time, changes in Circular A-21 seemed to move in that direction. The original ONR policies did call for the negotiation and payment of actual costs. But from 1950 to 1963, the Department of Health and Human Services did not even pretend to that goal. Its rules limited recovery on grants to 8 percent of total direct costs. In 1958, the maximum rose to 15 percent, and in 1963, to 20 percent. It was only in 1966 that the ceiling was removed, but that change was accompanied by an explicit requirement for cost sharing by the universities.

Circular A-21 can be read as an outline for full cost reimbursement, but as even this cursory history shows, it has never been interpreted that way by those on the government side who control most of the dollars, even though most of the changes in the rules through 1982 were in the direction of fuller reimbursement. The 1982 revision, the last one to favor universities, was especially fateful. In it, the government agreed to allow payment for the cost of interest on buildings and equipment. As much as any other single decision, this change triggered the burst of borrowing by universities for the construction of new research facilities. With the assurance of the government that the cost of borrowing—the interest in full and the principal in part—would be reimbursed, universities, for the first time, had a sure stream of income that would underlie their bond ratings and repay the debt. For those universities that availed themselves of the new opportunity—and this included virtually all of the private research universities—the stakes in the game of indirect cost recovery rose enormously. Any threat to reduce indirect cost recovery could have drastic financial consequences.

Throughout 1982, efforts by the government to change Circular A-21 were negotiated between experts on both sides, and the government negotiators typically based their arguments on the need to reform the system, tighten accounting practices, or bring greater uniformity into the calculations. In 1983, the basis of the conflict changed. That year, for the first time, the Department of Health and Human Services proposed to limit reimbursement to 90 percent of the negotiated rate. No substantive reason was given for the change or for the amount. It was simply a unilateral budgetary move. The Congress, which tends to be sensitive to arbitrary actions by the executive branch, refused to go along, and the provision was dropped, with instructions to the secretary to review the matter in consultation with universities and other concerned government agencies.

Armed with what it chose to interpret as a mandate to restrain the increase in indirect cost rates, in 1985 the Department of Health and Human Services (or the OMB—each claimed that the other was responsible) proposed to freeze indirect cost rates at that year's level and, in exchange, offered to eliminate the requirement for mandatory cost sharing. Since universities already contributed more than the required amount, this was a largely empty offer. Once again, the Congress rejected the proposal, but this time it instructed the Department of Health and Human Services to take vigorous steps during 1986 to restrain the increase in both indirect and direct costs of research.

In 1986, the government chose to implement half of the congressional instructions. This time, for the ostensible purpose of saving $100 million from the NIH budget, the president's budget proposed to limit recovery for administrative costs to 26 percent (later reduced to 20 percent). Nobody knew what such a change would cost universities or save the government. Some institutions would have lost a great deal of money, others would not, depending largely on how they had chosen to account for various administrative items. However, if the proposal were to be accepted, it would constitute a departure from the system of cost-based reimbursement that was so important to universities, especially those in the private sector, whose costs could not be met by state appropriations and whose rates, in part as a reflection of that fact, were considerably higher.

When the dust settled, the Congress had appropriated $1 billion more than had been requested for the NIH, dwarfing any possible savings from the cap, and a compromise had been reached in which a sub-element of the rate was capped, saving the government no money and costing universities none. But the wall of cost-based reimbursement had been breached, and the breach would be widened in the years ahead. This battle was instructive for other reasons. I later summarized it to AAU members as follows:

> It soon became clear that this attempt to reduce indirect cost recovery was, like its predecessors, motivated primarily by budgetary considerations, not by any particular zeal to reform the research support system. The alleged abuses in the latter were merely useful arguments in support of the former. There are, of course, those who would like to reform the system. For them, the budget pressures provided important support, just as their arguments buttressed the position of those whose goal was to make the budget look better.
>
> If the case had been solely budgetary, I believe that it would have been relatively easy to defeat it outright. . . . There was considerable sympathy on Capitol Hill for the argument that it is not good policy to try to save money by unilateral changes in the rules of the game, especially when the rules had always emphasized the notion that the participants were collaborators in a common enterprise and owed each other at least the obligation to consult before making important changes.
>
> However, it was not to be that easy. Doubts about the legitimacy of the administrative elements of the indirect cost rates increasingly were shared by key members of Congress, and their patience for doing battle yet again in a seemingly endless campaign was growing shorter. As in the past, they were willing to help, but this time the help was accompanied by a clear message: "Settle it, and try not to come back again." The instrument for conveying the message was the Yates Amendment to the Urgent Supplemental Appropriations Act, which prohibited OMB from spending any money to implement changes in A-21. OMB took the message to mean that they were expected to reach a reasonable result after consultation with the universities, and we took the message to mean that we could not expect the Congress to continue this extraordinary provision much longer or repeat it very often.

The real lesson of these repeated battles, and the other battles that followed, was that, pressed to the wall on budget priorities, the relevant officials of government had no qualms about changing the rules in order to relieve the pressure. Moreover, they would do so without warning or consultation, and largely without regard to the effects of their actions. That was brought home to me early in the 1986 dispute at a meeting in the office of an OMB official whose support was critical to the resolution of the issue. When it was pointed out to him that what OMB/NIH was proposing to do would have an especially large negative impact on private universities, his response was that the government ought to take its research dollars to the places that could do the work for the least amount of money. If private universities charged higher rates, then research funds should go to public universities. Moreover, he said, no damage would be done to research, because the best scientists currently at the private universities would go to the publics if that was where they would find funding.

It was a shocking comment from a senior public official. The least of the problems with it was its crude and erroneous view of the way in which labor markets operate in the academic world. Far more serious and more troubling was its indifference to the value of institutions whose sustained quality was a contribution to the nation that outweighed by far any conceivable budget savings. Even if the threat implied in the comment was an empty one, the willingness to use it was ominous beyond simply the dollars at stake in that year's budget.

Universities were clearly on the defensive, and we groped for a way to respond. The AAU established a committee whose charge was to examine all sensible ideas for reform and to recommend changes in the reimbursement system that would make it clearer, simpler, easier to explain, and therefore more stable and easier to defend.

The Pings Committee (named for its chair, Cornelius Pings, provost of the University of Southern California and my successor at the AAU in 1993) eventually proposed reforms that became the basis of university policy. The committee essentially conceded that charges for administration were hard to explain and unpopular. Since they were not rising in any event, it made sense to offer universities an incentive to accept a fixed allowance in lieu of the need to document and negotiate a new rate each time. In exchange for that concession, the committee proposed that facilities and instrumentation costs—interest, depreciation, and maintenance— be allowed to rise as those costs were shown through documentation to rise. In this way, the system would neutralize the most controversial parts of the rate and would focus on the main issue of public policy involved in the entire indirect cost debate, namely, the need of research universities to keep their facilities and instrumentation up to date.

These were sensible proposals, and they were widely recognized as such, although there were serious misgivings expressed in the AAU debate over adoption of the committee report. A significant minority feared that the report offered the government a road map of acceptable cuts, which it would gladly impose, without any assurance that the second part of the deal would actually come to pass. This was by no means a groundless fear. It was overridden, though, by a more general realization that failure to offer some reasonable plan would be likely to produce even worse results.

For a brief time, the Pings Committee proposals actually served as the basis for discussions with the OMB about changes that would improve the system. Those discussions, and all other rational consideration of funding the costs of research, ended abruptly with the hearings of the Dingell committee and the air of scandal that enveloped the whole topic of indirect cost policy. Government agencies feared being seen negotiating any agreement that might seem to be advantageous to universities, which were now widely believed to be cheating the public. The order of the day was to look strong and decisive and make it impossible for those items that seemed most scandalous ever to be charged to the government again. With an unerring instinct for the trivial and the political, and with an understandable eagerness to move out from under John Dingell's guns, the OMB announced that a series of trivial charges—the president's house and liquor for entertaining, for example—were prohibited, while a system that was unresponsive to important issues of research policy and vulnerable to political attack was allowed to continue unchanged.

By 1992, however, wise leadership in the OMB saw the need to examine the system more carefully and thoughtfully. Throughout that year, informal meetings were held between the parties, and a new set of proposals was developed that would limit recovery of administrative costs and continue to reimburse facilities costs, very much in the spirit of the Pings Committee report. Revisions to A-21 were written and for the most part agreed to. But something else was happening in 1992: a presidential election. During the course of the campaign, candidate Bill Clinton, speaking at a college in Maryland, promised to bring to an end the waste, fraud, and abuse of the indirect cost system, to take research funds from the wasteful university administrations and return them to the scientists' laboratories where they rightfully belonged. After a tidal wave of faxes, letters, and phone calls issued from every "friend of Bill" who could be found in university circles and aimed at anyone who might conceivably have the ear of the candidate's advisers, the Clinton campaign gave private assurances that the candidate did not mean exactly what he said. Upon taking office, however, the new leadership of the OMB refused to issue the revised rules that the old crowd had agreed to, and a new round of studies and negotiations ensued.

What matters here is not the details of a set of government accounting rules but what the process of arriving at those rules says about the relationship between universities and their governmental patron. It is not a pretty story. Contrary to the widely held belief in universities, the government recognizes no entitlement to research funding whatsoever. There is, and can be, no promise that funding for scientists or their universities will be sustained at any given level. That is not to say that the government will cease funding research or even that it will make sudden, drastic cuts. The former is impossible in the modern world, the latter improbable. What is certain, however, is that funding levels, the objects of funding, and the rules governing the use of the money are subject to change without notice and with few qualms about the consequences. University faculty and university officers who make commitments based on any other understanding of how the world works are liable to encounter some rude shocks ahead.

Faculty and the Myth of Community

Any generalization about the opinions and behavior of so large and diverse a group as university faculty is bound to do an injustice to some. To narrow the field to a fairer and more manageable size, some things can be said with confidence about those faculty whose research brought them into regular contact with the federal government. For one thing, it is fair to say that those who entered university faculties between about 1950 and 1975 came to view the availability of regular research funding as a natural part of academic life. For another, not very many of them had reason to inquire into the nature of government or to understand the underlying dynamics of the politics of representative government. Indeed, for most, the government was not an abstraction but the concrete reality of the program officers with whom they dealt or the study sections on which they served. The people in government whom they knew shared their goals and existed to serve them. They made common cause in seeking larger appropriations and generally succeeded; in the process they helped greatly enlarge the research enterprise, to the benefit and greater glory of all.

A second set of generalizations is in order. The first of this set is that most faculty do not understand the economics of their own universities, and, absent a crisis, they have very little incentive to learn. Second, it has long been the almost universal belief among faculty who receive government funding that their institution's indirect cost rate is too high. Third, there are those on every campus who are convinced either that they lose grants because their university's rate is too high or that, if it goes higher, they will be priced out of the market. One hears stories of faculty who believe that they failed to win a grant because their university's indirect cost rate was too high. Often, faculty are encouraged in this view by their agency program officers, who share with them an interest in maximizing the direct cost component of grants and minimizing the indirect. We frequently heard reports from campus research administrators that program officers of the National Science Foundation were pressuring applicants to persuade their universities either to waive a portion of the indirect cost rate or otherwise subsidize the grant with local funds. When we checked those reports, they were always denied. But the frequency of the reports and their common substance lent credibility to the stories. Notwithstanding faculty beliefs and agency pressure, however, there is no systematic evidence to support the belief in the competitive disadvantage, and universities with the highest rates remain at the top of the list of recipients of federal funds. Still, the belief remains strong.

So long as the system was expanding and appropriations were growing, university administrations were the third side of this triangle. The way to improve was to grow, and growth paid in both quality and prestige. Like so many aspects of that golden age, this combination of interests carried the seeds of its own disintegration. When funding leveled off and could no longer support the growth in the number of research performers that the preceding years had produced, what was left was a large number of faculty with a well-established sense of entitlement, government officials who identified with them, and university administrations having either to disappoint their faculty or to find money to make up for the shortfall from government.

That sense of entitlement was palpable. One manifestation of it was the growing conviction on the part of many faculty that their universities could help solve the problem by forgoing some of their indirect cost recovery. This made perfectly good sense, since it was never clear to many that this money was justified. So long as appropriations were growing, that issue was not worth fighting about; but with tight times at hand, indirect cost funds seemed a large and attractive pool of redeployable resources.

During my years in Washington, I argued this point with the leaders of scientific societies many times. Two things were clear: First, it was taken for granted by these very smart people that money saved by reducing indirect cost recovery would naturally be spent on increased direct costs. It was very difficult to get across the point that, regardless of what they said publicly, the budget makers were concerned about spending less money, not about giving them more money. Second, it was widely believed among this group that universities could make up for any reductions in research funding out of some unspecified source of money that administrators had available to them. As a result of these views, faculty were lined up against their universities at home, in conflicts over the size of the indirect cost rate and the way money recovered was used, and in Washington, through their scientific societies.

The on-campus conflicts were most intense in the private universities. Because the privates lacked state subsidies for their administrative and facilities costs, indirect cost rates among them were higher than in their public counterparts, although there is no evidence that the actual costs were higher in the private sector. To use Stanford as an example again, the threat of a substantial increase in the indirect cost rate was triggered in part by large building plans. Donald Kennedy later described what followed. "During the year before the [Dingell] hearing, Stanford announced that it would have to negotiate for a higher rate—78 percent—for 1991. That produced a very strong reaction on the part of the science faculty, which became public in a *Science* magazine article that contained angry statements by several prominent Stanford researchers. Unbeknownst to us, Paul Biddle (the resident representative of ONR) had already become involved in that developing discontent. He met over hamburgers . . . with a number of these faculty members, at luncheons whose purpose he would describe as 'to see if we can do anything about the indirect cost rate at Stanford.' At this time . . . he was already in regular contact with members of the Dingell subcommittee staff."

No doubt this is an extreme example of faculty disaffection—indeed, just about everything in the Stanford case was extreme—but it is not off the scale, only toward the far end. Public statements of faculty concern about their institution's indirect cost rate are not unusual, though meeting secretly with a government auditor to plot what to do about it is extraordinary. In this instance, the disaffected faculty got more than they bargained for. In addition to the opprobrium heaped on their university, Stanford's rate was arbitrarily lowered from 74.4 percent to 55.5 percent, costing the university about $15 million a year in recovery, and the university eventually spent roughly $35 million to pay consultants and lawyers to defend against what turned out to be unwarranted allegations of massive overcharges and to install a new set of accounting arrangements. It was an expensive protest. In the end, it should be noted, the central allegation of overcharges, in some accounts amounting to as much as $300 million, was reduced to a finding that the university actually owed $1.2 million for a ten-year period in which the government had failed to conduct audits. In short, a priceless national resource had been seriously damaged for no good reason at all.

The immediate effect of the Stanford case on faculty views was undoubtedly to confirm the beliefs of those who had thought all along that their universities had to have been misbehaving in order for their indirect cost rates to have risen so high. Such views were no doubt strengthened even further as additional universities examined their charges and offered to repay the government for those that were incorrect or gave the appearance of impropriety. However, second thoughts were not far behind. Some of the suggestions for clamping down on reimbursement were so draconian that the more sober members of the scientific community began to worry about the effect these changes might have on their institutions' ability to host high-quality science. As serious discussions began with the government about how to change the system, a group of individuals representing universities, led by William Richardson, president of Johns Hopkins, and Nobel laureate Harold Varmus, of the University of California, San Francisco (and later NIH director), held a series of meetings attended by a small group of faculty, administrators, and association heads that produced a statement of principles about research costs to which both sides agreed. The statement was less important for its substance, which was largely unremarkable, than for the change in the atmosphere that was brought about by the fact of the meetings and the agreement. During the negotiations with the OMB that followed, scientific societies and university groups were united as they had never been before.

It would be foolish to think that government-university and faculty-administration conflicts over the costs of research, who should pay them, and how they should be shared are over. So long as budgets are tight, government budget makers will find the institutional costs of research an attractive nuisance, too good a target for their savings. On campus, there is a natural conflict between faculty, who want the largest share of dollars for their own activities, and administrations, who must find ways to pay the bills that are run up by a large volume of research. During prosperous times, both the scientific enterprise on campus and the apparatus for managing and supporting it grew. It now seems that both grew beyond any reasonable expectation of sustaining them over time. The question that universities face today, when their budgets are under stress, is whether parties that have interests that diverge, as well as interests in common, can agree on a scale of operations and a distribution of resources that is sustainable and is consistent with the idea of the university as a community devoted to the collective aggrandizement of teaching and scholarship rather than the separate aggrandizement of its parts. We return to that question at a later time.

Chapter Four

THE RULES CHANGE
II

Matters of Principle

THE ISSUES DISCUSSED in this chapter—research fraud, conflict of interest, and conflict of commitment—all have at their core an ethical dimension. They deal with matters of responsibility, accountability, and obligation, both personal and institutional. These issues also have a common theme, which can be put in the form of a question: Is the modern university becoming simply a piece of land on which essentially autonomous scholars pursue their independent goals, seeking reputation and money in an institutional structure that is itself increasingly devoted to seeking reputation and money and with declining community norms that provide a common sense of purpose and obligation, either to scholarship or to teaching?

In reality, of course, there is no single answer, and surely no simple one, if only because universities are made up of differentiated communities with far-from-identical norms. Humanists are different from social scientists, who are in turn different from physical scientists, biological scientists, medical doctors, lawyers, architects, and so forth, all of whom are different from each other in material ways. The plea of complexity, however, is not an excuse for ignoring the question, for if the trend is in the direction suggested by the question, then there is good reason for concern, not to say alarm.

Fraud in Research

Americans have long had a somewhat idealized notion of academic life and the people who engage in it, although the ideal has taken different forms at different times: the endearing, absent-minded professor, the stern, fatherly taskmaster, or perhaps the university as a playground for engaging fraternity and sorority members. Whatever form the ideal may have taken, what lay at the core was a sense of innocence, of a place beyond the temptations and transgressions of ordinary life. Periodic athletic scandals sometimes challenged that view, but never for long, and in any case the public liked and wanted athletics. Certainly, it was no part of the American vision of the university that professors might falsify their research or enter into relationships for financial gain that conflicted with their obligations to their students and their institutions. Nor was it part of that picture that, confronted with evidence of both of those phenomena, university officials and faculties would be unable to take effective action to discipline offenders or that a university would promote highly dubious science for its own financial purposes.

By the end of the 1980s, few people in Washington or in the media any longer believed in the university as an island of innocence in an otherwise corrupt world. In their eyes, a land bridge had formed, and it was difficult, if not impossible, any longer to distinguish one from the other. Arguably, the change began in the 1960s when the student Left attacked universities for what they viewed as university complicity in an immoral war. The evidence cited for that proposition was the funding of research by the Department of Defense and the unwillingness of institutions to bar military and intelligence agency recruiters from campuses. That position had very little public support and even less among politicians. It did, however, put what universities do squarely in the middle of a major public debate. Suddenly, the metaphor of the ivory tower seemed much less apt.

The 1970s produced new developments that built on those doubts. The most important was the discovery of how to split DNA strands and recombine them into new forms not hitherto seen in nature. That extraordinary bit of science did two things immediately. First, it established the scientific basis for the biotechnology industry and made biochemists, geneticists, and molecular biologists hot economic properties. The gap between the basic scientist's bench and the production of products suddenly diminished to what seemed (an exaggeration, as it later turned out) nearly the vanishing point. In a remarkably short time, major companies were entering into multimillion-dollar agreements with universities so as to be close to those scientists who were likely to be at the cutting edge of the new science. Because of their size and their novelty, agreements between the Monsanto company and Washington University and Harvard provoked special interest, including congressional hearings, chaired by Congressman Al Gore. In addition, leading scientists were associating themselves with new companies or forming new companies to exploit discoveries made in their labs. As a result, universities were suddenly faced with the need to think through the wisdom and propriety of investing in businesses that involved their own faculty as principals and were based on work done originally in the universities' laboratories.

Second, it unleashed an amazing backlash against scientists in the field, spurred by largely hysterical stories in the media telling of the frightening new organisms that scientists would create if left to follow their own unrestrained ambitions. One cover of *Time* caught the spirit in its representation of a swarm of ghastly looking bugs pouring from a test tube presumably onto an unsuspecting and vulnerable public. That a group of the scientists involved in the research, meeting at Asilomar in California, called for a moratorium on certain lines of inquiry until their implications were better understood and their safety assured paradoxically served more to lend credence to the fears than to reassurance about scientific responsibility. The result, once again, was to bring home a new perception of the university as a place whose activities were not wholly benign, an institution that needed watching and even regulating. And regulation, in fact, followed. Universities whose faculties wished to do recombinant DNA work were required to establish formal committees, including members from outside the university, to review proposals for safety.

In some places, even that was not enough. Always alert to an opportunity to stick a thumb in Harvard's eye and bolstered by alarmist testimony from some biologists and environmentalists, the city council of Cambridge, Massachusetts, enacted its own three-month moratorium on recombinant DNA research within the city limits, after which it added restrictions on the research beyond those already required by the federal government. Mayor Alfred Velluci, a longtime Harvard nemesis, had no difficulty justifying the council's actions. "Who the hell do the scientists think they are that they can take federal tax dollars that are coming out of our tax returns and do research work that we then cannot come in and question?"[1]

In the end calmer heads prevailed, and what looked at first like a mad race by local jurisdictions to protect their constituents against threatened epidemics did not occur. But the reaction against the new research, reflecting a readiness to believe the worst of the doomsday predictions, left a different kind of residue. As one observer at a 1977 hearing in California put it, "If there was ever a time when you wouldn't want to even *appear* to be making life hard for concerned scientists, it would be the first time they timidly expressed their social conscience. But politics being politics, this is just what happened. Thus, [James D.] Watson wishes he had kept quiet. Next time he, or others, will remain silent. They are bright people who learn from experience, since that is what science is all about."[2]

The biological sciences had exploded with extraordinary speed and dazzling creativity, and among the unintended consequences of the explosion was the need to deal with the issues of conflict of interest and research fraud. Neither issue was wholly new. During the Kennedy administration, the government had required universities with research contracts to adopt

1. Quoted in James D. Watson and John Tooze, *The DNA Story: A Documentary History of Gene Cloning* (New York: W. H. Freeman, 1981), 122.

2. Letter from Lance Montauk to Jerome Lackner, director of the California Department of Public Health, March 18, 1977, cited in Watson and Tooze, *DNA Story,* 163.

a policy on conflict of interest. As it happens, I participated in writing Stanford's policy. It was what might be described as "an officer and a gentleman" policy. It said in essence that the university expected its faculty to behave like responsible professionals; if anyone had reason to be concerned about a developing relationship, it should be discussed with the department head or dean. That remained Stanford's policy until well into the 1980s, although the Schools of Medicine and Engineering adopted somewhat more pointed regulations.

Similarly, research fraud was by no means unknown. It was believed to be uncommon, a belief based partly on the fact that when it was detected, it was rarely made public. Rather, the matter would be handled quietly by the offending person's colleagues, and an arrangement would be made that might see the offender leave the university for another, typically with nothing on the record to warn the new employer.

How far that set of attitudes had changed by the end of the 1980s is illustrated by two pieces that appeared in newspapers, coincidentally, two days apart in 1989. The first, on July 30, was a letter to the editor of the *New York Times* from a professor emeritus at Harvard. The main point of the letter, which commented on an incident of misconduct associated with an article that appeared in *Science* magazine, was familiar enough. The writer argued that fraud in research is rare and that science is essentially "self-cleansing." Almost in passing, the writer wrote, "Scientists, regrettably, are no more honest than other people, and no one should be surprised if occasionally one of them steals the work of another." As for faking data, "Scientists refrain from faking data not because of inherent virtue, but because if the work is important, they will promptly be caught and exposed, and if the work is trivial, although the fakery may not be checked promptly, there is little to gain anyway." Whether or not any of these assertions are correct, they constitute a view of university scientists that would have been startling even a decade earlier. Even more startling was the fact that an eminent scientist would so casually say such things in public. University faculty were not accustomed to being thought of as no better than anyone else; and few of them would have thought that, as a group, they refrained from cheating because they feared being caught, not because they knew it was wrong to cheat.

Perhaps it should have come as no surprise to the public that scientists are not born with an extra gene for ethics; that they are in fact human beings who have chosen a scientific career. Or perhaps years of being seen by the public as larger-than-life heroes and role models produced a larger-than-life disillusionment when feet of clay were exposed. Whatever the reason, the reaction to the realization was sharp, as seen in this 1989 *Washington Post* editorial commenting on a report of the Institute of Medicine titled "The Responsible Conduct of Research in the Health Sciences." "The report," the *Post* said, "is evidence of the widespread agreement among scientists that the 'cultural' problems of their profession—the misplaced incentives and pressures that make cheating an easy option—urgently need attention. While the report takes the familiar academic stance that scientific misconduct is rare and the product of 'individual deviance,' it argues—a considerable concession—that universities' leniency can tolerate and foster such behavior."

What had produced this change was a series of very public allegations of fraud made by whistle-blowers at some of the most prestigious universities. In the most embarrassing of the cases, the universities had responded in a perfunctory or confused manner, typically rejecting the allegations without sufficient inquiry and in some cases blaming the whistle-blower for behaving irresponsibly. There is never a good time for treating charges of misconduct in that manner, but this was one of the worst. There now existed an eager audience for such stories outside the university. Investigative journalism was riding high, and congressional oversight committees were constantly on the lookout for opportunities to expose malfeasance. And as anyone knew who had paid the least attention to Watergate, the damage done by admitting the original offense may be trivial compared to that done by the exposure of attempts to cover it up. As a result, the issue of research fraud was transformed from an internal matter to be dealt with internally to a public matter for which the university needed to have in place policies and procedures to enable allegations to be dealt with quickly, thoroughly, and fairly. Few met the test.

It should be said that the government was no better prepared, making the problem even worse. As *Science* magazine reported in March 1992,

> NIH's Office of Scientific Integrity (OSI), born three years ago largely because of congressional complaints that the universities had proved themselves incapable of investigating allegations of scientific misconduct, now seems about to become a victim of similar complaints. For most of the past year, the office has taken a beating at the hands of nearly everyone who has come in contact with it, whether scientists under investigation and their lawyers, other researchers who want to see it police their profession more efficiently, university administrators, legislators, or the NIH director, herself. The office staff is incompetent, some say. The process denies constitutional guarantees and basic fairness to those it investigates, say others. The complaints go on: The office has succumbed to unwarranted political influence. It's too slow. It confuses investigations with adjudication. Now NIH's parent agency, the Public Health Service [PHS], has proposed yet another cure-all—in effect declaring that OSI's "scien-

tific dialogue," an attempt to settle misconduct allegations through a scientific approach instead of a legal one, has been a failure.[3]

Nobody seemed able to get it right, a condition that blunted all efforts to address the underlying issues: first, how much fraud and misconduct is there, and second, who can be trusted to deal with whatever amount exists? The first of those questions is probably unanswerable in a fully persuasive way. It rests on what is defined as fraud and misconduct, and that has been in constant dispute and remains so today. Most scientists argue for a narrow definition, one that is limited to falsification, fabrication, and plagiarism. Regulators have wanted a more expansive definition, including under the rubric of fraud and misconduct acts that seriously deviate from established scientific norms. Even the narrowest definition poses problems. Everyone agrees that error and fraud are not the same, but distinguishing between the two may be difficult indeed. A system that is careless about that distinction would not only be unfair to individuals, but it would also encourage a kind of risk-averse behavior on the part of scientists that would be disastrous to the conduct of science.

Difficult as it can be, distinguishing between error and fraud is not the only definitional problem. David Goodstein describes how scientists, even Isaac Newton, are likely to behave when theory and experiment do not quite fit.

> Because [Newton] was disturbed that his theory [about the propagation of sound waves in air] didn't quite correspond to the observation, he tried to cook up some explanation for the discrepancy. He came up with all kinds of things that sound hilarious to us now. . . . He made little fixes until he finally got the theory in agreement with the experiment.
>
> It's the sort of thing that every theorist does today; if you have a theory that doesn't quite agree with the experiment, you speculate on what might cause the small discrepancy. That's exactly what Newton was doing . . . and that's the way people really act. But it's not fraud.[4]

Repeated attempts to craft an acceptable definition have failed. A version proposed in September 1995 by the government's Commission on Research Integrity tried this formulation: "Research misconduct is significant misbehavior that fails to respect the intellectual contributions or property of others, that intentionally impedes the progress of research, or that risks

3. David P. Hamilton, "OSI: Better the Devil You Know?" *Science* 225 (March 13, 1992): 1344.
4. David Goodstein, "What Do We Mean When We Use the Term 'Science Fraud'?" *Windows* (Texas A&M University) (fall 1991).

corrupting the scientific record or compromising the integrity of scientific practices."[5] Ralph Bradshaw, president of the Federation of American Societies for Experimental Biology, said of this attempt that it was "overly broad, vague, and unclear" and that the commission's work reflected "a lack of understanding of the process of basic scientific research."[6]

The existence and prevalence of research fraud is, of course, not entirely or even primarily a definitional matter. But without consensus on a definition there is no way of knowing whether the cases that come to light are the whole iceberg or just its tip. Is research fraud limited to falsification of data and plagiarism, or should it include failure to keep adequate records, sexual harassment, or other forms of misbehavior, all of which have been proposed? Even with an agreed definition, we can only know of the instances that have been uncovered. But we can never prove that because we have no evidence of others, others do not exist.

Then there is the second question: Who can be trusted to monitor, investigate, and adjudicate allegations of fraud, however it is defined? It is certainly not a question unique to the scientific domain. Every significant social institution has been bedeviled by it. Lack of trust in institutions to police themselves has led to the creation of independent counsels to investigate suspected misconduct by high officials of the executive branch of government. It has brought congressional ethics committees under attack for suspected cronyism. Police forces are not trusted to deal with misconduct by police officers, and churches are suspect when they undertake to deal with charges of misbehavior by the clergy. Throughout American society, trust in established institutions to behave well or to find and punish misbehavior is at a very low level.

For most of their history, universities were near the top of the list of America's most admired and trusted institutions. However, by the close of the 1980s, scientists and their universities were no exception to the prevailing view. It was critically important that a strong sense of public confidence be restored, and so the AAU's primary focus during this period was on helping to insure that universities remained responsible for the conduct of their faculties and that they had the tools that would enable them do so. The latter was by no means a given. On the contrary, what seemed closer to the truth was that every university that found itself with a problem also found itself needing to invent, on the spot, a process for dealing with it. That is a recipe for disaster; it increases the chances of error, and it undermines the credibility of the results, even if they are the right results. Our

5. Jocelyn Carsen, "Commission Proposes New Definition of Misconduct." *Science* 269 (September 29, 1995): 1811.
6. Ibid.

first undertaking, therefore, in conjunction with several other interested associations, was to create and distribute a set of guidelines, based on best practice, for developing workable policies and procedures for dealing with cases from the moment a charge is made to the point of its disposition, whether that be dismissal of the charge or punishment of the offender.

It was a modest enough undertaking, but it was essential. It is impossible to overestimate the size of the stakes here. Nothing could be more corrosive to public confidence in science, and the public support that follows from it, than a belief that scientists cannot be trusted to do honest science and the corollary belief that when fraudulent science occurs, scientists and their institutions cannot be trusted to find it and discipline the offenders. It was not a concern to be taken lightly. A 1989 public opinion poll conducted for the American Medical Association reported that 17 percent of those interviewed believed that research fraud happens a lot, and an additional 41 percent believed that it happened fairly often. A particularly vivid example of the treatment of the topic in the popular media can be seen in a 1991 *Time* magazine essay by Barbara Ehrenreich, called "Science, Lies and Ultimate Truth." She began, "If there is any specimen lower than a fornicating preacher, it must be a shady scientist. The dissolute evangelist betrays his one revealed Truth, but the scientist who rushes half-cocked into print or, worse yet, falsifies data subverts the whole idea of truth." She went on to compare her own experience as a graduate student in biology with what she saw as the modern ethos:

> There were mistakes, but mistakes could be corrected, which is why you reported exactly how you did things, step by step, so others could prove you right or wrong. There were even, sometimes, corners cut: a little rounding off, an anomalous finding overlooked. But falsifying data lay outside our moral universe.
>
> . . . This was the ideal, anyway, but Big Science costs big bucks and breeds a more mundane and calculating kind of outlook. It takes hundreds of thousands of dollars a year to run a modern biological laboratory, with its electron microscopes, ultracentrifuges, amino-acid analyzers, Ph.D.s and technicians. The big bucks tend to go to the big shots . . . whose machines and underlings must grind out "results" in massive volume. In the past two decades, as federal funding for basic research has ebbed, the pressure to produce has risen to dangerous levels. At the same time, the worldly rewards of success have expanded to include fat paychecks (from patents and sidelines in the biotech business) as well as power and celebrity status. And these are the circumstances that invite deception.

. . . If a Nobel laureate in science could sink to the moral level of a Milli Vanilli or a White House spin doctor, then maybe the deconstructionists are right and there is no truth anywhere, only self-interest masked as objective fact.[7]

The case that occasioned these strong words involved Nobel laureate David Baltimore, who was coauthor of a paper whose primary author was a junior colleague. A research assistant in the latter's laboratory charged that the data in the paper had been fabricated. Her allegations were dismissed as without foundation after inquiries that later seemed to be less rigorous than the charge required. What followed was a political-scientific circus played out in congressional hearing rooms, the press, the courts, and a series of inconclusive scientific reviews. It would be hard to imagine a worse way to try to resolve a controversy involving a highly esoteric piece of research. That point is made strikingly clear in an excellent summary of the so-called Baltimore case by historian of science Daniel Kevles.[8] In it he recounts the way in which small differences escalate to irreconcilable conflicts as professional reputations and egos are tested in the public spotlight. He also describes what can only be judged the dismal performance of John Dingell's congressional investigating committee and its staff and of the NIH machinery for investigating allegations of misconduct. Nor does he spare the media and its apparently irresistible temptation to give undue weight to leaked documents, its rush to premature judgment, and its tendency to overplay the easy-to-describe charge of fraud and to underplay the necessarily more complicated defense.

In the end, the Department of Health and Human Services' review board concluded that no case of fraud had been proved. It had been a largely empty exercise in which a dispute about extremely esoteric points of science had been transformed into a morality play in which the stage was a congressional hearing room—surely the worst possible venue for determining the merits of a scientific dispute—and in which the critics, like Barbara Ehrenreich, felt free to make outrageous ad hominem attacks against protagonists who, when the facts were in, turned out to be innocent of wrongdoing.

The Baltimore case should be taken as a warning, if any were needed, about the potential for damage that fraud allegations contain—damage to individual reputation, to institutional reputation, and to the reputation of science as a disciplined and ethical profession. It is a warning, too, about

7. Barbara Ehrenreich, "Science, Lies and Ultimate Truth," *Time*, May 20, 1991, 66.
8. Daniel Kevles, "The Assault on David Baltimore," *New Yorker*, May 27, 1996, 94–109.

what can happen when the institution in which the controversy arises is unable to resolve the matter definitively with its own processes.

Virtually all of the dramatic allegations of research fraud that came to the public's attention emerged from the biological sciences, where the close connection to the public's health enhanced the sensitivity of the issue. A study by sociologist Patricia Woolf of twenty-six cases of misconduct between 1980 and 1987 found that twenty-one of them involved the biomedical sciences, and that seventeen of those involved M.D.'s, who are typically not trained in research until their postdoctoral years. But the damage was not field specific. It extended broadly to the conduct of science and to universities, in which most basic science takes place and whose reputation for integrity was placed in jeopardy.

It would be a serious mistake, however, to think of this as simply a matter of public image. Far more important was the question of how universities define themselves, what kind of institutions they purport to be. Universities are mixtures of hierarchy and autonomy, competition and collegiality, individual entrepreneurship and collective effort, openness and secretiveness. Changes over the years had been in the direction of greater hierarchy, less collegiality, more entrepreneurship, less openness. Within a reasonable range, such changes are tolerable, even if not desirable. What cannot be tolerated, however, without calling into question the very basis of the institution, is default of its responsibility to define and enforce standards of intellectual quality, one of which, surely, is a high standard of intellectual honesty and professional integrity. If universities and their faculties cannot carry out that responsibility, then it is hard to know what else they ought to be trusted with.

By 1989, the main issue in dispute from the point of view of an organization representing universities was whether the primary responsibility for investigating and judging allegations of fraud would reside in the universities or be shifted to the federal government. The 1986 reauthorization of the National Institutes of Health had instructed the secretary of health and human services to issue regulations specifying how allegations of fraud and misconduct were to be dealt with. The next three years, and indeed the years since, were occupied with battles over virtually every element of the issue.

Those who wanted a more active role for the government did not find it in the halting efforts of the National Institutes of Health to assume a more aggressive role, and no one seemed to have any real appetite for creating another instrument. What emerged is still a work in progress, a work with which none of the participants is especially pleased. Primary responsibility for investigating and judging charges of fraud and misconduct lies with the university in which the charge is brought. A university is obliged by regulation to inform the government if its preliminary investigation reveals sufficient evidence to warrant a full-scale inquiry, and then it must report the results of the process in a timely manner. The government may review the case as it sees fit, it may hear appeals, and it has a general auditing function.

In its broad outlines this is a workable arrangement, but its separate parts are shaky. There is no agreement on a workable definition of fraud and misconduct, the respective roles of government and universities are not sharply defined, and the appeals process in the government, because it must, like all appellate processes, focus on procedure over substance, may reach conclusions that have little to do with the merits of either the charge or the defense. Neither whistle-blowers nor those charged by them can embark on this journey happily.

It is important to understand, though, that no system can insure against bad behavior. We may confidently expect that new instances of egregious misconduct will come to light. Can we now expect that scientists and their universities are prepared to treat such cases seriously and to respond in a manner that inspires confidence? Doubts remain. With something less than full confidence but with more than would have been justified in the past, we may expect that the universities in which these episodes occur will deal with them in a forthright, careful, and expeditious manner. Should they fail to do so, they will have lost their most precious asset, the trust of the public.

There is still another sense in which the manner in which universities accept their responsibility in this area will tell much about their character. Fortunately, it is the easiest of all possible remedies for the ailment of unethical conduct in research: education. To put the matter as charitably as possible, the virtually complete absence of instruction about what constitutes ethical behavior in research—or, indeed, in academic roles more generally—may be ascribed to the assumption that the mentoring process that naturally accompanies graduate education would teach the young, by example if nothing else, what is expected of them. But that assumption is increasingly open to question. In the first place, the growth of large laboratories, with their complement of postdocs, research associates, technicians, and managers, increases the distance between faculty members and graduate students. With the best will in the world, it is difficult to reproduce in the modern laboratory the close personal relationship that once prevailed—or that nostalgia invents for us—between the graduate student and his or her mentor.

In the second place, as we have seen, some of the primary performers of research in the biomedical sciences have not completed their training in research by the time they enter a laboratory as a postdoctoral fellow. There they meet all of the pressures that accompany high performance expectations and high career rewards for a productive research output.

And in the third place, it is surely optimistic to believe that all people learn by example or that exemplary learning cannot be improved by instruction. It is an especially strange assumption to find in an educational institution.

Prodded by government—formal instruction in research ethics is now a required part of all NIH-funded training grants—and by the urging of national scientific organizations, more universities have organized courses for their graduate students and postdoctoral fellows. As a result, a growing literature exists to inform practice by sharing both successes and failures. It would be foolish to think that courses in ethics guarantee ethical behavior. Strong laws do not eliminate crime, and professional codes of conduct, even when enforced by strong sanctions, do not prevent all unethical conduct. The pressures of career and life sometimes interact with individual character in ways that education is powerless to reach. But for many, one hopes for most, knowing what is expected and what is unacceptable is all that is needed to prevent the errors of judgment that one can slip into easily when good fortune comes in too easy a package.

Conflict of Interest

My own opinion about the incidence of significant research fraud, and it is based on as much data as anyone else's opinion, is that it is not common and does not constitute a serious substantive problem in science, but that for all of the reasons given, it is terribly important that it be taken seriously and dealt with accordingly.

Conflict of interest is of quite a different character, even though it is sometimes swept under an overly broad definition of fraud and misconduct. On occasion it may even be a cause of overt research fraud. Conflict of interest, unlike inventing nonexistent data or stealing another's work, is endemic in the research university. It cannot be attributed to character defects or the eternal condition of human nature. Rather, it is inextricable from the fabric of the university, because that fabric has been woven of a mixture of activities that are conducted by the same persons in the same place and that give rise to real, apparent, and potential conflicts among them. The question is not whether the conflicts can be eliminated—they cannot—but whether they can be managed in such a way as to minimize the likelihood that they will do damage to individuals, institutions, and the public. The conflict of interest issue became visible toward the end of the 1970s, grew in importance in the 1980s, and remains unresolved today. It has this in common with the issue of fraud in research: it touches institutional values, and the way it is handled will tell much about the character of the modern research university in the future.

In ordinary usage, the term *conflict of interest* is understood to refer to circumstances in which an individual cannot fulfill the demands of one role without compromising the demands of another, or at least appearing to do so. That is, indeed, the case to which most attention is directed and which most regulation is aimed to control.

Nelson Dong has provided a useful list of the real and alleged evils, from the points of view of both universities and government, that conflict of interest regulations are supposed to prevent.[9]

An investigator and his or her company profit at the public's expense by using federal or nonprofit foundation funds to pay for research to create a valuable product owned and controlled exclusively by that company.

An investigator deflects the research, teaching, or even clinical care missions of the university for private gain.

The "profit motive" inhibits an investigator from sharing research freely and detracts from the open communications that are at the heart of university life.

An investigator out for "private gain" exploits his or her students, postdoctoral fellows, or collaborators.

The enriching of an investigator creates "hard feelings" and pangs of jealousy, envy, and resentment within faculty departments or schools.

Conflict of interest is also generally understood to involve cases in which money is one of the interests in conflict. There is no reason why it should be limited in that way, except that in American life money is thought to move people in ways that deeply held beliefs, for example, do not. Thus a scientist who is receiving money from a pharmaceutical company will find his opinions on an issue of drug safety challenged for bias, whereas another scientist who believes that companies in a capitalist economy cannot be trusted will not.

Finally, although efforts to regulate conflicts of interest are generally aimed at individuals, institutions, too, can face conflicts. There are few laws or regulations governing those conflicts, but they are real, and the way

9. Nelson G. Dong, "University-Industry Symbiosis: The Passing of an Era?" BIO-TECH '95, November 3, 1995. American Law Institute/American Bar Association, San Francisco, 4. For this, and other parts of the following pages, I am indebted to Dong for his lucid and thorough coverage of the ground.

in which they are resolved reflects institutional values and establishes the climate from which members of the institution take their own behavioral cues.

With such concerns, it is not surprising that conflict of interest became an issue on the public agenda, and therefore on the university agenda, as science and commerce came closer together and as scientists and their discoveries became valuable assets to business. Here, too, the defining event was the discovery and subsequent exploitation of recombinant DNA. Prior to that, other faculty had connections with industry. Particularly in engineering fields, in chemistry, and in computer-related fields, consulting arrangements were common, and in the last of those it was not unknown for faculty to hold corporate positions in companies whose products were related to their work. Those relationships sometimes raised questions about whether government-sponsored discoveries were finding their way inappropriately to corporations and whether graduate students were being seduced or coerced by their professors into work that was of greater interest for the professor's corporate connection than for the student's education.

Those were and are important questions, but neither they nor any other such question had great force as a public concern until two things happened at about the same time. First, fundamental biology met the biotech industry. Suddenly, scientists whose closest acquaintance with a balance sheet or a business plan had been the annual budget and work plan of their NIH grant found themselves involved in new businesses, corporate structure, marketing plans, stock options, and proprietary information. Second, the leveling off of research funds from the government, together with the discovery of America's competitive deficit in international markets, put universities on the lookout for money and put business on the lookout for new ideas, developments that were encouraged by rhetoric and action from Washington throughout the 1980s.

It all happened very quickly. The method of recombining DNA was discovered by Herbert Boyer of the University of California at San Francisco and Stanley Cohen of Stanford University in 1973. At first, neither thought to protect the discovery by seeking a patent for it. They were not alone in that. While patents were common in engineering, they were much less common in biology, and especially in fundamental biology. As a result, the time allowed by law to seek a patent had almost expired when the director of Stanford's patent office became aware of the discovery and undertook to persuade the inventors to allow the university to seek patent protection for it.

At Stanford, that was not an easy sell. A group of senior faculty, including three Nobel laureates, expressed deep misgivings about the wisdom of allowing commercial concerns into the university's laboratories. Their worries were weighty ones: If economic gain were to become an important motive for the scientist and the university, what was to prevent an unhealthy and destructive secretiveness from inhibiting the free flow of information among scientists? If scientists were seen to be profiting from the commercial exploitation of their work, would they not be ruled out of public debate about how their work should be used? If the university were to profit from the discoveries of some faculty, would it not favor those who produced the profit with resources that would be denied to other valuable, but not predictably profitable, scientific work? In sum, would not the introduction of economic motives into the university corrupt the values and habits that made them such valuable institutions?

Before a patent was sought the inventors had agreed to forgo any royalties, which, at Stanford, were to be divided among the university, the medical school, and the inventor's department. Moreover, the university agreed to inform the NIH of its intention to patent the discovery and of its requirement that all licensees abide by the safety rules established by the government for recombinant DNA research. If the NIH were to object, the patent would not be sought. The NIH did not object. The patent was ultimately issued, and licensing royalties from it reached the millions and became the single most lucrative patent that Stanford ever owned. By 1993, it accounted for $20 million out of Stanford's total of $33 million in royalties from licenses on patents. Moreover, it was only the first of many patents to emerge from basic biology and genetics. Both Boyer and Cohen associated themselves with major biotech companies, and within a relatively few years, virtually all of the dissenting scientists had themselves entered into arrangements with corporations. It may not have been the rising tide that lifts all boats, but it surely was the wave of the future that swept all before it.

There was, from the start, something amiss in these new connections between universities and business. It was the wish of the government, promoted by the Reagan and Bush administrations, that these relationships be seeded widely. Eric Bloch, the director of the National Science Foundation and a former IBM scientist, was an especially enthusiastic and effective advocate of closer relations, in which he saw the only real hope for growth in the foundation's budget. Indeed, he made these joint enterprises the centerpiece of an ambitious effort to double the size of the NSF budget.

As a general proposition, Republicans do not like "industrial policy," which they scorn as an inherently self-defeating process by which the government undertakes to identify favored technologies and encourage them with subsidies, attempting to outguess the market and override the decisions that business would take for sound business reasons. In spite of that general bias, they were perfectly prepared to support programs that brought businesses together with universities in centers of technology and research as well as development in fields deemed by officials at the National Science Foundation to be economically promising. Through the 1980s, the executive branch of the federal government, state governments, businesses, and universities acted together to make universities instruments of economic development. In the process, how could scientists not become closer to business, and how could the perception, if not the reality, of scientific decisions made for financial reasons be avoided? The question answers itself.

Democrats, however, controlled the Congress. Since they are, as a party, much more disposed to think that it is right and proper for government to make economic decisions, they were inclined to encourage efforts to use government to stimulate economic development through industry-university collaboration. The NSF programs aimed at that goal grew disproportionately compared with other NSF activities.

However, as a party, Democrats, especially liberal Democrats, are also disposed to be suspicious of concentrations of economic power and to be more quickly outraged at suspicions of shady dealings. It is no accident, then, that the issue of conflict of interest came alive in the 1980s, with investigations led by such liberal Democrats as John Dingell (Dem., Mich.), Ron Wyden (Dem., Ore.), and Ted Weiss (Dem., N.Y.). They had fertile fields to plow. As connections between faculty and industry were expanding rapidly, so too were occasions for at least the appearance of conflicts and, in some cases, the reality. It was a short step from that discovery to legislation and the pressure to regulate. It was a much longer step to the understanding that their own party's policies were helping to produce the behavior they deplored. Most never made that leap.

By 1989, both the NIH and the NSF were busy devising policies for the regulation of conflict of interest among their grantees. Since all universities and many scientists received funds from both agencies, one might have thought that they would collaborate on a single set of policies for both agencies. Government, however, rarely works that way, and so each eventually produced a separate set of regulations, using somewhat different definitions, covering somewhat different sets of personnel and activities, and imposing somewhat different procedures.

In 1989, the NIH, in a series of meetings and semiformal statements, announced its intention to develop guidelines for the regulation of conflicts of interest. In the fall of 1989, it released a statement setting out what it considered appropriate guidelines for handling conflicts. As Dong describes it, "The September 1989 NIH proposal envisioned that grant-receiving institutions would collect massive amounts of detailed financial information from individual investigators and would then report that information to NIH. Furthermore, the proposal would have effectively banned investigators from holding any equity stake in companies that would profit from NIH-funded research." [10]

The reaction from academics and industry was immediate and vehement. The NIH received a flood of comments, which ran ten-to-one against the proposals. Dr. Louis Sullivan, the secretary of health and human services, instructed the NIH to withdraw the proposals and return to the drawing board. The next three years saw the floating of a series of narrower proposals but no closure on the issue. Unhappy with the absence of action, the Congress, in 1993, in its annual appropriation for the NIH, instructed the institutes to issue regulations within 180 days of the passage of the act, and it prescribed some elements that the regulations must include.

The NIH missed its deadline by a good margin, but in June 1994, it did finally issue proposed regulations in two parts. One part dealt with the obligations of grantee institutions; the second dealt specifically with individual scientists. The latter set of regulations were called "Objectivity in Research" guidelines. Their purpose was this:

> The value of the results of [Public Health Service–funded] research to the health and economy of the Nation must not be compromised by any financial interest that will, or may reasonably be expected to, bias the design, conduct or reporting of the research. The proposed regulations seek to maintain a reasonable balance between these competing interests, give applicants for PHS research funding responsibility and discretion to identify and manage financial interests that may bias the research, and minimize reporting and other burdens on the applicants. [11]

After a period of public comment, regulations were finally issued, and in the end, the NIH probably got it about as right as it is possible to do in such a murky area. The principal remedy proposed was disclosure of possibly entangling relationships to the scientist's institution, with the university held responsible for recognizing actual and potential conflicts and acting to mitigate them. In spite of the false starts and the congressional impa-

---

10. Nelson G. Dong, "Government Regulation of Academic Entrepreneurship in Federally Sponsored Research," BIOTECH '94 American Law Institute/American Bar Association, Boston, 1994.

11. *Federal Register* (June 27, 1994): 32997, microfiche.

tience, the general good sense of these regulations is an instructive example of why, in government, it is usually more important to get it right than to do it fast. So broad is the scope of the government's reach, so blunt are the regulatory instruments at its disposal, and so limited is its knowledge of the vast variety of circumstances its regulations must embrace that government is capable of doing great damage with none but the best intentions. The long gestation period for these particular regulations served the public well.

Institutional Conflict of Interest

Universities advocated and won the primary responsibility for monitoring and mitigating individual conflicts of interest. The question remains whether they are up to the job. Massive amounts of information will be collected from faculty detailing their outside engagements and their financial ties, and those of their families, as well. Knowledge may be liberating, but in this case it is also a burden. What does one do with all of those reports? Who is responsible for analyzing them? What standards should be used to determine when a particular association crosses the line into questionable territory? What kinds of mitigation fit particular cases? How does the institution process appeals on decisions that emerge from the answers to those questions? What sanctions are available for dealing with egregious violations of the rules? The questions go on and on. I do not know how many universities are prepared to answer these questions today, though I suspect that those that can are in the minority.

Recognizing the likelihood that universities could use help in framing effective policies and procedures, the Association of American Universities, in May 1993, once again published a framework to help universities construct the system required by law. The framework document suggests alternative approaches to many difficult questions that arise when dealing with individual financial conflicts of interest. It is explicit, however, in noting that it does not address one question that it urges universities to attend to: "The document does not address the development of policies for institutional conflicts of interest, which develop out of links between institutional financial interests and the commercial application of faculty research results. However, universities are strongly encouraged to establish such policies, as well."[12]

The fact that the AAU did not attempt to offer suggestions on this topic suggests, among other things, that no consensus existed among its members. That is in fact the case. There are widely varying ideas about

12. *Framework Document for Managing Financial Conflicts of Interest* (Washington, D.C.: Association of American Universities, 1993), 2.

what kinds of relationships are appropriate when universities enter into arrangements with industry. Within a single university, interests are in conflict, and since those conflicts will almost always involve the activities of faculty, they can be extremely difficult to disentangle. The trouble is that the failure to think the problem through clearly can result in the exercise of bad judgment on a large and very public scale.

The NIH found itself in the middle of one such problem when a proposed deal between the Scripps Research Institute in La Jolla, California, and the Sandoz Pharmaceutical Company of Switzerland provoked loud outcries from the press and the Congress. In exchange for a large grant, Scripps gave Sandoz primary rights to virtually every discovery in the institute. Since Scripps was a major NIH grantee, the obvious question was whether it was appropriate to grant to a private corporation, and a foreign one at that, the fruits of research paid for by American taxpayers. The agreement was ultimately significantly amended, and in its new rules, the NIH insisted on tougher reviews of the large, long-term agreements that would constitute a large proportion of the institution's total research funding.

The NIH rules addressed a particular problem, but one that was unlikely to be repeated very often, simply because companies do not very often offer funds in the amount that Sandoz was prepared to pay. There are other, more common, problems, and their answers are not so easy. Early in the development of the biotech industry, for example, Harvard's investment managers decided to invest in a company that grew out of the work of Mark Ptashne, one of Harvard's most eminent biologists. The university subsequently reversed the decision after receiving significant criticism from the Harvard faculty, including a pointed and public complaint by Walter Gilbert, another Harvard luminary who thought it unfair that the university proposed to invest in a company that might be in competition with one with which he was associated. The underlying question was addressed in the report of the Pajaro Dunes conference in 1982. The report noted

> the growing tendency, especially in the biotechnology field, for professors to own significant blocks of stock in commercial enterprises, to assist in the formation of such enterprises, or even to assume substantial executive responsibilities. Conflicts of interest may arise through combinations of public funding, private consulting, and equity holding in companies engaged in activities in a faculty member's area of interest. These developments underscore the need for universities to consider the rules and procedures needed to insure that faculty members fulfill their responsibilities to teaching and research, and to avoid conflicts of interest.

At times, the research or entrepreneurial efforts of a faculty member may have the potential materially to affect the economic condition of a company. (In such cases, the faculty member is often a substantial stockholder in the firm.) Under these conditions, investment by the professor's own university in the firm gives the institution a financial stake in the activities of its faculty member. This situation may cause others to believe that the university encourages entrepreneurial activities by its faculty. Moreover, it may cause, or appear to cause, the university to extend preferential treatment to the professor, for example, in such matters as promotion, space, or teaching loads and thus to undermine the morale and academic integrity of the institution. Hence, it is not advisable for universities to make such investments unless they are convinced that there are sufficient safeguards to avoid adverse effects on the morale of the institution or on the academic relationships between the university, its faculty, and its students.

Those are measured, thoughtful, even wise, words, but they read today as if they were discovered by an archeologist on the walls of a cave. There hardly exists a major university, including Harvard, that has not found a device for investing in promising companies whose promise derives from the work of its own faculty. These devices frequently isolate academic officers from the investment decision. There is no way, however, to separate academic officers and other faculty from the knowledge that university funds have been invested in the for-profit work of a colleague, a circumstance that may give rise to the suspicion or even the conviction that preferential treatment is being accorded the favored individual in order to protect the university's investment. Whether that actually happens is impossible to say without knowledge that could come only from within schools and departments, but it would be foolish not to consider the possibility and to wonder, still, about the wisdom of the practice, notwithstanding the money that might be lost if universities were to forswear it.

There are other dangers from overly enthusiastic efforts by universities to exploit the work of their faculty. The episode that serves as a paradigm for all others exploded on the public in March 1989, when officials of the University of Utah called a press conference to announce that two of its scientists had produced a fusion reaction at room temperature. If this were true, they were leading the way toward a technology that would free humanity from dependence on fossil fuels and would provide cheap, pollution-free energy. This technology would obviously have profound economic implications, not the least of which was the possibility that licensing the technology could bring the university between $100 million and $200 million in licensing fees in the first year, according to estimates reported by a university official.

With visions of sugarplums dancing in their heads, university officials set out to protect the dream. The first step, according to James J. Brophy, the university's vice president for research, was to persuade Professors Stanley Pons and Martin Fleischmann to announce their findings eighteen months before they were prepared to do so. The *Chronicle of Higher Education* reported that "University of Utah officials, concerned that news of the research might leak out and possibly jeopardize the prospects of commercializing its results, advised the scientists to scrap their schedule, prepare a preliminary paper on the work, and hold a press conference even before it was published."[13] There could be no better description of the practice of "science by press conference" that, for the same reason, had become common in the biomedical sciences.

The Utah announcement generated a storm of publicity, a $5 million appropriation from the State of Utah, and a congressional hearing arranged by lobbyists retained by the university at which officials of the university suggested that about $25 million from the federal government would help the next stage of the work. It also set off a storm of controversy among physicists. Attempts to replicate the work were unsuccessful, though no one could be sure if they were replicating the experiments exactly, because the university was unwilling to allow Pons and Fleischmann to release their experimental methods for fear of jeopardizing their patent position. Most physicists were scornful of the research findings on both experimental and theoretical grounds, and it did not take long for the media to turn away from the initial claims and, as is their wont, turn on those who had exploited their gullibility. Leading the opposition to the cold-fusion finding were scientists at MIT, a fact that did not prevent the institute, along with several other universities, from applying for patents on their own room-temperature-fusion work, an academic example of hedging one's bets.

Officials at Utah took some comfort from this, and even found in it a way to grope toward higher ground. Said Vice President Brophy, "Everybody is doing what they criticize the University of Utah for doing—science by press release." What sets the University of Utah apart, he told the *Chronicle of Higher Education,* was the fact that Pons and Fleischmann had worked on their research for five years before making an announcement. "Everybody else has been working on it for five weeks. You don't push science this fast" (ibid.).

13. *Chronicle of Higher Education* (May 17, 1989): A5.

It is hard to find even a single redeeming feature in this sorry episode. The scientists involved, the officials of the university, the state government, the Utah congressional delegation, and the media—none of them had reason to be proud of their performance. What is most disturbing, though, is the likelihood that this case is not unique, only extreme. There are many good reasons why universities should be actively trying to move the discoveries of their scientists into the stream of commerce, not the least of them being that it is one powerful way to provide the public a return on its investment in universities. If, however, economic return becomes the purpose of the enterprise rather than a by-product of it, then alleged concern for the public is nothing but a rationalization for behavior that subverts science itself and that distorts the institutions in which it takes place. That would be a bad bargain. One president interviewed for this book put it this way:

> I am not persuaded that universities have done enough thinking about what the limits ought to be. The pressures to get money, to sign things that would bring research funds into the university, are so strong that you really need to be prepared in advance to know what you stand for and what is for sale. And if you are not prepared, and you just do it in the context of a deal that is suddenly offered, and you have to decide whether to accept it or not, then it is not going to be an equal contest. The people who stand to gain money are going to be so much more insistent than the people who are scratching their heads wondering about abstract principles. And the principles will go right down the drain.

Embedded in that paragraph is a phrase that resonates: "what you stand for and what is for sale." Questions of institutional conflict of interest come down in the end to two questions: What is for sale? What is beyond price? As Derek Bok put it,

> In a world in which so much of what we do has commercial value ... what is there in a university that is *not* for sale? An institution that cannot answer this question doesn't know what it really stands for. Yet the commercial temptations are everywhere, and they are everywhere gaining ground. We say that we won't sell paintings. But will we rent them to a corporation on a long-term basis? We say we don't sell places in our entering class. But will we admit that fantastic point guard with substandard grades, who might just take us to the Final Four and gain us a share of those lucrative TV revenues?[14]

---

14. Derek Bok, "A Matter of Accountability," *Bulletin* [of the American Academy of Arts and Sciences] 48, no. 4 (January 1995): 37.

It has never been easy for American universities to answer those questions because, historically, their purposes have been so much bound up with the economic, social, and political forces swirling around them. They have been highly permeable institutions, and any institution that competes in the market for students, private philanthropy, and public funding will find the line between its own purposes and those of its patrons and consumers sometimes hard to detect. Indeed, tight finances can render the line invisible, can tempt institutional leadership, in the words of W. H. Auden, into "Greening after the big money / Neighing after a public image" ("The Garrison"). If university leaders, administrators, and faculty together cannot demonstrate the discipline that clear and consistent answers to those questions require, it is hard to imagine governments and businesses being more restrained in their demands for immediate returns on investment, or more understanding of the uncertainties of fundamental inquiry, or more confident of its ultimate rewards.

Conflict of Commitment

A new term has found its way into discourse about academic life, *conflict of commitment*. In the "premodern" university, there was little need for such a term. A professor's job was well understood. For all but a very few, it consisted of teaching and doing such scholarship as time and inclination permitted. There were few calls to service off campus and few competing claims on a professor's time. Clearly, that has changed. Today's research university professors are nothing if not worldly. That is most obviously true for scientists, engineers, and the faculty of professional schools, but it is true, too, for social scientists. Even humanists have become involved in public discourse and debate as controversial critical theories and what are called "cultural studies" have entered the curriculum, the literature, and public consciousness. The demands on their time and attention, and in many cases the variety of competing rewards available to them, can severely strain their commitment to the institution that pays their salary and claims their first loyalty.

Loyalty is the essence of the issue of conflict of commitment. Conflicts of commitment are not the same as conflicts of interest, they are more encompassing in their causes and in the areas of the university affected by them. Conflicts of interest, as we have seen, have generally to do with money. The lure of money may also be the cause of a conflict of commitment, but there are many other reasons why faculty members may fail to meet their primary institutional obligations. For most faculty in most universities, those obligations include undergraduate teaching, graduate teaching and mentoring, original scholarship, university service, and to a greater or lesser degree, depending on the nature of the institution, public service.

This is a formidable array of responsibilities, and it is easy to understand how shifts in the balance among them might occur. One such, the one that is probably of greatest public interest, is the balance between undergraduate teaching and all of the others, but primarily scholarship. People who know little else about universities are likely to have been persuaded by what they have heard: that undergraduates are short-changed because faculty are chasing the rewards that come from successful scholarship and that the system—that is, the universities in which they work—encourage and even require that they respond to those incentives.

That perception is essentially true. The balance has changed. In principle, universities have always been about research as well as teaching, but in practice, until World War II, the scarcity of funds for research meant that most faculty spent most of their time teaching. The top universities have always sought to recruit the top scholars, but teaching was the institutional bread and butter, and those who could supply it were rewarded for that ability.

The vast increase in research funds that followed the war changed the market, and personal and institutional behavior changed with it. The availability of money made choices possible, and it turned out that most faculty wanted to do more research. Their predisposition matched institutional ambitions. Research funds that bought faculty time, in the form of reduced teaching loads, necessitated the addition of more faculty to deal with the rapidly growing student bodies, and these new faculty also came with reduced teaching loads. More faculty more engaged in doing and publishing research brought publicity and prestige, larger state appropriations, and private gifts, which in turn helped fuel the expansion. A 1992 study by the American Council on Education reported that research university faculty spent a majority of their time on activities other than teaching. Research accounted for 29 percent, administration 12 percent, and outside activities, including consulting, 13 percent. Moreover, those aggregate figures mask wide discrepancies among fields. Disciplines that benefit from heavy research funding or are subject to intense competition for faculty would show a considerably lower commitment to teaching.

There was nothing sinister about all of this. Indeed, the result was, without doubt, stronger universities and more of them. The modern American university is an enormously powerful collection of intellectual talent arrayed across a breathtakingly wide span of fields. There has never before been anything like it. By any measure, the patrons of research, both public and private, have gotten their money's worth, and the American public has been the major beneficiary. But there was a price to be paid for those benefits. One part of the price was a shift in the balance of emphasis within universities from undergraduate teaching to research and related activities. To think that it could have been otherwise is to engage in childish fantasies in which everything in the world we want is given to us and nothing is ever taken from us.

It is important to be clear about what this means. Compared with the situation of fifty years ago, the typical university faculty member today teaches fewer courses, interacts personally with fewer undergraduates, and is under greater pressure to engage in scholarship and publish the results. In the same comparison, more teaching is done by graduate students than was previously the case. That is especially true at large public universities that have heavy freshman and sophomore enrollments and the need to break large classes down into smaller ones, but private universities show a similar pattern in their introductory courses, and teaching loads at all universities are lower now than in earlier times. It is also true, however, that alarmist reports of the demise of teaching and the abandonment of the undergraduate are greatly exaggerated. There is much good teaching still, including by many graduate teaching assistants, and students get an excellent education at some universities and have the opportunity for one at all universities.

Assuming for the moment that this reasonably cheery assessment has some merit, what is the problem? The simplest answer is that the balance has shifted too far in the other direction. These are not, after all, finely calibrated matters. When prices move in a market, they do not stop moving until they encounter resistance. Since faculty and administrations profited from the movement, there was no reason to expect resistance from those quarters, and there was, in fact, little of it. In the mid-1980s, resistance began to emerge from outside the university in the form of hostility to rapidly rising tuition, political and ideological attacks on universities, and tighter government research budgets. Once again, as the market began to shift, so did behavior. Faculties began to engage in serious debates about the nature of the undergraduate curriculum; greater attention began to be paid to training and supervising graduate teaching assistants; various kinds of rewards for good teaching were devised—some institutions tried seriously to find ways to credit teaching more in decisions about promotion and compensation, and virtually all at least paid lip service to the idea. There is every reason to expect this rebalancing process to continue. Since there is little likelihood that research funding will return to its previous state, keeping classes full will be an important priority.

Some things will not change, however. They have been built into the culture of the modern university, and they will continue to work against a fair balancing of the competing interests. Chief among them is the faculty role and the expectations that go with it. The modern faculty role is badly fractured. For many faculty members, loyalties are divided among their disciplines, their corporate affiliations, their research sponsors, and, finally, their students and their institutions. The potential for conflict is high, and so is its cost. After leaving the Harvard presidency, Derek Bok spoke about the conflict:

> For both universities and faculty members, the temptations to stray from our primary mission are constantly growing stronger. For professors, opportunities to consult, travel, go to conferences, and make money are greater than ever. In these circumstances, who will enforce the rules? University administrators are reluctant to intervene. After all, they are trying to attract and retain outstanding professors, not to irritate them by trying to police their behavior. Besides, what authority do administrators have? The ultimate power lies with those who are hardest to replace, and they are not the presidents or deans. Besides, administrators are in an awkward position to complain, as they are more intrigued by new opportunities to engage in commercial ventures of their own.[15]

There are no easy answers. Indeed, there may be no answers at all. Few people would wish to unmake the modern university, even if it were possible to do so. And it may be that the dynamics of these institutions, and of the society that created them, produce conflicts of commitment that are unavoidable and must be counted as a necessary cost of the benefits received. I think that is the truth of the matter, but I also think it is irresponsible simply to leave it at that. There must be some force, moral if not legal, behind the proposition that faculty owe their primary loyalty to the institutions that employ them and that when those primary obligations conflict with others, the conflict should be resolved in favor of their university duties. There must also be force behind the proposition that the primary role of universities, and what they do best, is to educate students and, through scholarship, to enlarge the body of knowledge that provides the substance of their teaching.

This is a task of moral suasion, not regulation and enforcement. It would surely be helpful if universities had unambiguous policies governing consulting, for example, and took steps to see that they were adhered to—neither of those conditions is currently being met in most institutions—but that is only part of the matter, and not its heart. The heart of it is the underlying attitudes that inform the academic career, both faculty and administrative, and those are matters best addressed by education, discussion, and debate; in other words, by the tools that constitute the core of the academic process. The principal educator in this classroom is the university president. He or she occupies the lectern, and if the syllabus does not in-

15. Ibid., 35.

clude instruction on the obligations of individuals and of the community, then those issues will not be raised, and their resolution is most likely to derive from individual and institutional self-interest, defined in the most elementary terms.

Chapter Five

FACING THE FUTURE

I

The Capacity to Govern

W E TURN NOW from the issues and politics of the outside world as those bear on universities to the internal politics that affect the ability of each university to deal with its problems and its opportunities. We turn, in other words, to the issue of internal governance, understanding that term to mean the processes by which goals are set, the means toward their accomplishment are agreed to, conflict is managed, and commonly held values are made real through day-to-day decisions.

American universities are, on the whole, self-governing entities. We have no national system presided over by a Ministry of Education, as many countries do, and the existence of strong private institutions has been, by example, a protection for public universities, as well. Thus, self-government is the literal truth for the privates, and it is close to the truth even for those that are subject to state control. In Michigan and California, for example, the independence of the state university is written into the state constitution, and even though a central university office, in the case of California, and active governors and legislatures in both states exercise considerable influence over university affairs, the tradition of deference to the university on academic matters is a strong restraint when the temptation to meddle is hard to resist. For other major public research universities, that tradition imposes similar restraints on political interference, even though those restraints are not constitutionally guaranteed.

Because universities have been granted the power to govern themselves, their capacity for self-government is of more than passing interest. As we shall see, the early failure of governance structures to meet the challenge of the student antiwar movement made a difficult situation even worse than it needed to be. As it turned out, when put to the test, many university administrators could not summon the will, and perhaps lacked the legitimacy, to resist the demands of angry students supported by a large segment of the faculty. Eventually, the challenge was met, and basic rules of civility and order were restored and enforced.

A different kind of challenge confronts universities today, and the ability of universities to meet the test will rest in large part on the ability of their governance systems to forge a common conception of what the university ought to look like. The alternative is a war of all against all over shares of a too-small pie. Before turning in subsequent chapters to the substance of the present and future challenge, I examine in this chapter the processes through which decisions must be made.

The University as a Political System

According to an old saying, if the only tool at hand is a hammer, then everything begins to look like a nail. So it is in the literature of higher education. To economists, higher education is an industry, and the university is a firm. Both are understandable using the tools of microeconomics or macroeconomics, depending on the specialty of the writer. To the anthropologist, the university is a culture, best approached with the tools of that discipline. The sociologist sees groups, and the psychologist no doubt sees psychopathology. All are legitimate ways of looking at a university, and all can yield important insights into institutions that are, after all, economic entities and cultures, composed of groups and rich with opportunity for social, experimental, and clinical psychologists alike. Misunderstanding arises, however, from believing that any of those approaches discloses the whole truth about so complex and odd an organization as the university.

In the interest of full disclosure, I must report that I was trained as a political scientist to use the hammer of that discipline. It leads me to the conclusion that, whatever else they are, universities are without doubt political systems, and the failure to understand their peculiar characteristics as political systems is a source of much confusion and even serious error. Donald Kennedy makes an analogous point with respect to one dimension of a political system, its methods of "public administration" or, as yet another discipline would have it, its "management style."

> Universities are complicated places. To many observers—some disaffected faculty members and students and more than a few trustees—they look like other kinds of corporations: there is a chief executive officer, a group of fiduciaries (who try on occasion to be managers), a chief operating officer (the provost), and a group of divisions each with its own relatively independent leadership. Certain services are needed by all the divisions, and these are often managed centrally—development, some version of public affairs, legal services, human resources, and the like.
>
> But there are terribly important differences. Perhaps the most significant in our present context is that the intellectual direction and even the leadership of the divisions is not controlled by the center. Nor is it really *managed* at the local level, where the putative "line managers" scarcely

want to manage at all. Indeed, the equivalents of what would be called product and line services in a corporation—the teaching and the knowledge-gathering missions of the institution—depend entirely on local divisions within which there is little or no management culture of the traditional corporate kind.[1]

What is true of management is at least as true for the university's political system as a whole.[2] Considering the most obvious of the university's governing arrangements, it is a wonder that it is governed at all. The university is nominally headed by a group of absentee landlords, its lay board of trustees. In all but a small number of institutions, its members are geographically distant from the institution except at meeting time, and that distance stands as a useful metaphor for their connection to the work of the institution. The board necessarily delegates broad authority to the president for administration and to the faculty for academic decisions. If they are seen to be interfering with those delegations, it is likely to be either a cause of or a response to trouble in the institution.

It would be hard to find a chief executive officer who, judged in conventional political terms, is weaker than a university president. Although the president is the board's principal agent of governance, he or she has little or nothing to do with the most important personnel decisions, those having to do with faculty. Indeed, the fact that Derek Bok was an active participant in every tenure decision during his term of office at Harvard was so unusual that it is widely cited in books on the university presidency with some wonder. Virtually no one outside the president's immediate office and a few senior administrative officers is appointed by the president or can be fired by the president. The president leads no political party, has little if any patronage to dispense, and if caught using that little for political advantage would be seriously damaged in the eyes of the university community.

There is more. The most numerous class of persons on the campus, the student body, once stood in awe of the president. As an undergraduate at the University of Michigan from 1948 to 1952, I would not have recognized President Harlan Hatcher if I had run into him on the street, and to the best of my knowledge, I never saw him on the street or anywhere else. Certainly, it never occurred to me or my friends that we might have business with the president or any claim at all on his time. Needless to say, the

1. Donald Kennedy, "Making Choices in the Research University," in *The Research University in a Time of Discontent,* ed. by Jonathan R. Cole, Elinor G. Barber, and Stephan R. Graubard (Baltimore: Johns Hopkins University Press, 1994), 90–91.

2. In this section, I have drawn on Robert M. Rosenzweig, "Governing the Modern Research University," in Cole, Barber, and Graubard, *Research University in a Time of Discontent,* 299–308.

1960s changed all that. Students learned a good deal about their ability to put items on the university's agenda and force their consideration. Presidents learned that they ignored the expectation of students' access to them at their peril and that being seen as remote or unresponsive could be a serious political liability. Yet students, as a group, are largely unreachable by the president. He or she does not admit them, cannot dismiss them, and generally has only limited appellate authority over discipline. The result is a president who is hired and can be fired by the group that is most remote from the day-to-day work of the job but who can be undone by angry faculty or rebellious students and has no constituency or support group whose well-being and success is linked to his or hers. I have described the university presidency elsewhere in this way: "The president issues few orders, has no real political constituency, and few powers beyond those of persuasion. The president may be a more potent person off campus than on."[3]

Yet, notwithstanding all of the above, not only have universities existed for a long time, but they have, by and large, flourished. Clearly, decisions are made, resources are allocated, and the apparent weakness of the presidency does not seem to deter good people from seeking and accepting the office. Why, then, does it matter how universities govern themselves? Is it not sufficient to note that somehow or other they do and then turn to other matters? I think not. There is one quality that all successful universities must have in the modern world. One president described it this way: "The question is how to redefine our leadership and how to lead change in our institutions to a point where an institution's capacity for relatively rapid adaptation becomes one of the telltales of being a great institution, while maintaining the core of how we perceive ourselves, namely, the ability to adapt to rapid change without sacrificing what is truly important at the core."

That ability requires strong and supple governing structures, and America's universities, until now, seem to have passed the test. It is worth trying to understand why, if only in the hope that by doing so, we will learn something about what present and future changes in the environment may require.

Universities, like all successful social organisms, have developed political systems fitted to their intrinsic characteristics. The dominant characteristics of the modern American university in this context are the extraordinary degree of autonomy of individual faculty members and the strength of the academic disciplines and the departments and schools into which they are organized. Successful political institutions must, therefore, balance

3. Ibid., 301.

the intrinsic dispersion of authority in the university with the need for some collective decision-making mechanisms—another example of the classic problem of how to balance liberty and order, in this case in a setting in which liberty is highly valued, order considerably less so.

Although traditions of faculty autonomy and strong departmentalism are frequently criticized, they are in fact well suited to the basic work of the institution. They make the university unique among major social organizations in that the policies and practices that govern the main work of the institution—teaching and research—are set by the people who actually do that work. While details may vary from place to place, faculty determine what is to be taught and how to teach it, what is required in order to complete a course successfully, and what number and sequence of courses need to be completed successfully in order to earn a degree. The faculty in their departments make the critical judgments about appointments to their ranks, and faculty, as individual scholars, are the sole deciders—subject to resource constraints—of what research they will do, how they will do it, and where and in what form it will be published. The faculty, individually and collectively, are responsible for the substance and the standards of the institution. It is in that sense, and probably only in that sense, that the commonly held belief that "the faculty are the university" has meaning. Thus, in spite of the fact that these powers are delegated to faculties by boards of trustees, and, in theory at least, can be withdrawn, in reality these are virtually plenary powers. Boards and administrations rarely challenge them, and turmoil is the result when they do.

Any political system that fails to take into account the way in which its "society" actually operates will surely fail. But it is also true that no organization as complex as the modern university can survive without some legitimate central authority, some way of generating agreement among separate dukedoms and independent dukes, some way of facing the outside world and responding to its demands, some capacity for dealing with issues that cut across the separate units. Typically, the arrangements that make these things possible take the form of an implicit bargain between faculty and administration. The latter agree not to intervene in matters that are essentially academic, and the former grant substantial authority to administration to deal with budgets, fund raising, infrastructure, business functions, and the implementation of such important academic matters as the admission of students. In real life that is not as simple as it sounds, and conflicts at the borders are common. And, of course, the specific arrangements by which the basic elements of the agreement are translated into practice vary widely. The University of California, for example, has long had an elaborate scheme of shared governance in which the powers of the faculty and the administration are spelled out in considerable detail. Private universities are typically not so formally structured in their arrangements.

After many years of viewing universities from close range and from a distance, I have concluded that when things are going well, when the institution is not under stress, one set of arrangements works about as well as another. So long as resources are reasonably adequate, faculty are reasonably content, and students reasonably placid, almost any political structure will do the job. Bad decisions may be made because the right people are not involved and potentially dissenting voices are not heard, but money is a great lubricant, and so long as there is more each year than the year before, almost any system will move things along in a way that is acceptable to all parts of the community. As one president put it, "When you're raising money, all is forgiven. You know, when you're ready to sprinkle out money into the place, enabling them to do things they want to do, why should they get into a fight with the president of the university?"

However, when stress is introduced into the community in any of the many forms it might take, the situation changes quickly and dramatically, and weaknesses in the decision-making structure—that is to say, the political system—compound the problem. The stress may come in the form of any sudden, discontinuous change—financial stringency, or attack from outside forces, or internal disruption. Whatever its source, stress produces controversy, controversy produces factions, the struggle between factions produces winners and losers, and the absence of authoritative and legitimate decision-making structures makes the acceptable resolution of disputes difficult to achieve. An example will illustrate the point. It is taken from the experience of Stanford University at the start of the antiwar movement.

The Antiwar Movement at Stanford: A Failure of Governance

When I arrived in 1962 as a young administrator, Stanford was clearly a place on the way up. Under the leadership of J. E. Wallace Sterling, a superb Mr. Outside, and Frederick E. Terman, a tough-minded and visionary Mr. Inside, Stanford had been one of the first universities to seize the opportunities afforded by the new government research funding and had moved quickly to strengthen its science and engineering programs. By the time I arrived, an aggressive recruiting campaign had already moved its programs in the humanities and the social sciences toward the front rank. Not surprisingly, a freewheeling, entrepreneurial spirit dominated the campus. Subject to strict quality control standards governing faculty appointments (hawkishly enforced by Provost Terman), faculty had license to pursue good ideas. The test was the marketplace: good ideas were ones that were academically sound and that found financial support. If, after start-up help, it was not possible to attract outside funding, then it was time to move on to something else.

In such an atmosphere, it is not surprising that faculty governing institutions were quite rudimentary. For one thing, faculty were too busy building their programs to worry much about larger questions of governance. For another, times were good, resources were growing, students were reasonably placid, and so there was every reason to leave most matters to the administration to solve. Stanford was hardly unique; on the contrary, it exemplified the spirit of the times.

The only instrument through which the faculty participated in university-wide policy matters was as an assembly of the entire faculty called the Academic Council. The council consisted of all tenure-track faculty, and it met once a quarter to hear a report from the president, read memorial resolutions for recently deceased faculty, confer degrees, and from time to time debate such matters as the merits of the quarter and semester systems. Attendance was typically small, questions were rarely asked, and the peace was hardly ever disturbed. The Academic Council had an elected Executive Committee that was responsible for setting the council's agenda and managing its affairs, such as they were, and an elected Advisory Board that played a key role in appointments and promotion to tenure and in faculty discipline and in an advisory role to the president on matters affecting the faculty.

This was the governance structure that existed at the start of the student disruptions of the 1960s; it was one that seemed to meet the faculty's needs and interests at that time. But even at the time, not everyone was convinced of that. A small group of faculty, working with the Executive Committee of the Academic Council, had been developing plans for a Faculty Senate, an elected, representative, legislative body. Those plans were not complete in the spring of 1968, when Stanford's first major sit-in took place and showed what can happen when unexpected events overwhelm the capacity of existing structures. In this case, the unexpected event was a sit-in at the Old Union, an administration building in the center of the campus. Compared with later events, this first major disruption was a peaceful affair, and its cause—a protest over minor penalties to seven students who had obstructed CIA interviews and the alleged illegitimacy of the judicial system under which they had been tried—was not the stuff of which great drama is made. However, the university's business was disrupted for three days, and there was no end in sight. The Executive Committee had put together a set of proposals for changing the student judicial system and for retrying the seven students. The committee's proposals were different from the demands of those sitting in, and they did not include amnesty either for the seven or for the sitters-in.

The full Academic Council was the only instrument through which those proposals could be enacted, and a meeting was called for late on a Wednesday afternoon. The meeting was a shambles. The tone was set before the meeting was even called to order, when it could not even be determined for certain who was a council member and therefore entitled to enter the hall, participate in the debate, and cast a vote. The recommendations of the Executive Committee for breaking the impasse and ending the sit-ins were summarily tabled and therefore could not even be debated by the full body. After tumultuous, not to say riotous, debate, the council rebuffed the president, the provost, and its own Executive Committee and voted to accede in substance to the demands of the sitters-in, to reverse the suspensions of the seven students—four of which were for the summer quarter only—and to offer amnesty to all those who had sat in.

Seated at the back of the hall that afternoon, I watched that parody of participatory democracy—a debate with no rules, no structure, and little order. It was clear that if the faculty could not find a way to organize itself to play a part in university policy, then the university's capacity to respond to disruptive behavior was at the mercy of any faction that could bring enough of its members to a meeting to dominate what would inevitably be a chaotic process. Stanford had experienced, as many other universities soon would, a radical change in the environment, and its political institutions were found wanting. For the first time, students had demonstrated that, by their actions, they could be a part of the governing process, at least to the extent of forcing consideration of their agenda, including bringing into the university an outside political agenda. That development, in turn, activated elements of the faculty that had never before shown any interest in governance issues outside their own departments and schools. Only after the event did the magnitude of these changes and their implications begin to be understood.

Two evenings later, Herbert Packer, a distinguished member of the Law School faculty who was also serving as vice provost, addressed the Stanford chapter of the AAUP at their annual dinner meeting. Packer, along with the rest of the academic administration, had been on the losing side of the vote, and he used the occasion to deliver a withering attack on the behavior of the faculty majority at the Wednesday meeting. He noted, among other things, that the winning side had been led and dominated by a bloc of Medical School faculty, most of whom had never before demonstrated interest in the issues in dispute and who gave no sign that they knew the facts of the case on which they were voting. "What many faculty members don't realize," he said,

> is that next year's issues may touch them a little more closely than this year's did. Many faculty members couldn't care less about the integrity of the university's judicial processes. Up to a couple of weeks ago most would have had trouble telling you what the initials IJB [Interim Judicial Board] stood for. I doubt whether there are more than a handful who even now can claim to understand the history, and thus be in a position to judge the merits, of that controversy. That is the administration's business, they say, although they are strangely reluctant to trust the administration's judgment when their own peace of mind is threatened.

It was a deeply pessimistic and, as subsequent events sadly demonstrated, prescient assessment of events and their consequences. "Faculty members who voted yes last Wednesday in the belief that nothing of importance was being given away will find themselves in for a rude awakening. Student activists have very different ideas about the appropriate role for students in university governance [from those of] their comfortable, liberal, but essentially bourgeois followers on the faculty." Packer went on to speak of his "deep foreboding about the troubled future of the university in its relations to the worlds outside—the Congress, other agencies of government, the alumni, the general public." In the end, the one significant element of hope he saw was the coming decision to create a Faculty Senate. "The senate will, I hope and believe, provide government by reason and deliberation, rather than by mob scene."[4]

He was right in that, too. After some early rough moments and some tests of the body's legitimacy through referenda on its decisions, the Faculty Senate came to be accepted as a legitimate decision-making body for the faculty, and on such issues as ROTC and the ending of classified research, its ability to speak for the faculty with clear authority was critically important.

It would be a mistake to overstate the importance of institutional arrangements. The history of the twentieth century provides many examples of allegedly democratic constitutions that were on their surface exemplary but were in reality nothing more than fig leafs for totalitarian rule. Institutions work when the underlying political will exists to make them work. Without them, hard times are even harder, but even the best set of institutional arrangements will be tested by major changes in the environment or shifts in the culture.

4. The quotes are from the author's copy of the text of Professor Packer's speech to the annual dinner meeting of the Stanford AAUP chapter.

The Faculty Look Outward: A Challenge to Governance

Challenges come in different forms. At Stanford, events precipitated a direct challenge to the existing governance structure, and Stanford failed the test. Not all tests are so visible and clear. The dramatically changed perspectives of faculty in the modern university provide a different example of the way in which change produces stress, stress provokes divisions, and divisions require acceptable arrangements for their resolution. The primary source of the change is the growth of science as the dominant driving force in the postwar university, the growth in the cost of science, and the consequent dependence of the university on external funding for scientific programs and therefore on the faculty whose work brings the money in. One president charted the change from his own experience:

> I came on the faculty in 1960. I vividly recall that the facility into which I moved my biology laboratory didn't have hot water in it. They had to plumb it to put hot water into it. It's easy to forget that science exploded in the late fifties and through the sixties and the early seventies.
>
> The thing that happened that I think was part and parcel of that, and it extended beyond science to other disciplines, was that the best faculty members became citizens of invisible national academies of their disciplines, primarily, rather than of a single university. . . . In a few big science disciplines the existence of national facilities has pulled loyalty away from the institution and into national organizations. But it's happened without that as well. If you really look at how the leading faculty members in our institutions behave now, as compared with the early 1960s, much more of their time is spent on activities whose primary locus isn't the campus. It's the NIH study section, or the international conference on whatever.

While science and technology led the shift in faculty identifications from institutional to disciplinary, other fields followed. Universities will tolerate a certain degree of differential in pay and perquisites from department to department—as a law professor friend once said, "If English professors think they're underpaid compared to me, they should go out and practice English"—but there is, in fact, a limit to the acceptable differences. Salaries in the humanities and social sciences were carried upward along with those in the sciences and engineering, and teaching loads moved downward, as well. Lessons learned by scientists were not lost on their colleagues in other fields. Government support of research not only fostered research but gave the receiving disciplines clout on the campus, and strong national disciplinary organizations were useful in generating support for greater government funding. Indeed, megadisciplinary organizations grew, at least in part to maximize political influence. Experimental biologists of various kinds came together to form the Federation of American Societies for Experimental Biology and became a major force in biomedical research policy, sometimes in cooperation with university groups and sometimes in opposition to them. The Modern Language Association and the American Council of Learned Societies, each representing many humanistic disciplines, came to play important roles in support of the National Endowment for the Humanities. And when the Reagan administration threatened to cut funding for the social sciences, the individual, relatively weak professional associations of social scientists joined together to form the Consortium of Social Science Associations in an effort to increase their influence on policy.

Nor was this fragmentation of institutional loyalties limited to faculty. Following a great American tradition in which government's touch spawns group action on the part of those who seek either nurture or protection from it, university administrations moved along with faculty in that direction. One president described his administration in this way:

> Another thing that I did not anticipate was the professionalization of the administration itself in segmented ways. We've always had this with faculty. But admissions officers now belong to the same kind of national organizations that professors of economics do. It's a fascinating point. When I became president I used to walk around the administration building which was newly built, and it was built for the purpose of containing the administration. And for a couple of years it did, before the administration outgrew it. Then I knew everybody. Well, that became just impossible, because we soon had legions of people, and when you talked to them they had their own language, their own professional criteria, and so on. They were still loyal to the institution, just as a professor of economics or history or medicine was loyal to the institution, but there was also that other world out there which had become incredibly complex and with which of course by the time I left they were all in touch electronically. So that it was a world that was not out *there*, it was, Goddammit, in their office all the time.

It may be too harsh to think of these new allegiances as a weakening of institutional loyalty on the part of faculty and administrators. Most university faculty and most administrators genuinely care about their institution, wish it only well, and would not knowingly act in ways that damage it. It is probably more accurate to talk about a fragmentation of interests. In earlier and simpler days, the interests of faculty were overwhelmingly identified with their institutions. In fact, there was very little competition. If the university was healthy, so, too, was its faculty, and staying healthy was largely a local matter. Events outside the university had far less impact on the ability of faculty to do their jobs, which in any event consisted largely in teaching their classes. Professors might, as individuals, be asked in private universities to help in fund raising or in student recruiting, but they were not expected to earn their salaries by winning grants and contracts, to support graduate students and postdoctoral fellows, to serve on peer review panels, to organize or even attend international meetings, except rarely, or to do the myriad other things that make up the life of today's successful faculty member. The ability of a faculty member to do his or her job now depends on the appropriation level of the sponsoring agencies, the ability of professional associations to bring pressure to bear, and the network of professional connections that help produce important committee assignments, peer and public attention, and greater success in getting grants. A healthy university is, of course, highly desirable, but the possibilities of generating very different definitions of what is required for institutional health multiply as the sources of faculty well-being multiply. To put it differently, it is no longer clear in today's world that the interests of faculty and the interests of their universities coincide.

Chapter 3 gives a clear example of such a divergence of interests, namely, the very different ways in which faculty and administrators view the indirect costs of research. There is a natural and, if one believes in the efficacy of checks and balances, not altogether unhealthy, tension between the two views. Faculty tend to view indirect costs as a deduction from the money they have won for their research in fair competition. Many faculty have never liked indirect costs or believed that they are real, and in times of budgetary stress they like them even less. As faculty see it, they are a tax on research, and we have ample evidence from the world around us that there are few public acts as unloved as a tax. Administrations, on the other hand, see the reimbursement of these costs as additions to grants and contracts whose purpose is to pay for the institution in whose absence there would be no faculty research. The goal of university administrations has been to maximize recovery.

The disastrous events involving Stanford's indirect cost claims can be viewed as a failure of the institution's governance mechanisms to deal with a particularly acute case of the faculty-administration tension that everywhere accompanies the issue of indirect costs. One of the main precipitating events leading to the debacle was an article in *Science* magazine in which several Stanford faculty members complained bitterly about the university's exorbitant indirect cost rate and suggested that it was not solely a function of high costs. To the best of my knowledge, no one publicly accused the faculty involved of disloyalty, much less suggested that any action against them was appropriate, even though in the end the president resigned and the university lost perhaps a hundred million dollars, was plunged into budget cuts and layoffs beyond what would have been necessary simply from the effects of a recession, suffered a major public embarrassment, and wound up with elaborate and expensive new systems of accounting controls whose effects will be felt for years to come in increased administrative costs and more burdensome bureaucracy.

It is the function of governance systems to provide a structure within which such conflicts can be resolved short of domestic strife. Clearly, Stanford's system failed that test, and it was not alone. Indeed, the inability of universities to come to agreement with their faculties on what constitutes fair indirect cost reimbursement necessarily poisoned policy making at the national level, as well.

Tensions of the kind that exploded at Stanford have their counterpart at the national level. The most persistent and effective advocates of restraints on indirect cost recovery during my time in Washington were scientific societies, especially those in the biomedical sciences. These groups represent their members as researchers interested in maximizing the numbers of grants available and the dollars within them that can be used for the direct costs of their laboratories. The health of the universities in which their members labor, while not a matter of complete indifference, is not their primary concern. More than once in the various set-tos over indirect cost policy during my years in Washington, I testified on behalf of universities before a congressional committee or an executive agency and was preceded or followed by someone representing organized faculty testifying on the other side. For members of Congress, indirect cost recovery is a marginal issue, at best. On such a matter, they are looking for a quick answer, not a dogfight, and they were understandably puzzled and frequently irritated.

It should be clear, therefore, that the inherent weaknesses in university political systems are not theoretical; they have consequences. That was not clear for most of the postwar period because prosperity, that great lubricator, worked to ease most strains. When that was not possible, as in the case of the antiwar movement and the indirect cost fight, institutional processes broke down in painful and destructive ways, some of whose consequences have not, to this day, been overcome. What happens, though, when prosperity is no longer available to help smooth over problems, when opportunities to expand are replaced by the need to contract? Since that is the present condition of most universities and the likely future prospect as well, it is not encouraging to hear the views of at least some presidents.

I came to work at [my university] two months before school began, and I've been with the place for nearly forty years since. Over that period of time, I would characterize the evolution of the place in phases. . . . The three periods were first, that period of the enormous explosion of federal involvement with research—financial support for research programs, to be sure, but perhaps more importantly, support for facilities development, encouragement to undertake new activities in materials, research centers, in that period of time, all through the 1960s.

Things changed in the 1970s. We thought at the time, "Well, that was part of the Nixon dysfunction," and [we thought] it would go away. In fact, the change was the beginning of a change more profound than that. We spent that decade and probably into the eighties jiggling things a little bit to accommodate to what was at its root a fundamental change in the relationship between government and universities.

And it seems to me we're now in that third phase in which the recognition is pretty well understood among trustees and administrators that we evolved over thirty years of enormous growth a structure in which the responsibility for the finances of the place devolved to the faculty to a remarkable degree. At the same time, we developed a sense of how responsibility and power are allocated within the institution, which is quite incapable of dealing with the likely future. The folks who are most important in developing and encouraging the flow of research dollars to the institution do not have a well-developed sense of the needs of the institution as a whole. When the time comes to address declining research support, or the problems of infrastructure, there is a remarkable degree of insensitivity to institutional concerns versus departmental concerns.

There is nothing new about the presidential view that faculty do not understand the institution as a whole or the corresponding view of some faculty that presidents, no matter how stellar their past faculty service, turn into corporate executives and politicians the day they take office. Indeed, both views contain a measure of truth. However, even against that normal level of suspicion, I was surprised by some of the views I heard while talking to presidents. One put it this way:

We are frightened of the faculty, and with good reason, because they can discharge us more readily than our boards in many ways. But I sometimes think we're out there as shills and salesmen, more because we're frightened of our faculty than because we really believe that everything we're doing in our institutions is being done as efficiently as it could be and is being done as much in the interests of students and parents and the public as it possibly could be.

Here is another view, stimulated by the preceding comment:

I think you find a lot of timidity in our leadership because we are frightened of faculty. Fear of faculty is a major problem. Maybe the biggest single problem is, how well trained are we for the positions to which we come? If the training ground is to come up through the faculty, which it tends to be . . . I'm not sure it prepares us for the kind of worldview I think you need to do these jobs well. Maybe that's why we don't have an awful lot of institutions that do very good strategic thinking. We look to the past. We remember where we've come from, and we're not focused enough on where we're going.

Another president recalled sharing a speaking platform with the late A. Bartlett Giamatti, president of Yale University:

> We were all sitting on this platform, and I had a manuscript prepared. Bart was on my left, and he said, "Are we supposed to say something?" I said, "Well, that's why we're here." Whereupon he took out a yellow pad and started writing quickly, all of which makes the point that he was saying what he really thought.
>
> He got up, and I was stunned because . . . it was a cry of anguish on what a horrible time he was having, how the faculty was not supportive, and I guess he was going through that strike.

I would not say that these views represent anything like a consensus among the leaders of America's major universities, but neither are they rare or idiosyncratic. They are, in fact, perfectly understandable if they are seen as coming from political systems under stress, in which older forms of behavior no longer meet the needs of the organization and whose structures will not support the painful new behavior required.

Analogies can be misleading, but it is worth observing that the situation on many campuses is not unlike what we have seen in the politics of the larger society. Since the 1960s, the American political system has faced repeated challenges to its legitimacy—not fundamental challenges of the kind that lead to revolution but a steady stream of smaller ones that ultimately produce declining faith in the capacity of institutions to govern, of political leaders to lead, and of citizens to participate effectively. A distance has grown between a professional class of officeholders and the citizens they are elected to govern. Powerful entrenched interests have the power to block action, at the very least, and often to achieve what they want at the expense of larger but weaker parts of the community.

The belief that legislatures are not capable of disciplining themselves has led to the imposition of tax and expenditure limits on state governments by popular vote, to the force behind proposals for a national balanced-budget amendment, and to the term limit movement. Discontent with the two major political parties led to a third-party candidate, Ross Perot, winning nearly a fifth of the popular vote in the 1992 presidential election. While the percentage of the vote for Perot dropped in 1996, many observers of the political scene believe that significant support exists for a third party that is properly organized and led. Political leadership seems in disarray, lacking in confidence, unsure of the basis for or the strength and durability of public support, and both the public and the politicians are increasingly inclined to blame "the system" for their own discontent. We have seen longtime representatives and senators leave office, announcing as their reason that they can no longer be effective because the system is broken and cannot be fixed from within.

Acts that were unthinkable a generation ago now seem to occur routinely. Senator Bill Bradley, a respected three-term member of the Senate, announces that he will not run for reelection because the Senate is no longer a place from which he can accomplish his goals. Even more surprisingly, Thomas Kean, president of Drew University and popular former two-term governor of New Jersey, declines to run for what would be a near certain Senate seat as Bradley's successor because he sees Washington and the Senate as "mean and ugly" places.

Without unduly pressing the analogy, I would say that much of the foregoing can be seen in universities to a greater or lesser degree, although it is probably the case that the points of similarity are greater at public universities than at private. Presidential tenures are shorter in the public sector, where the ordinary university problems are often exacerbated by pressures from partisan political masters and by the closer scrutiny of reporters and editors to whom universities represent a fresh lode of scandals waiting to be mined.

Boards of Trustees

In one respect the governance structure of universities is closer to that of business than to government, namely in the existence of boards of trustees. The lay governing board is an American invention and remains a unique American institution. It is "in" the institution, in the sense that its members are committed to the institution's well-being, but it is not "of" the institution. Rather, its members are members of the community; they are outside the internal governance structure. Therefore, board members can bring to the university a sympathetic but dispassionate view of its activities, as well as advice and counsel from their varied perspectives and experiences. Most of all, they are the president's natural supporters. Having appointed the president, they have a personal stake in seeing to it that their choice works out well. They might be expected to be aids in governance, detached but concerned, critical but loyal. Clark Kerr and Marian Gade put it this way in their 1989 study of college and university boards,

The care of the presidency is particularly in the hands of the board, and the presidency is the most important single position in a college or university. A board cannot perform much better than its president, although it can be a good deal worse.

... Boards should realize that when they evaluate a president's performance they are also evaluating their own performance in selecting, advising, and supporting the president. Also, they should realize it is harder for a good president to survive a poor board than for a good board to survive a poor president.[5]

That, at least, is the theory. The practice is often rather different. Some boards do all these things well—advising, evaluating, and supporting the president they have selected. Those that do are most likely to be found at private universities. Generally, the members of private university boards have demonstrated their attachment to the institution by long service to it in various volunteer capacities and frequently by their financial contributions. They are not appointed by an authority outside the institution, and so they should have no conflicting loyalties. While the boards of private universities can be overly intrusive and reach beyond their appropriate duties and competence, it is far less likely that they will do so than is the case in public institutions.

If excessive intrusiveness is a fault, so, too, is excessive deference, and too many boards of trustees have been too deferential to the academics to whom they have delegated the management of the institutions for which trustees are legally responsible. Private institutions are especially vulnerable to a situation in which the president comes to dominate the selection of new trustees, ending up with a board that is beholden to the president and not disposed to challenge presidential judgment. When that happens, the usual and proper governance relationship is turned on its head. The case of Adelphi University, in which the high salary and lucrative benefits given to the president were challenged by the university's faculty and the New York State authorities, is a case in point.

In good times, the temptation to shine in reflected glory and to avoid asking potentially awkward questions is all too human. Few, if any, boards can claim credit for anticipating the harsh public criticisms of universities that came in the 1980s, accompanied by the challenges to the research culture of universities and the alleged denigration of teaching, or even the problems in the system of indirect cost recovery that produced charges of scandal. Nor was there much visible resistance from boards to the rapid run-up of tuition in the 1980s. Few trustees and fewer boards used their

5. Clark Kerr and Marian L. Gade, *The Guardians: Boards of Trustees of American Colleges and Universities* (Washington, D.C.: Association of Governing Boards, 1989), 94.

detachment from their institutions and their places in the community to bring hard messages to their administrations and faculties. Furthermore, I think it is doubtful that much more can be expected in the future. Businesspeople and lawyers are as likely as academics and political reporters to be captured by the reigning conventional wisdom. Those who argue against it are rare at any time.

There is a case to be made for more active boards. One president, for example, commenting at our symposium of former and current presidents on a paper I wrote in preparation for the meeting, saw the growing activism of some boards as having some saving virtue:

> The life of a president is indeed hard, constrained from all sides. But we haven't yet heard much talk about what may be either a specter or possibly the U.S. Cavalry coming over the hill to save us.
>
> I was much struck by a sentence in your paper that says, "Boards of trustees are important instrumentalities, but they do not govern." That is changing, particularly in the public sector. One of my colleagues has written about what he sees happening in governing boards. . . . It's following some of the rather spectacular industrial examples in which boards observing a company that had become hidebound and constipated and was not responding to the needs of the market simply marched in and took over, fired the CEO, reorganized the company, set it on a new track.
>
> We're beginning to see evidence of that in public boards as well; boards that, for example, no longer rely on the CEO, the president, as their sole source of information about what's going on, but boards that actually go out and seek information from students, from your administrators, and make up their own minds about what's going on.
>
> You may think of that as a specter, a horrible thing
>
> [Voice of a private university president:] Yes.
>
> [Laughter.]
>
> [Speaker:] But there it is. There's another reality, and one might just conceivably imagine that for our institutions, maybe not for us as presidents, but for our institutions in the long run, that may be a good thing.

One symposium participant, a longtime observer of college and university boards, went even further: "Particularly in private higher education . . . I think boards have got to realize with their presidents that they've got to govern more than they have in the past. Hopefully, they'll do it in the right way."

In the public sector, at least, governing boards have discovered an appetite for governing. There is little doubt that the boards of public universities are less willing to defer to the judgment of their presidents than they once were, and the reason why that is so raises some troubling questions about the balance of governance in those important institutions. To put it simply, universities have grown to be too large and important to be immune to the influence of outside political forces any longer. Both public and private universities are affected by swings in national political fortunes, and they will continue to be so long as they are dependent on federal government funding. In the public sector, a university, through its board, may be embroiled in a political dispute at any time. Members of public university boards come to their positions in one of two ways. In a small number of states they are elected in their own right, in most they are appointed by the governor. In neither case do they come to the university as political free agents. They bring their own agendas or those of the governor who appointed them.

In earlier years that was not a serious problem because, to put it bluntly, universities were rarely important enough to generate political agendas. Moreover, exceptions such as the antiwar movement notwithstanding, the state university was an unambiguous source of pride within the state, and the dominant political goal was to make it bigger, better, and more useful. The politics of today's public university are considerably more complex. The public university has become a main gatekeeper to personal economic success, and so its admissions policies are a matter of political controversy. It is seen as a key to local economic prosperity, and so its research policies and priorities are now on the political agenda. It is expensive, usually one of the largest single items in the state budget, and so issues of tuition charges, faculty productivity, and administrative efficiency are likely to be raised in every budget cycle. Partisan differences over these and other issues are not uncommon, and whether or not the issues become partisan, the careers of politicians have become increasingly bound up in matters of university policy, and their political allies—their appointees on the university board—are among the weapons in their political armory.

The clearest recent example of this phenomenon was the vote of the University of California Board of Regents in June 1995 to end all programs of affirmative action within the university. Historically, in most universities, admissions policy is considered an academic matter and is delegated to the faculty for setting admissions standards and to the administration for execution of policy. The 14–11 regents' vote was heedless of this practice, and it was taken over the explicit opposition of the university president and vice presidents, the chancellors of all nine campuses, the faculty senates of the university and its individual campuses, the student governments, and the university's alumni bodies. On the winning side was the governor, a candidate for the Republican nomination for president, and his appointees and allies on the Board of Regents. Quite apart from the merits of the issue, which are certainly a subject for legitimate debate, this was a decision that never would have been taken were it not for the governor's political ambitions.

The University of California case is instructive because its very clarity illustrates the phenomenon of politicized boards and its potential on issues of less public visibility. The University of California, because of its independent status under the California Constitution, is better protected than most other public institutions from political intrusion, but it was unable to protect itself from the ambitions of a determined governor.

There are good reasons for protecting universities from shifting political winds. Protection of academic freedom obviously is one, but, paradoxically, academic freedom is so well protected today that threats to it find ready and effective opposition. What is less well understood, though, is that the values and the practices that make good universities require longer time horizons than politics ever provides. For any given university, there is no natural constituency or organized interest group to resist the imposition of bottom-line, short-term considerations. Universities calculate in decades or generations; a single tenure decision commits resources for thirty or forty years. By contrast, the calculations of politicians run to the next election. If boards of trustees are to serve their universities, there is no more important responsibility they can take on than to explain the importance of that difference to the public and to elected officials. If, on the other hand, they are to serve their political masters, they cannot at the same time be faithful to the trust in which they hold their universities.

Boards of trustees are not the answer to the intrinsic weakness of institutional governance systems. They are important devices for some purposes, but it remains true that they cannot govern, and the most likely result of their attempt to do so is to undermine the authority and legitimacy of those whose job it is to govern. Since universities, especially those in the public sector, are not likely to become less important, less visible, or less costly in the future, the temptation of public officials to use their influence on university boards to advance political agendas will remain strong. It should also remain a source of active concern.

Governance and the Job of the President

On one point of governance virtually all observers are agreed: presidents are supposed to lead. At a minimum, that is understood to mean that they should be able to articulate some goals and formulate programs that, if enacted, would lead to fulfillment of those goals. Simply stating goals and proposing programs, however, is not enough. The real test of leadership consists in the ability to persuade others to adopt one's goals and support one's programs and to put them into practice with enthusiasm. That test applies to presidents of the United States and presidents of universities, although the circumstances under which each labors and the tools at their command vary greatly.

Beyond these basic elements of leadership, agreement tends to break down—with one exception: there seems to be fairly general agreement that yesterday's leaders were better than today's. Steven Muller, former president of the Johns Hopkins University, put the question with conscious irony this way: "Where are all the great university presidents of today? Why do we not see the likes of Eliot, Butler, Lowell, Harper or Hutchins towering over their institutions and raising mighty voices to address society? The most obvious answer, of course, is that the men and women who serve as university presidents today simply lack the greatness of their predecessors."[6] Or, as another president put it,

> I think if you looked at the really unprecedented barrage of criticisms, beginning with Bill Bennett and Alan Bloom and then a series of books, reports, investigations, lawsuits, and so forth, that followed and then said, where were the clear strong voices speaking out trying to educate the public to what was going on, it is really quite remarkable how little was done. And so then you cast around and of course the conventional explanation is that we have a race of pygmies in charge of these institutions where giants once strode the land. It sort of implies that there's been some failure in the gene pool for university presidents.

We live in an age that is hard on the possibility of heroes. In politics, business, and education, no sooner does a strong figure emerge than the apparatus of exposure discovers some past flaw that reduces the individual to human scale. Heroes, though, are supposed to be larger than life, and so another candidate is lost. Even death is no bar to this apparently inexorable process of modern life, as witness the decline of John F. Kennedy from near mythic status at his death to that of a mere mortal with uncontrolled appetites.

Daniel Greenberg is a shrewd and experienced journalistic observer of science and its practitioners. In a *New York Times* column headed "The Vanishing Heroes of Science," Greenberg marked the death of Jonas Salk in terms that are often applied to university presidents.

> With the death of Jonas Salk, we have run out of scientific folk heroes. On the public roster of the majestic and the revered, he was on the scale of Benjamin Franklin, Marie Curie, Louis Pasteur, Albert Einstein and . . . J. Robert Oppenheimer.
>
> Given the economic, cultural and technical transformations that have

6. Steven Muller, "Presidential Leadership," in Cole, Barber, and Graubard, *Research University in a Time of Discontent*, 115.

remade the scientific community since Dr. Salk developed his polio vaccine 40 years ago, the emergence of another universally worshipped scientist seems unlikely. During these decades, science and the neighboring fields of medicine and technology have been demythologized from within and blemished by allegations of fraud and glory-stealing.[7]

He is right, though he is curiously unreflective about the reasons for the condition. One, certainly, is the growth of investigative journalism and of a generation of reporters, of whom Greenberg is one, who have never met an allegation of misbehavior they didn't like or a whistle-blower they didn't want to believe. One can argue about whether the nation is better or worse off for this development, but there can be no doubt that few people in any walk of life have lived lives so exemplary that they are invulnerable to the work of an aggressive reporter or a sharp-tongued columnist. Small wonder, then, that heroes are hard to find.

There is no reason to believe that lesser mortals occupy positions of high responsibility today than in the past, but there is every reason to believe that the institutions of the 1990s are vastly different from those of the late nineteenth and early twentieth centuries, that the environment for leadership and the demands on leaders are also different, and so the styles of leadership appropriate to each age are different, as well. It is still possible that today's university leaders and scientists should be judged failures by today's standards, but it is surely unfair to judge them against historical icons whose reputations have grown with the distance from their performance.

What has not changed is the need for leaders who are deeply grounded in the purposes and values of the university and who are skilled enough to operate in a society that professes to want leadership but is suspicious of leaders. Without exception, the presidents interviewed for this book were keenly aware of the need to lead and of the problems in the attempt to do so.

The first requirement of leadership is to have an agenda, a set of goals that command the respect and support of key elements of the community. Those goals may, in fact, come out of the community itself, and the task of the leader is to identify them and articulate them. One president put it this way:

A president with a good, strong positive relationship with the faculty . . . is able by persuasion and patient coalition and consensus building to move some change. The president can at least change the vector of the

7. Daniel Greenberg, "The Vanishing Heroes of Science," *New York Times,* July 4, 1995.

institution by speaking to its values in an effective way and by reflecting everybody's values back to them and saying, "Here's how we need to fulfill our own vision of ourselves." That sounds a little corny, but I think that presidents do that. And I think it's an important ingredient in directing the institution, giving it more energy in a particular direction.

Without exception, every president with whom I spoke entered office by articulating some fairly clear goals for his or her institution. With few exceptions, the matters they put at the top of their agendas were specific to their own institutions and would have made less sense at another. For one, the list included rebuilding the arts and sciences, making faculty selection procedures and standards more rigorous, improving faculty salaries, and building relations with the surrounding community. Another spoke of the need to rebuild the sciences and the need to help rebuild the community around the university. A third put his own outside activities high on his agenda, both because of his own interests and background and because he saw those as a visible way to build institutional reputation and pride. For a fourth, setting his medical center in order was the most urgent problem. For a fifth, it was to rebuild his institution's base of support after many years of hostility from the state's governors. Still another emphasized the importance of addressing issues of racial and ethnic diversity. And so it goes. The single item that appears on the agendas of as many as three presidents is the need to build strength in the modern biological sciences, without which no research university can stay in the front ranks.

All entered office with some fairly clear ideas about what they wanted to achieve. The goals they articulated, while in some cases quite specific, tended on the whole to be middle-range goals, doable within the reasonable expectation of presidential tenure. Moreover, all of them felt that they had been at least partially successful, and most believed that they had largely fulfilled their initial agenda.

Not surprisingly, as a group they were thoughtful about what constitutes presidential leadership in a modern university. All of them had thought deeply about how one exercises leadership in an institution with such weak and dispersed lines of authority. In the words of one:

> Well, partly it's to make people feel more responsible for themselves and their colleagues and the people that they're put in charge of—students or whatever. . . . The second thing is to try and create a community of learning in the university which is sufficiently vigorous and sufficiently integrated that everybody in fact wants to be taught. And that means being a cheerleader, being a headmaster. I always felt like a pretty good headmaster. I thought of the job as having kind of two functions—polar functions. One is like the CEO of a large corporation. You could stay in your office

and meet on the budget or do all that stuff and feel like that. The other was being a headmaster. Helping to find the new faculty member. Helping to recruit this or that. Going to the student residence. Showing up at night during a crisis. . . . And that assemblage of things can seem quite miscellaneous, but in fact it's all devoted to the purpose of creating a community in which there is enough additional mutual stimulation and inspiration so that the lack of authority matters less.

One president offered a specific recipe for accomplishing an objective: "You needed three ingredients to get something done. You needed some leadership from the top. You needed funds. And you needed faculty members who really believed in the enterprise, not just intellectually but to the point of being willing to really devote a lot of their time and energy to getting it done well." Another president found a source of influence in his ability to speak for the institution: "I always felt I had the authority to speak for the university. Obviously that's an authority to be used with discretion and judgment, but it seemed to me to be part of my job."

Another tool of leadership is the ability to define the spheres within which one chooses to exercise it. Of course, some are imposed by internal or external exigencies, but a surprising amount of latitude is often available. This president compared his choices thoughtfully with those of his predecessor:

Now, [he] spent a disproportionate amount of his time dealing with academic senate committees, faculty, and educational issues. . . . I did the reverse. I weighted it more heavily on the side of political parts of the job, but tended to the other part of it as best I could. When you're getting over $2 billion from the state it is by definition political. I don't mean partisan. But I think anyone in these positions needs to understand how the political process works. How to get along with both parties while telling them the same thing. How to know where the line is between advocacy and unseemly activism. How to obtain and sustain the confidence of the board so they won't be second-guessing you on these issues. How to get the university's other officers to work with you instead of being at odds with you when it comes to legislative matters. How to assure one's credibility with the legislature, whatever the disagreements may be. How to manage the conflict between the governor's office and legislative leaders of both houses. How to take account of egos involved without being obsequious or demeaning your own position. And I think anyone who is not willing to play in that arena is going to find these jobs to be highly unattractive. . . .

Now, one other point I'd like to make, though, to give some balance . . . I think it's equally true that a president cannot succeed without a sophisticated appreciation of the subtle inner life of these institutions.

One president, whose experience encompassed both the political and the academic worlds, found the tools that bred success in the two quite similar.

When I arrived, after a few months I could see very quickly that the experience of being a member of Congress was enormously valuable to being university president. If you look at the two worlds, you'll see what I mean. In both one deals with a diversity of constituencies. One is a public person making speeches, articulating a cause. One raises money. One resolves conflicts. One wrestles with massive egos. There are two very important differences, however. One is that a university president does not seek reelection every two years as does a member of the U.S. House of Representatives. And the other difference, perhaps more substantive, is that a university president is the chief executive officer of a large complex institution. And so one must be much more preoccupied with fiscal and budgetary concerns in a daily, existential, practical way, as distinguished from a member of the House. It doesn't make any difference how senior you are in the House, you simply don't have to deal with such matters.

I also found it very natural to give credit. When I would make a talk or a speech I would say, "I'm so pleased to see so and so here because I know the great leadership he's given in this," et cetera.

And it's very natural for an elected politician to recognize people. And I remember very well what Isaiah Berlin once told me when I called on him when he was at All Souls and I was still in Congress and went back to Oxford from time to time. We were talking about what motivates people in politics and Isaiah said, "Recognition drives it all."

After all, even a precinct committeeman back in one's home district is delighted when you say, "Al, how's Suzy doing?" And the same is true of a member of Congress who goes through a White House reception and the president of the United States says, "John, how does Notre Dame look on the football field this year?"

As a congressman, obviously, I'd gone out to raise money for my own campaigns and though we're now talking in much different sums, the style of what you do, the nature of what you do, is not all that different. Indeed, it's probably easier to raise money for a university than for your own campaign, because it's not quite so self-serving.

When I became a university president, my former colleagues in Washington told me, "John, you're really now going to get into serious politics." I'm not going to say that there weren't times when the faculty may have had some disagreement with me on something or other, but I guess my own attitude—I hope not arrogant—was listen, you guys, I've fought with presidents of the United States; you're amateurs.

There are some inherent obstacles to the exercise of presidential leadership. One of them is analogous to the public alienation from politicians that has accompanied the growth of a professional political class, a group whose life consists in occupying political office and whose career consists in moving from one office to another. Just as the life experiences and role requirements of doctors and lawyers can produce a distance, even an antagonism, between them and the public, so too does the life of politicians. The harder it becomes for voters to imagine, much less empathize with, the political life, the easier it is to be cynical about the motives and behavior of those who live it.

Something like that has happened in universities. The university career, like the political career, has become more professionalized. The decision to become a dean, for example, is more likely than it once was to be a shift to a new career track than to be a period of institutional service in the midst of what is still basically a career in teaching and research. As that has happened, the tension between faculties and their administrations—always a feature, even a healthy feature, of academic life—has become less a dispute among colleagues who share the outlook of a common career and more a battle between a working class and a ruling class.

At the presidential level, it has become unusual to the point of rarity for a new university president to be drawn directly from the ranks of the faculty. Universities are too large and too complicated to be entrusted to anyone who has not already had the responsibility for running at least a large part of one. Thus, presidents are likely to be drawn from the ranks of deans or provosts or, as in a growing number of cases, from among those who have been presidents at other places. Distance from the faculty life is a de facto requirement for becoming a president. The idea, then, of the president as someone who comes from the community to lead the community and then returns to it has about as much connection with reality today as the idea of the citizen-politician who serves for a brief time out of civic duty and then, having done his duty, returns to a quiet private life among neighbors and former constituents.

The problem is compounded by the life that a president leads, a life that, over time, produces even further distance from the community over which he presides.

I would hazard a guess that in some cases, by no means all, the great problem we've run into is that presidents get so distracted in these areas that they can't spend enough time to really worry about issues—intellectual issues that concern their faculties. And then they get into a crisis situation where you have to say, "We've got to tighten our belts together and make some massive cuts. We've got to close down a department or two. We've got to do some other tough things." Those are tough calls under the best of circumstances. Then, they look around but they have not put down enough roots into their faculty, which doesn't really pay much attention to fund raising or administration. And as a result the support isn't there, and then their position becomes untenable, their proposals are rejected, and they have to move on, or feel they need to move on.

That was the rather detached view of one long-term president who probably suffered less from the condition he described than most. The two views that follow have more of the bite of personal experience.

In the early days I really was a leader. In the later years—and here some themes come together—the demands of the government relations part of the job and the fund-raising part of the job caused me to focus much more outside. I had a first-rate provost, and in my last years I left a lot more to him than I had left to his predecessors. And in that mode you do get much more of the feeling of riding the tiger. You're not hands-on with critical things that were happening, so that in some ways my last years were not nearly as interesting or satisfying as the early years.

There were a lot of factors that led me to conclude that I should stick with my commitment to serve ten years and be done. There was my wife's feeling about what the job was doing to her and our relationship. But part of it was that by that point, after three years on the road for our fund-raising campaign, I felt really out of touch with the reality of the place. And I turned over to the provost the chairmanship of promotion and tenure meetings. I was an infrequent attender at visiting committee meetings. The great continuing education program for the president is to go to visiting committee meetings and find out where the dogs are buried. I had to stop all of those things because I was away so much. I was out of touch with students; I was no longer an adviser. And so, I felt really quite disconnected intellectually. That was the consequence of the campaign.

As both of the foregoing suggest, the external demands on presidents' time and attention accumulate as they move deeper into their tenure in office. The observations that follow connect that phenomenon with the inevitably debilitating process of decision making.

It can happen that, as a presidency goes along, the president is increasingly pulled outside the institution. That certainly is true, and it happened to me because we started a fund-raising campaign, and I did get drawn more and more outside the institution. But I think there is something more important than that. The president makes a certain number of decisions that faculty don't like. Some of them are budget allocation decisions, some are decisions about difficult personnel matters. Some of them are decisions on positions that the institution qua legal entity is taking. I jokingly said at one point, about ten years in, that I believed in the silver bullet theory of management: that they gave you *N* silver bullets at the beginning, and when you look down and there aren't any left, then it's time to go.

The longer you stay in office, the more it is true that, while you will have said yes to many, many people at least once, you are much more certain to have said no to almost everybody more than once. And it is human nature that people don't have big, strong, vivid memories about the yeses, but they never forget the nos.

The key to the success of the American university in the last fifty years has been its ability to adapt to new demands and new opportunities while maintaining its core strengths. Governing systems that are fluid enough to permit the former but structured enough to protect the latter have been an essential element in that success, and leadership is a central part of governing. In universities, as in other organizations, effective leadership is contextual. The older models of heroic academic leadership operated under a conception of the university community as a seamless whole, consisting of harmonious interests that could be represented by small groups or even single individuals. Even then, that view of the university required suspension—willing or otherwise—of disbelief, and it was sustained for so long only because the constituent elements of the university were either powerless or indifferent to how the institution was governed. None of the heroes of old would succeed in the modern university without becoming a modern president.

It may seem unrealistic, as it sometimes does to me, to expect strong and effective presidential leadership, given the obstacles that the modern university puts in its way: faculties that are fractured into separate, outward-looking disciplines, trustees whose agendas are too often not those of the institution, pressures from strong and competing interests, and the lack of a reliable presidential constituency. But it is no more unrealistic than it is to expect strong leadership from the president of the United States. That, too, is an office with structural weaknesses that often seem to make a strong presidency a contradiction in terms. Yet it is possible to have an institution that is structurally weak but politically strong. Abraham Lincoln, after all, took the same office that James Buchanan held before him, and from an extraordinarily weak position he performed prodigies of accomplishment.

The fact is that the president of the United States and the president of a major university have one advantage not shared by other participants in governance: the ability to set an agenda and require others to react. Except in highly unusual circumstances, the Congress cannot do that; it cannot muster the sustained coherence that agenda setting requires. Faculties are similarly disabled. Legislatures, and it is fair to think of faculties as legislatures, are reactive bodies. They can amend and they can shape, and occasionally they can create; but without executive leadership to rub up against, they are likely to flounder.

There lies the essential presidential role, without which effective governance is not possible. It was captured well by one president in a somewhat off-hand way when he said, "It always seemed to be a key part of the president's job to articulate the values of the university, and presumably, if you get it wrong, somebody will say so, and you can have an argument about it."

The modern university requires its president to be a skilled politician and a competent manager of a large, complex enterprise. Like all truly first-class political leaders, the first-class university president also needs to know the central values and fundamental purposes of the polity he or she leads and must find ways to preserve those while helping the organization adapt to changes imposed by a changing environment. In good times universities will move forward on the energies of their faculties and students. The absence of strong and skilled leadership might produce less than optimal results and might help to lay the groundwork for troubles ahead, but the United States, after all, seemed for a while to be doing pretty well under the leadership of Warren G. Harding and Calvin Coolidge. In times of stress, however, when what needs to be done for the best will impose pain, there is no substitute for leaders who can recall the institution to its central purposes and lay out a program that is faithful to those purposes while addressing the institution's problems, leaders who have the courage to risk rejection and the skill to construct a winning coalition. Those are not easy requirements to meet, and in recent years American life has seen few such leaders in any realm. As I argue in the next chapters, the future of the American research university depends in significant measure on whether its leaders will do better.

Chapter Six

FACING THE FUTURE

II

The Decade Ahead

I F THE 1950S AND 1960s were the golden age, the seventies the period of the steady state, and the eighties the age of borrowed growth, what can be said about the progress of American research universities in the 1990s and forward into the new century? No one can know, but everyone is entitled to a guess. My own is that we are in a period in which the practices and the role of the research university will be subject to searching review, both on individual campuses and as matters of national policy. The main stimulus for this rethinking will be continuing resource constraints combined with demands for increased productivity and service to society. With those urgent pressures, nothing can be taken for granted, and few institutions will be able to drift through the period successfully.

In this and the next chapter, I examine the effect of resource constraints both locally and nationally. I also consider the questions that underlie all of the others, namely, why do we need these expensive and often troublesome institutions? Is there something so important about them that they are worth their cost and bother? If so, what might that worth be, and can it be preserved in the face of pressures to become something different? I treat these as open questions. Just as few people in 1940 predicted the future course of the American research university, so there is no inevitability about its course from this point forward. It would be melodramatic to say that all things are possible, but it is no exaggeration to say that there are many possible alternative futures and that which future actually comes to pass is not wholly beyond the capacity of humans to influence.

The Problem of Resources and the Dreaded P(riority) Word

In his inaugural address as the tenth president of Cornell University (October 12, 1995), Hunter R. Rawlings III made the following observation about his new institution, an observation that is surely of more general applicability:

Cornell has, throughout its history, taken proper pride in the number and variety of its academic programs. With the passing of each new decade and the rise of each new discipline, we have seen the creation of more departments, graduate fields, centers, and institutes—most of them vibrant and rich with ideas—contributing not only to our students' education but also to the world's store of knowledge. But as this process has unfolded ever more intricately, the composition has lost some of its cohesion and motivating force. Academic divisions become more isolated from one another, intellectual energy becomes ever more dissipated, and redundancy becomes ever more likely. In an era of expanding resources, devolution of academic authority is natural and even positive in many instances. But as state and national support tightens, we can ill afford to see this process continue. . . .

In designing new programs and evaluating current ones, we should take a broad view of our academic strengths and weaknesses and plan together our future directions. To some extent, this effort will require a change in our culture, but it is a mandate we share with all research universities, confronted as they are with the explosion of knowledge, the expansion of societal demands, and the erosion of public support. Those universities that can think their way into greater curricular coherence and more collaborative research across departmental and college barriers will be best prepared for the twenty-first century.

This is an inaugural address for the nineties. It raises questions and suggests possibilities that were not on the agenda in previous decades. It questions the wisdom of the broad devolution of authority that characterizes universities and suggests the possibility that greater centralization of authority might better fit the times. That, in turn, raises a question about traditional forms of academic governance that place faculty in the central position in decisions about academic matters. Rawlings also suggests that the old pattern of change and improvement by accretion is no longer possible. What new ways, then, of improving academic quality can be substituted, and what changes in the university culture will be required, as all research universities confront the reality of increasing demands and limited resources?

This is the heart of the 1990s agenda. Questions like these were entirely absent from the inaugural addresses of the presidents interviewed for this study. A major change has come over American universities. Of course, resource problems are not new. As one president told me, "In all my years as president and provost, no one ever asked me to spend money on anything stupid. They just asked me to spend ten times as much money as I had." The inevitable result is the condition described by Thomas Ehrlich, former president of Indiana University: "Expenses rise to exceed revenue. That is an inexorable rule of university administration."[1]

Every university, probably in every time, has faced ambitions that outrun resources. That is a problem but not a critical one, so long as the general condition is one of growth and the expectation that growth is the natural condition of life. What is different now is the widespread sense that this is no longer the case—that it is not reasonable to expect continued growth. If the new circumstance and the expectations that arise from it are to be dealt with satisfactorily, it will require important changes in old habits and ways of doing business.

The probable absence of significant growth in revenue sources for universities is one conclusion on which most observers agree. The line of argument that leads to this conclusion is straightforward and based on readily observable conditions in the economic and political environment. Harold Shapiro, president of Princeton University, provided a succinct and powerful statement of the case at a symposium held to honor the 100th anniversary of the University of Chicago in 1991. "Intellectual imperatives," he said, "arising out of our improved understanding create certain economic imperatives for the continued vitality of the enterprise." As an example, he pointed to the rapid and growing sophistication of scientific instrumentation that has led to "*qualitative* changes in the scholarly agenda. However, these changes contain within them a specific economic imperative as they require us, for example, to associate a lot more capital (facilities, equipment, technical support, etc.) with each student, each scholar, and each teacher if they are to operate at the forefront of scholarly and educational frontiers."

There may well be improvements in productivity brought about by such devices as computers, but they are most likely to take the form of greater output, accompanied not by less but by more cost. "New developments in computation have dramatically increased costs. Associated productivity gains, *if any,* have been taken in quality improvement and/or agenda expansion rather than cost reduction." This leads to the conclusion that, "unless their resource base can rise very quickly, most research universities will find themselves with a large number of underfinanced efforts. That is, we may not be able to generate the resources, institution by institution, to carry forward the full complement of our existing activities and sustain a position of leadership."

What, then, are the prospects of significantly increasing the resource base to support new demands for resources?

1. Thomas Ehrlich, foreword to *Responsibility, Center Budgetry,* by Edward L. Whalen (Bloomington: University of Indiana Press, 1991), 4.

Recall that the principal source of support for the core academic activities of the university are the following: tuition and fees, state appropriations . . . federal appropriations (primarily for the support of research and student aid), corporate support of research, gifts, and endowment income. In addition, meaningful revenues supporting academic activities can flow through academic health centers for those universities with medical schools and associated clinical activities. . . . My own conclusion is that unless the economy experiences both a sustained and [an] unusually rapid rate of economic growth, none of these revenue sources can be expected to be unusually robust. . . . Indeed, my own view is that in the aggregate we may be facing a long-run situation where the overall rate of growth in revenues to higher education will be somewhat lower than would be necessary to maintain the *quality, scope,* and *method of production* of the current system.

It should be noted that Shapiro reached this conclusion before the Contract with America, the seven-year balanced national budget, cuts in student aid and research, and the major reductions in Medicare and Medicaid spending that are profoundly affecting the nation's medical schools and hospitals. Some programs will fare better than others in the annual budget struggles—student aid and biomedical research were favored in the early budget-cutting skirmishes—but no university has been untouched by these developments. Some have been and will be hurt worse than others due to their particular mix of programs, the size of their endowment, the health of their state's economy, and a variety of other local circumstances. But it is safe to say that all universities need to face the likely conditions that Shapiro described and that those that fail to do so will be leaving their future to chance in a situation where the odds are against them.

Each institution must ask itself a number of questions: What do we do that is central to our definition of ourselves as a university? Are we supporting activities that are below the level of quality that we expect of our programs? If those programs are not central to our purposes, can we afford the resources required to bring them up to speed? To what extent should marginal activities, even if they are of good quality and real value, be allowed to drain resources from our core programs? How can we assure that we will be able to seize future opportunities for real improvement?

Those questions no doubt sound familiar; they are ones that have been asked by virtually all private and public sector institutions in this decade. Answers to these questions have produced substantial downsizing in business and industry, major efforts to substitute capital for labor, a succession of budget-balancing initiatives in governments at all levels, cuts in services, and enormous stress on all counts. Thus, there is no excuse for failing to recognize the problem—limited resources and unlimited demands—and the difficulty of dealing with it. Nor is there any reason to believe that universities will be exempt from its discipline.

It is a painful fact of life that the decisions required by the inability to grow, and even more by the need to contract, are the most difficult and divisive that organizations are called on to make. They test the skills of leaders and the loyalties of those they lead. Failure to come to terms with those decisions is not necessarily dishonorable, but it is almost always disastrous, and more painful in the end than making the decisions in the first place would have been. Before examining the problems that lie ahead for universities, it will be instructive to look at a closely related example from the national level. While the scale is larger because it involves the federal government, the issues are very much like those that are being played out on campuses across the country, as are the difficulties of resolving them.

Federal Science Policy and the Great Priorities Debate

Concern about continuing federal budget deficits and the growing national debt began to surface politically early in the second Reagan administration. They took shape in the Congress in 1985 in the form of the Gramm-Rudman-Hollings Act (GRH), which set a course toward a balanced budget and presumably bound the Congress to abide by its terms. For all of the ballyhoo and chest thumping that accompanied it, some said at the time that GRH was doomed to failure, that no Congress could bind future Congresses unless the political will existed to keep the pledge, and that there was no real evidence that it did. The skeptics were right. The GRH limits on domestic spending were consistently evaded by various tricks of the budget and appropriations process, with the result that annual deficits grew at even faster rates.

Notwithstanding its weaknesses and its ultimate failure, GRH was a wake-up call. For one thing, it focused on the category of domestic discretionary spending as the target for expenditure reductions. Since all university programs fell into that category, that focus was in itself cause for concern, if not alarm. For another, it demonstrated that there was sufficient political pressure behind the concern about deficits to produce some kind of response, and that unless something substantive were done, other steps would be taken. In short, the days of automatically rising appropriations might well be numbered, and groups that depended on the civilian, domestic portion of the federal budget would be prudent to consider that possibility. Pursuing that thought led to an unexpected conclusion.

In a year-end letter to the AAU members in 1985, I offered a message that was not really in keeping with the spirit of the season.

As the year draws to a close, one can detect in the air an almost palpable sense that the new year will bring with it new ways of looking at old matters. The proximate cause of the change is money, or rather the widely shared conviction that we are spending more as a nation than we are prepared to pay for through taxation. That conclusion has not yet produced a political coalition that is strong enough to enact a tax increase, and so the focus inevitably has turned to spending reductions. The result is Gramm/Rudman/Hollings.

... Although G/R/H would allow Congress and the President time to reach agreement on the distribution of cuts, its key provision makes reductions automatic, by formula, in the (expected) event that they will be unable to do so,

What difference will it make? To give you one example, NIH is under instructions to reduce this year's budget by 5 percent—$300 million—and next year's by 10 percent—$600 million. That is nearly $1 billion in two years, and that translates into a very large number of grants. All agencies will be under similar discipline.

It seemed clear that this development signaled a new dynamic in the politics of science and higher education, one in which competition for scarcer funds would overwhelm the expression of common interests, disciplines would be pitted against one another, and science and education would become adversaries. That unhappy prospect seemed to me to argue for a serious effort to come together with other groups to find our common ground and to identify points of difference.

Unless we know more than we know now and understand better the circumstances that lie ahead, consultation and debate will be sterile and frustrating. In that event, we may expect policy to be determined solely by battles between battalions of advocates whose purpose is to win as much as they can for those they represent and whose practical concern for the system as a whole extends no farther than the boundaries of their membership.

Of course, there is a respectable case to be made that what I saw as an unhappy prospect is exactly the way the system is supposed to operate, that diverse interests perform their highest function when they forcefully articulate their needs in competition with others, leaving it to those who hold elective office to sort out their claims. The Hobbesian war of all against all is, in that view, not only the way it really is but the way it should be.

There is, in fact, much to be said for that view in a somewhat more refined form. Those who serve in representative institutions need robust articulation of competing views of public policy to inform their decisions. Political interest groups are one principal means of providing that. Seen in this way, they are not simply an unavoidable nuisance but a necessary part of the democratic process. But there is also much to be said, on both practical and theoretical grounds, for coalitions among those who have a common interest in addition to their separate ones. Perhaps the system works better if accommodation among interests is made prior to entering into legislative battles. That might lower the decibel level of debate and open the opportunity for more thoughtful deliberation.

This, at any rate, was the line of reasoning that led me to get behind efforts to develop priorities for science funding. Tracking that effort is a record of unreasonable expectations eventually altered by an education in the way the world works. It begins in March of 1986 at the annual Colloquium on R&D Policy of the American Association for the Advancement of Science. The title of the session at which I spoke was "R&D Community Responses to the Budgetary Situation: Charting a Course for the Stormy Future." The stormy future of the title was the one precipitated by the recently enacted Gramm-Rudman-Hollings Act, and I, like everyone else, was at a loss to know where it would all end. I described the situation in words that had recently appeared in *Science* to describe the emerging theory of chaos. According to the article, "In chaos, a little bit of uncertainty in initial conditions is quickly and enormously magnified. The system is unpredictable because the initial conditions can never be specified so precisely that you can tell where the system will end up." I had not seen any political commentary that better described the federal budget prospects.

That said, serious people were not relieved of the need to make the best guess possible as to how the most likely future events would affect universities. Those events, I argued, would constitute a triple whammy, if they came to pass. One part consisted of probable budget reductions, a second part consisted of likely attempts to limit indirect cost recovery, and a third part could be seen in the tax reform bill then working its way through the Congress. Losses on those three fronts constituted a nightmare vision for university presidents, whose concerns necessarily went beyond next year's R&D budget. Their world included humanists and social scientists, lawyers, doctors, and business schools, and, not least of all, large numbers of undergraduate students, many of whom could not enroll without some form of financial assistance. Who, I asked, would provide that if the government scaled back its student aid programs? And how will it be decided whether the next $10,000 of general funds should go to student X to stay in school or to professor Y to pay the summer salary that NSF will no longer provide?

In the real world of budgeting, decisions do not come in such neat packages; they are hidden in decisions that are made in larger aggregations. At some point, however, knowingly or not, the consequences of the macro-decisions produce the microresults described above. Whether they are the intended results will depend on how honest those involved in budgeting are in facing the consequences of their choices and how thoughtful they are in weighing them. While I could not speak for what was happening on dozens of university campuses, I could report that in Washington I saw "a pervasive inability to look beyond the budget function or appropriation line that includes one's own programs. In the various meetings I attend, I have not heard scientists worrying about what effect severe cuts in under-graduate student aid might have, even on the future of their own fields, and whether it might make educational as well as political sense for them to lend at least their names to efforts to protect those programs."

I applauded Eric Bloch, the director of the National Science Founda-tion, for taking on the issue directly. In an announcement describing the GRH-induced cuts in the foundation budget, he said that the NSF would protect programs for graduate students, postdoctoral fellows, instrumenta-tion, and equipment. Bloch suggested that future cuts might well produce reductions in investigators' salaries and indirect cost recovery, as well as increases in other forms of institutional cost-sharing so that the priority items could be protected. I did not think that all of those were wise deci-sions, but Bloch had performed one of a leader's vital functions: he had set out an agenda that would focus debate on the important questions.

In conclusion, I said that I saw only two likely choices. One was to shrink the size of the scientific enterprise to a level that the nation was prepared to afford—in other words, to do less science. The second choice would be to subsidize scientific research at the expense of other intellectual or educational activities. I thought it would be truly unfortunate if we were simply to stumble into either choice because we were unwilling to think hard thoughts.

Although the budget limits set by GRH never fully took hold, the pressure on science and education budgets continued, and the possibility of serious cuts was an always looming prospect. Two years later, I returned to the same forum with a talk I called "Thinking about Less." I began with an elementary civics lesson:

> As a nation, we have always had a hard time with priorities. The task of setting priorities is never easy, but it seems to be even harder for us than for others. . . . We are a society of dispersed, divided, and shared power. Even with the growth of the power of government in this century, the private sector retains a considerable degree of autonomy, and many im-portant instruments of policy remain outside the reach of the more cen-

tralized instruments of public decision making. Moreover, governmental power is divided at the national level and dispersed further among states and localities. . . . Authoritative priority setting goes most easily with planning; planning goes most easily with centralized political, economic, and social institutions; and none of that describes the United States of America.

In science, I noted, the task of priority setting was especially difficult because of the very success of the scientific enterprise. The past had been a time of extraordinary growth, the present was one of enormous productivity and exciting new breakthroughs, and the future held dazzling prospects across a broad array of scientific fronts. Our ambitions were high. They included megaprojects like the superconducting supercolliding accelerator (SSC), the project to map the human genome, superconductivity, the space station, AIDS treatments and vaccines and other biomedical research, and others almost too numerous to list.

The difficulty, it seemed to me, lay in the fact that our ambitions far outstripped our willingness or our ability to pay for them. Someone would need to make difficult decisions. Who would do it, using what criteria? The answer to the former was easy. Decisions about funding would be political, and they would be made through political processes. Political decisions need not be bad ones; whether they are or are not frequently turns on the balance between consideration of narrow constituency interests and a conception of some broader set of interests. Attempting to provide that broader conception could be risky business. It would certainly be divisive. No one since Abraham has willingly offered up a child for sacrifice to a larger good, and most people will fight like fury to protect the interests of their children. Yet three things seemed clear enough. First, the broader and better-informed the considerations that lead to decisions, the better those decisions are likely to be. Second, that goal cannot be achieved without the constructive participation of scientists and those who are responsible for the institutions in which science is conducted. And third, neither of those groups was prepared to participate constructively in such a process. There was no lack of passionate advocacy for every item on the agenda, but there was a virtually total absence of help for any serious-minded government official who was willing to consider how to think about the decisions that had to be made. The conclusion of this sermon was that "choices that are made without regard for the opportunities that will be forgone are not serious choices. We are drifting in the direction of just such easy, unserious thinking in our own counsels, thereby encouraging uninformed and dangerous decisions by government."

As it turned out, the spring of 1988 was the high point of the interest in talking about priorities. Several weeks after my appearance at the AAAS meeting, Frank Press, president of the National Academy of Sciences (NAS), addressed the annual meeting of his prestigious organization on the same subject and urged them to consider its seriousness. At about the same time, the Senate Budget Committee asked the NAS to look at the subject of science priorities and propose to the committee ways of thinking about it that could be used to inform their difficult decisions. The NAS complied, proposing a sensible set of categories that might serve as at least a starting point for decisions. Even the press showed a momentary interest in the issue. The *New York Times* ran a long story under the headline, "Two Leaders Challenge 'Big Science' Trend," which was inaccurate but close enough for newspaper work.

The NAS's report provided the occasion for a hearing by the Senate Budget Committee in March 1989. Ironically, it was that hearing that taught me my final lesson on the subject of science priorities. The NAS had identified three categories of science projects that were analytically distinct and to which policy makers could assign different values, according to their own ordering of priorities: investments in the science and technology base; science and technology (S&T) activities that contribute significantly to national economic, social, and political goals; and new S&T initiatives, including but not limited to those that are heavily capital-intensive. It was fairly clear in context that the NAS assigned the highest value to the first category and the lowest to the third. In my testimony, I indicated support for that ordering, while recognizing that the debate on S&T policy was precisely about what weight should be given to each of them and that different views were perfectly legitimate. I said that I was confident that an annual debate that began along those lines would produce better results than the project-by-project and program-by-program tussles that had dominated the system. I applauded the NAS for giving us a framework for a more orderly consideration of science policy and science funding priorities.

Had I stopped there, my education would not have been complete. However, I went on to suggest that one of the elements of the R&D enterprise badly in need of serious review was the network of national laboratories that had grown up since World War II and that were, by most reckoning, of mixed quality. This was hardly an original thought, since several reports had reached the same conclusion. I noted that all of the laboratories had strong advocates in the Congress based as much on their local economic impact as on their place in a high-quality scientific enterprise. I suggested that, in that respect, they had much in common with military bases, and since a process had been invented that enabled the closing of unnecessary military bases, something similar might be adapted for reviewing national laboratories.

As I reached that point in my testimony, Senator Pete Domenici (Rep., N.M.) entered the room, just in time to hear what he took to be an attack on the national labs, of which two of the largest, Los Alamos and Sandia, are located in his state. Senator Domenici is one of the most thoughtful and decent members of the Senate. Moreover, he was a leading advocate of spending limitations in order to bring the budget into balance. Clearly, though, I had hit a nerve, for he interrupted my statement and proceeded to give me a tongue-lashing that would have been remarkable coming from an ill-tempered senator, and all the more so from one ordinarily so reasonable. He accused me and my member universities of hypocrisy for attacking these fine labs, some of which, he said, employ as many as five thousand people, while at the same time we were unwilling to make sacrifices ourselves. I was, to say the least, stunned, both at the source and the vehemence of the attack and because the first part of my statement had been about the need to set priorities that would embrace everyone.

Shortly after this outburst, I saw a staff member approach the senator and ask him to step outside. Upon his return, Senator Domenici asked for the floor. He explained that he had missed part of my testimony and apologized for jumping to the wrong conclusion. In ten years, I cannot recall hearing a senator apologize to a witness for an unfair attack. It certainly had never happened to me. The senator's apology was, of course, a tribute to his decency. But it should also be said that he did not forget the incident. Several days later, addressing a higher education meeting in Washington, he recalled the testimony of "one of your association leaders" who seemed to think that the Congress was about to close some national laboratories. He just wanted it to be clear that such innocence would not be rewarded in this life—or words to that effect.

By this time, the message was clear even to me: Notwithstanding all the talk, including my own, there was to be no serious effort to come together on the question of setting priorities. That conclusion was reinforced later in the spring, when Frank Press, again addressing the annual meeting of the National Academy of Sciences, said that the answer to the priorities question was to persuade the Congress and the administration to double the size of the science budget.

As appealing as that "solution" to the problem would have been, it would not have solved the problem but would only have deferred it for a while, and not for a long while. It is perfectly predictable that demand would have increased to exceed supply as new scientists were trained with the new money and came into the market with the expectation that they were as entitled as their mentors to support for their research. To be sure, more research would be done, and the nation would profit from it; but a policy of doubling the science budget whenever it is insufficient to meet the demands placed on it is hardly a long-term solution to the problem of how much science the nation should support and how that support should be distributed.

In fact, of course, decisions about spending are made every year; rarely, if ever, though, are they the product of a considered judgment among a set of well-understood alternatives. There are structural and political reasons for this. Structurally, the executive branch, starting in the Bush administration, has made some progress in taking a crosscutting view of science spending and proposing in its annual budget an easy-to-grasp picture of the whole. The congressional process, however, is hopelessly fragmented. A veteran observer of the process, Albert H. Teich, describes it this way:

> The budget for the National Science Foundation, which is part of an appropriations bill for independent agencies as well as for the Departments of Veterans Affairs and Housing and Urban Development, thus competes against the National Aeronautics and Space Administration (since both are "independent agencies"), but it also competes against housing and veterans programs, which are much larger components of that bill. The National Institutes of Health contend with health services, labor, and social-welfare programs. The Department of Energy's research is pitted against other DOE programs and river, harbor, and dam-construction projects. Thus research programs in NSF, NIH, and DOE do not face off directly against one another, and none of the civilian research programs competes directly with Defense Department research.[2]

One obvious consequence of this fragmentation is that there is absolutely no incentive for advocates of these programs to do anything but ask for the maximum number of dollars for them. A public-spirited concern for the well-being of the whole research enterprise would not be served by asking for less money for the NIH, since none of the money not spent on the NIH would go to the NSF or necessarily to any other research or education program.

Moreover, both academics and politicians, for all the complaining about it, like the system the way it is. Science has fared well under arrangements that disperse program responsibility in the executive branch and in the Congress. Under such a system, alliances involving specialized scientific

2. Albert H. Teich, "Discussions of Setting Priorities Are Filled with Misunderstandings," *Chronicle of Higher Education* (January 22, 1992): A52.

groups, their supporting agencies, and the relevant committees of Congress are easier to hold together and carry more weight than they would in a more consolidated system. Members of Congress like it because it gives more of them an opportunity for a major role in a significant, even if relatively small, area.

The history of the National Institutes of Health provides an especially instructive example of these reciprocal benefits. The growth of the NIH is intimately associated with the careers of a succession of senators and representatives whose influence over appropriations and whose dedication to biomedical research and training defeated persistent efforts of presidents of both parties to restrain that growth. Their names constitute an NIH honor roll, and in several cases their names can be found on buildings on the NIH campus or at research centers in their home states: Lister Hill of Alabama, Warren Magnusen of Washington, Lowell Weicker of Connecticut, and Mark Hatfield of Oregon—two Republicans and two Democrats. On the House side, the list of patrons begins with John Fogarty of Rhode Island and includes such others as Joseph Early of Massachusetts, William Natcher of Kentucky, and most recently, John Porter of Illinois—three Democrats and a Republican. The National Institutes of Health, an agency without a large constituency in the ordinary sense of that term, prospered through constituencies of one in the appropriations committees of each house. Only in a system in which the parts were more powerful than the whole could an agency prosper as the NIH has done.

Periodically, someone will call for the creation of a Department of Science, as Robert Walker (Rep., Pa.), the chairman of the House Committee on Space, Science, and Technology, did. Such proposals have gone nowhere in the past and are unlikely to fare better in the future because, while greater centralization would make a few people more powerful, it would make a larger number less so. Teich concludes:

> Does all of this mean that scientists have nothing to contribute to priority setting for research? Not at all. Scientists have a great deal to contribute, but not by pursuing the unattainable goal of a consistent set of priorities for all of science. . . .
>
> Discussions of priorities among researchers need to be recognized as a means of informing decision makers, of providing balanced information on the prospects and limitations of various areas of research, and of moderating irresponsible claims. Such input from researchers can help decision makers block "end runs" by those who choose not to play by the rules.
>
> While scientists' participation in budgeting and priority setting should not be expected to yield comprehensive reforms and ultimate answers, it

can result in better incremental choices. But ultimately, political decision makers must make final decisions.[3]

Those are sensible words, and not excessive expectations, to which might be added the observation that the political decision makers will make their decisions in their characteristically political ways. The decision to authorize the SSC was in larger part a political than a scientific decision, while the decision to end it was wholly political. Similarly, the emphasis of the Clinton administration on research that will have an economic impact came out of the doctrine of the Democratic Party, just as the determination of the new Republican congressional majority in 1995–96 to end those programs came from Republican doctrine. In neither case was the opinion of scientists used for any purpose other than to buttress positions already held by the politicians.

It must be said that hope dies hard. In 1995, the Senate Appropriations Committee, now under Republican control, asked the National Academies of Science and Engineering and the Institute of Medicine to revisit the question of how to make science funding more rational and systematic than in the past. The academies' answer, issued in a report in December 1995, was to call for a new definition of what should count as federal science and technology. It recommended counting the roughly $35 billion that goes for "expanding fundamental knowledge and creating new technologies" and excluding the roughly equal amount that goes for "demonstrating, testing, and evaluating existing technologies"—mainly for military and space use. The former would be called "federal science and technology" and would be given priority over the latter, which would be called "research and development." The report goes on to say that S&T spending "should generally favor academic institutions because of their flexibility and inherent quality control, and because they directly link research to education and training in science and engineering." Each agency would need to identify its obsolete or ineffective research programs, so that more money would be available for new initiatives. The report does not identify specific areas of science that should be cut. Instead, it calls on the administration to identify which scientific and technical areas are so important to national needs that the United States should spend enough to maintain worldwide leadership in them and which are less important areas, for which the government should try to sustain work at a "world-class" level.[4] The report was greeted with cautious commendation by officials in the administration and the Congress.

3. Ibid.
4. *Allocating Funds for Science and Technology* (Washington, D.C.: National Academy Press, 1995).

This is a report that academic scientists could only love. If it were possible to eliminate competition from such technological public works programs as the space station by consigning them to a different and lower category, science funding would probably fare better in the annual battles. Moreover, if the primary goal of science and technology policy were to maximize high-quality scientific output, as perhaps it ought to be, this would be the right thing to do. The report, of course, gives no guidance as to what the priorities should be within the science budget. Nor can it give assurances that decisions about which areas are the most important can be made with confidence in their integrity, much less in their substantive merit.

Any thoughtful contribution to the debate over how to make science policy and how to spend limited dollars most effectively is welcome. Back in the real world, though, the same issue of the *Chronicle of Higher Education* that reported on the academies' study also reported, "Pentagon Budget Gives Priority to Purely Military Research: The FY 1996 Department of Defense Budget Increases R&D Spending by 6 Percent, But Refocuses the Programs on Strictly Military Applications." According to John C. Crowley, MIT's representative in Washington, the research areas slated for increases are not those for which universities typically win grants.

As is so often the case when it matters, policy priorities in science and technology are made in the heat of battle out of considerations that have little to do with the merits as those merits are judged by working scientists or university administrators. What will be the effect of the new DOD approach? The *Chronicle* reported two conflicting views:

> Stuart W. Leslie, a professor of the history of science at the Johns Hopkins University, argues that universities should resist a shift back to military-dominated agendas, even if that means less money overall for research. His own institution and others could use this as an opportunity to focus more on teaching, he adds.
>
> Still, some policy experts say universities and their researchers are likely to follow the government's leading research priorities.
>
> "In the long run," says Al Teich, director of science and policy programs for the American Association for the Advancement of Science, "if civilian R&D is going down and military R&D is going up, then people at universities are likely to look more carefully at what's available on the DOD side of things."[5]

A more diplomatic statement of the reality principle would be hard to find.

I expressed my own conclusion on the subject of priorities in an inter-

5. *Chronicle of Higher Education* (December 8, 1995): A26.

view in February 1992 for the publication *Science and Government Reports,* a cranky but always lively newsletter that is widely read among people interested in the politics of science.

> I think that all the talk and hopes about setting research priorities has probably been wrong. I now think that priorities are not going to be set nationally. What's going to happen nationally is that large decisions are going to be made about the level of funding, and that will be constrained by macro-economic considerations. And within that, large decisions will be made about large projects. And those will be determined, in large part, by political considerations, not primarily scientific considerations.
>
> The rest of the money is not going to be enough to do what everybody wants to do. And that's going to require that institutions make their own decisions about tailoring their programs. What will turn out to be scientific priorities in retrospect, 10 or 15 years from now, will be the accumulation of a large number of institutional decisions made in response to the fact of constrained resources. That seems to be the way we do things in this country. We don't do very well—in fact we hardly do at all—central planning of the kind that would enable us to establish scientific priorities.[6]

If that is an even approximately correct assessment of the situation, then it is another case in which the context for educational policy, and a fairly broad set of parameters in which to operate, is set by large national forces over which no single institution, or even higher education as a whole, has much control, leaving critical decisions to be made at each institution. Thus, the future shape of the enterprise, its health and vitality, will be the product of decisions widely dispersed over a large number of institutions, each reacting in its own way to the forces that are operating on all of them. The important question to ask is, are they up to the job? On that question, the experience of the presidents, both those who have left office and those who are still serving, is illuminating.

Universities and the Dreaded P(riorities) Word

It is sometimes hard to tell whether a message, especially an unpleasant one, is being heard. Even when it is heard, it may not be believed. Denial is one of the primary human responses to bad news, and there are always persuasive-sounding reasons to believe that one's own circumstances are different from those of other potential victims. In the case of the message of constrained resources, ignorance of the message was not a defense for anyone in higher education as the 1990s opened. The popular

6. "A New Nastiness Prevails in Federal-Academic Ties," *Science and Government Reports* 22, no. 3 (February 12, 1992): 5.

media were filled with stories about the hard times ahead. Here is a cover story in *Time* magazine from April 13, 1992: "The College Crunch: Strapped for Money." *Time* even knew how to do it, or at least where to end up. "By the year 2000, American colleges and universities will be lean and mean, service oriented and science minded, multicultural and increasingly diverse—if they intend to survive their fiscal agony." The *Chronicle of Higher Education* reported, "Public Colleges Expect Financial Hardship in 1991, as Budget Crises Imperil State Appropriations" (January 9, 1991).[7] Stories about institutional efforts to deal with the problem became news: "Rutgers Feels Cuts, but President Won't Cry" (*New York Times*, January 9, 1993); "Short of Money, Columbia U. Weighs How Best to Change" (*New York Times*, May 23, 1992).

Some advice was freely offered: "The Cost of Higher Education: Lessons to Learn from the Health Care Industry" and "Cost Containment: Committing to a New Economic Reality" appeared in *Change* (November/ December 1990). Other advice was anything but free, as management consultants, sensing a large new market for their services, set about selling to universities the experience gained in reengineering and downsizing American business.

Some universities plunged into the water, if not with a will, then at least with a sense of grim determination. In January 1993, the *New York Times* reported that

> the University of Connecticut has devised a system that intends to measure how productive its professors are. The plan . . . could revolutionize the way the university administrators decide how to spend state money. The plan would give each academic department a set of scores. The departments would be scored on a scale of zero to five in each of ten categories. . . . Progress in the categories would be measured against goals set by the professors themselves, and would be taken into account in budget decisions. . . . Lewis B. Rome . . . chairman of the school's board of trustees, said the plan will help the university examine what it can afford to offer or pursue.[8]

In November 1991, Brown University reported in the *Brown Alumni Monthly*:

> Over the past year, the national economic turndown, recent government decisions affecting research funding, and a decade of near-euphoric

7. *Time*, April 13, 1992, 54–60; "State Budget Crisis Threatens Funds for Public Colleges," *Chronicle of Higher Education* (January 9, 1991): A1.

8. "U. Conn Devises a Point System to Rate Professors' Productivity," *New York Times*, January 10, 1993.

growth at Brown [leading to a surfeit of economic commitments] combined to undermine seriously the university's economic health. . . . This was brought home during the May meeting of the Brown Corporation, when the Budget and Finance Committee refused—for the first time in anyone's memory—to approve the budget submitted by the administration, and sent it back with a mandate to balance it. Over the next several weeks, Brown's senior administrators were immersed in the painful task of trimming nearly $3.5 million from a budget already notable for its lack of fat.[9]

In January 1992, William Richardson, then president of the Johns Hopkins University, addressed a letter to the university community. He began, no doubt on the sound psychological assumption that misery loves miserable company, by placing Hopkins' budget problems in a national context of similar institutions.

For months, the news has been full of reports of how the country and its institutions—public and private—have been affected by, and are coping with, adverse economic conditions. Many universities are planning or have already taken actions to help solve serious budgetary problems. Some examples: Columbia is reducing faculty positions by 45 by the end of the fiscal year; Chicago suspended all faculty appointment initiatives directed toward the next academic year; Cornell withheld one day's pay from each of five consecutive paychecks for faculty and staff in state-supported schools; Harvard reduced departmental budgets by up to 6 percent, and Yale by 5 to 15 percent; and Stanford canceled external searches for department chairs and reduced operating expenditures by academic departments by more than 7 percent.

He then went on to project a budget deficit at Hopkins during the current fiscal year and a substantially larger one for the next year if nothing were done to prevent it. It was too early, he said, to know the amount with any precision, but the most likely projections of revenue and expenditures would see financial deterioration of $3.1 million in the School of Arts and Sciences, $2.4 million in the School of Hygiene and Public Health, $2.5 million in the School of Engineering, and $6 million in the School of Medicine. The remainder of the letter outlined some cost-cutting possibilities and expressed confidence in the future of the university and in its ability to weather hard times.

One last example will suffice. In January 1991, the *New York Times* reported:

9. Ann Duffy, "The $8 Million Question," *Brown Alumni Monthly,* November 1991, 1.

The president of Yale University has ordered all schools and departments to trim their budgets by between 5 percent and 10 percent next year and to consider long-range cuts in faculty and possibly entire departments to help the university offset declining revenues and steadily rising costs.

Yale's president, Benno C. Schmidt, Jr., has been warning the university community since November that cuts were inevitable because of the national economic slowdown, reductions in federal grants, increasing competition for faculty stars and the need for half a billion dollars in repairs for aging buildings that have been put off for too long.

"Yale for many years has been consuming its capital resources to live beyond its means," Mr. Schmidt said in a letter to the university last November.[10]

The story closed with these brave words from Donald Kagan, dean of Yale College: "We're hoping to find something that can be expendable, rather than try to bleed everybody."

The Problem of Selective Cuts

In fact, it is no harder to cut some parts of a university's budget than it is to make similar cuts in a business. All organizations need an administrative apparatus, and it is quite likely that, after years of largely unexamined growth in the organization, the administration has grown, too. In universities, the growth of administration considerably exceeded the growth of either faculty or student enrollment through the 1980s. This was largely the result of regulation and demands for accountability from government and a rapid growth in student services, as the competition for students grew more intense. Whatever the reasons for the growth, it was apparent that administrative functions were the first place to look to solve a budget problem. Moreover, unlike faculty, administrative staff do not have tenure and, no matter how important their services may be, they are not the reason for the institution's existence. Thus, virtually every institution that saw a financial problem ahead looked first to its administration to bear the heaviest load of cuts.

It is, of course, important for universities to be well managed. However, since efficiency is not the highest institutional value, university administrative arrangements may not look like their counterparts in business. Functions that may be highly centralized in business—personnel for example—may, in a university, need to respond to the fact of departmentalism and substantial faculty autonomy. Still, within the constraints imposed by

10. Anthony De Palma, "Yale Plans Cuts as Income Falls and Costs Rise," *New York Times,* January 30, 1991.

their character, there is no excuse in university management for ineffi-
ciency or redundancy, and those were logical first targets.

They were rarely sufficient. Even the most rigorous, indeed ruthless,
approach to administrative cost-cutting could not come to terms with the
central problem, which was, in the words of the Brown story, "a decade of
near-euphoric growth ... [leading to a surfeit of economic commit-
ments]." Dealing with that problem presented an altogether different kind
of challenge. The reason for that is embedded deeply in the nature of the
university. Growth is the natural condition of the university. It emerges
from the energy and creativity of the faculty. The ability of American universities to give free rein to those qualities has been the basis for their
flowering in the last half of this century. It is obviously not the case that
the emergence of molecular biology or computer science or biomedical
engineering makes history or classics or language and literature expendable. As knowledge grows, divides, and grows again, universities expand
to accommodate the new requirements for teaching and research. As one
president said, "I'm not very sanguine about the way a place like MIT, or
Stanford, or Cal Tech, or Harvard is going to respond to these [con-
straints]. The good thing about [this university] is that most of what it
does is of high quality; the difficulty ... is that most of what it does is high
quality. And there's very little that you can look at and say, that's a candidate for shutting down."

With growing resources, it is in everyone's interest that the process
continue. Moreover, at most institutions it is a process that is "managed"
in only a rough sense of the word. The institutional impulse is not to
restrain growth but to find the resources to support it. Indeed, one test of
the value of a new idea may well be its ability to attract resources for its
support. Standing still, on the other hand, is contrary to the nature of
the beast, and contraction is simply an abomination. Moreover, neither
condition is in any obvious way in the interest of anyone in the institution.
Some may profit from the suffering of others, but that is always a risky
proposition and not a very stirring rallying cry. And, of course, future
generations of students and faculty may profit tomorrow from today's
hardships, but they are not at the table, and vague future benefits have
tough sledding against real present pain.

One strategy for mitigating divisive internal struggles over smaller
budgets is to share the pain through uniform, across-the-board cuts. Virtually everyone despises that as a strategy, on the grounds that it is a recipe
for mediocrity. But it may not be a bad strategy to meet a short-term
problem. Avoiding conflict is not a trivial accomplishment, and the belief
that every budget has some fat in it is close enough to the truth to support
one or two rounds of evenly shared pain. As a longer-term strategy, how-

ever, it surely is a downhill slide. Thus, most would agree with Dean Kagan: "We're hoping to find something that can be expendable, rather than try to bleed everybody."

Therein lies the problem. As one president who had been through the fire put it,

It's extremely difficult for at least institutions of the kind I am familiar with to cut selectively, to identify areas in which they're weak or anachronistic. Indeed, the biggest decision I made in response to the need to make some fairly modest cuts in the size of the faculty was to try to do that selectively rather than across the board. Faculty members told me that I was clearly right to try to do it selectively, clearly right, but that it would be a disaster politically. And they were right about that. . . .

It just proved to me that no rational president out for his or her own interests will do that again at [my university]. And I would be surprised if it's not very similar even at a place that I've always imagined to be far more rigorous and hard-nosed about these matters, such as MIT.

If that's right, what we can expect to see from these institutions is a systematic avoidance of hard choices having to do with systematic judgments on their merits. What that means is that inertia is in the saddle. And at a time of static resources, that the capacity for innovation that we've come to associate with our great institutions is not going to be anything like what it has been for a lot of the period since World War II.

While this is the darkest view of the matter that I encountered, it is not hard to find others like it. Here is one more:

The faculty are inclined to look at these questions starting with great skepticism and say, well, these financial problems will go away if we can just get that bloated administration. And when they do think about the necessity of cuts, they say, don't cut you, don't cut me, cut that guy over by the tree. And there's very little willingness to think in larger institutional terms, to transcend one's department or profession, one's personal interest, and think in institutional terms.

This president also spoke from hard experience:

[The Provost] and I had decided that the time had come to close department X, which was one of the newer departments here. It split off from another department and [over the years, it changed its identity several times]. It had in it some very excellent activities. . . . It also had a lot of quite pedestrian work and it made a series of appointments, junior faculty appointments, which were by and large folks who had already been turned down by other first-rate departments. And we concluded that the time had come to close that department. Save some of the activities and terminate others. And I guess you have to say, with the benefit of hindsight, that we did it badly. I'm not quite sure how we could have done it better. But we did it badly. And it led to much unhappiness. Terrified the faculty that we were about to close down mathematics or physics or economics. And it left big scars for both of us.

The Role of the Faculty in Budget Cutting

There is one point on which most, if not all, of the presidents interviewed would agree, and that is the central role of the faculty in designing a strategy for dealing with scarcity. Having said that, though, they would probably also agree that while it cannot be done without them, it is devilishly hard to do it with them. On this point there is ample testimony, some of which we saw in chapter 5, on governance. Faculty are the most powerful single force in the university. Their activities carry the institution forward, their resistance can stop it in its tracks. The first problem, as many presidents see it, is to get faculty to understand that there is a problem that needs to be addressed and that a temporary patch will not do the job. That problem, as the president of a public system of mixed institutional types saw it, was especially acute at the system's large research university.

> What we've seen in many institutions over the last ten or fifteen years was the result of the first impact of really needing to behave differently, to think differently, to look differently at what we do in higher education, and at our budgets. In my state, for example, we have four campuses. The differences are dramatic among those four campuses in terms of their response to today. At the research university, the faculty have never had to deal with it. The reason they never saw it before is that they had the capability when things got tough financially to find other revenue streams. The first and most important was out-of-state tuition. We learned just how high you can push out-of-state tuition in a public university. And we learned just how many students you can take from out of state before your legislature screams, and the people scream. It's fifty-one percent.
>
> My other campuses have been struggling with these issues. They couldn't generate the out-of-state revenues. They couldn't look to increasing their research revenues. They couldn't look to private fund raising. So I have a very interesting study in which I've had three campuses dealing with this, restructuring, reallocating resources, finding ways to connect and deal with the expectations, and to get very high on the state's list of priorities. And I've had one campus digging in its heals, unwilling to think and talk and deal with the issues.

The president of a private university, reflecting on the major budget reductions over which he presided, concluded, "Well, in order to get faculty to pay attention you've got to give them the message like a cold bath. When you do that, the modulation that causes them to respond responsibly and not panic is very difficult to achieve. And I think for a little while we did not achieve it, and so we got a negative reaction."

This president had only dire concerns about the response of private universities:

> Private institutions are facing resource pressures no less than the publics. How have they responded to them? I believe they've responded on the whole irresponsibly, by attaching themselves to a set of tuition policies that don't work out mathematically. You cannot raise tuition the way [my university] raised tuition over the last twenty-five years for the next twenty-five years. There is no one who can pay it. When you embark on that, your financial aid costs are going to skyrocket compared to your tuition costs. Where once high-tuition institutions were claiming 20–25 percent of an average family income, they're now up to 50 percent and beyond. It's just not going to work.
>
> The other way I think we have done it is by letting our physical plants fall apart. What happens when you get inertia in the saddle is that present consumption will just dominate relative to investment for future needs.
>
> Survival is not the question. These [institutions] are too important not to survive. But it's hard not to be pessimistic about the combination of resource constraints, internal governance difficulties, and, in the case at least of the institutions I am familiar with, a pretty substantial accumulation of problems that has come about because of their political preference for present consumption over future investment.

Another president pointed to a generational divide that made governance, generally, and resource constraints, specifically, more difficult.

> The faculty who lived through the golden age have different attitudes and expectations [from those of] the newly tenured faculty, who represent the trailing edge of the baby boom and who had a totally different order of difficulty in their own personal lives in getting to where they are. And even within the same departments, there is a gulf of understanding between those cohorts that makes the whole problem of faculty governance, even at the departmental level, much more difficult.

Experience breeds expectations, expectations are translated into interests, and interests are to be protected. In those respects, faculty are no different from the rest of the population, except that they are somewhat better able to protect their interests, if not against so large a force as the federal government, then at least within their own institutions. In contrast to industry, for example, universities cannot downsize by laying off faculty. The conditions of tenure require a financial emergency before that can be done. Few universities could make a plausible case for that, and fewer would wish to, even if they could. Furthermore, to a large extent faculty control the conditions of their work. They are responsible for establishing the curriculum, and they choose the instructional methods for carrying it out. Their initiative brings in research funds, and their mobility provides powerful leverage on institutional decisions. Finally, traditions of collegial governance that exist to some degree in all universities make top-down decisions unwise and generally ineffective.

Examples, If Not Models

There is no set of rules, no guidebook, that institutions can turn to when financial problems require something more than administrative re-structuring, when the opportunities for greater revenue have been fully exploited, and when it finally becomes necessary to take a hard look at academic commitments. There are more successful cases to look at and less successful ones, but the lessons learned from either are not readily applicable to other circumstances. At UCLA, for example, an institution character-ized by a large, underfunded College of Arts and Sciences and an excess of small, expensive professional schools, a major restructuring of its profes-sional schools was undertaken in 1993 in which the School of Library Sci-ence merged with the Graduate School of Education, the School of Archi-tecture and Urban Planning was divided into its component parts and both parts merged with other schools, the School of Nursing was put under the direction of the Medical Center and its budget drastically reduced, and something similar was done to the School of Public Health. As a part of the package, a new School of Public Policy was established. In the process, a yearly savings of about $8 million was achieved, no tenured faculty were let go, and though some would surely disagree, the university was arguably better for the exercise.

There may be some lessons in the way the changes were accomplished, but it is more likely that what others have learned from the UCLA experi-ence is that major change requires unusual tenacity and a high degree of tolerance for abuse. The affected schools, with one exception, mounted campaigns against the changes, and each of them had friends in high places. They were not, in all cases, polite. The state legislature became in-volved, letters were generated from members of Congress, and, of course, the alumni of the affected schools mounted campaigns to save their schools. In the end, the day was carried by a combination of the determination of the leaders of the administration and the faculty senate to make deep rather than wide cuts; confidence in the chancellor, built over twenty-five years of successful service; three successive years of forced reductions amounting to 25 percent of the state's subsidy; and the stark picture facing the university in the future.

At Yale, in contrast, everything seemed to go wrong. Following the announcement of the need to make reductions reported earlier in this chapter, a faculty-administration committee was established to recommend how to do that. Following Dean Kagan's injunction not to spread the pain evenly, the committee proposed, among other recommendations, to eliminate the departments of linguistics, sociology, and engineering. In response, large segments of the faculty rose up in outrage. That was understandable, coming from the units that had been singled out for reduction or elimination, but the anger went far beyond those few. Clearly, there was more involved than simply disagreements about where to cut the budget. One suspects that some old scores were being settled, and that confidence in or affection for the president was not sufficient to overcome misgivings about the recommendations or fears of what they might portend for the future. Shortly thereafter, President Benno Schmidt left the university, and after several years of an interim presidency, Yale appointed as its new president a member of the faculty who had, ironically, been a member of the committee that had made the despised recommendations.

One of the more dramatic responses to the problem of financial constraints was announced in late 1995 by the University of Rochester. Over five years, undergraduate enrollment will be allowed to decline from 4500 to 3600, graduate enrollment from 1100 to 850, and the faculty, through attrition, will shrink from 343 to 306. A revamped undergraduate curriculum will be installed, and more money will be spent on merit aid for top students and on new investments in library and computer and networking resources and on campus facilities. Doctoral programs in modern languages and comparative literature, mathematics, linguistics, and chemical engineering will be closed.

By any standard these are major changes, a refocusing of an institution described by the late Ernest L. Boyer as belonging to the "middle ground [of institutions] that have not achieved world-class research status nor a reputation for the best teaching. For this ... group to make themselves distinctive, it calls for this sort of boldness." Not surprisingly, not all aspects of the plan met with universal approbation. According to the *New York Times,* "Sanford Segal, a professor of mathematics and chairman of the faculty senate, said that while he supported a number of the initiatives, he thought the discontinuation of the doctorate program in math was 'ill considered.' As a result, we will attract fewer science-oriented students.' "[11]

Significantly, the reaction from outside the university seemed even more intense than the inside response.[12] Leading the charge was the organized mathematics community, which went to the barricades in support of its threatened colleagues. A fact-finding committee sent to Rochester by the American Mathematics Society (AMS) found that Rochester may become the first "major institution with a physics graduate program that doesn't have a mathematics graduate program." Fearing to risk subtlety, the AMS established a task force consisting of scientists and mathematicians, and it was reported to be drafting a letter to Rochester trustees saying that the proposed action would be "a tragedy for American mathematics." To which Rochester's Dean Richard Aslin responded, "Give me a break. . . . This is being viewed by AMS as a test case, and it must be because they're fearful of it happening elsewhere."[13]

The result was a compromise in which the university agreed to save a smaller Ph.D. program and cut the mathematics faculty from twenty-one to fourteen, with one additional faculty position created by the transfer of two physics professors, each on a half-time status, to mathematics. For its part, the math faculty agreed to concentrate on improving its undergraduate courses. The three other departments slated to lose their doctoral programs, perhaps lacking the cohesive and energetic support of their national disciplines, had to accept their fate. The point of the story is not who won and who lost, still less who was right and who was wrong. The point is to illustrate how difficult it is to cut back on academic programs as resistance from important national organizations is brought to bear in support of the threatened locals. Inertia, alone, is a powerful obstacle to change. The conditions of the modern university, specifically, in this case, the existence of a strong national disciplinary group, multiply its effects.

It is too soon to know for certain how any of these efforts will turn out or whether the radical surgery practiced at UCLA and Rochester was better therapy than the more cautious and incremental approaches adopted by other institutions. Indeed, describing individual institutional responses is a little like studying military strategy by sitting in the American Legion Hall on a Friday night and listening to the vets recounting their war stories. Somewhere among them all there lie some truths of general applicability, but it is terribly hard to figure out exactly what they might be. If there are

11. William Horan, "Rochester University Plans More Spending per Student," *New York Times*, November 17, 1995.

12. The following was reported in *Science* 271 (January 19, 1996): 284.

13. Constance Holder, "Does Rochester without Math Add Up?" *Science* 271 (January 19, 1996): 284.

lessons here, they are not obvious ones. Every university, it seems, must find its own way to heaven or to hell, and the sum total of their choices will determine the shape of America's universities in the future.

But it is unsatisfying to leave the matter there. Perhaps there are a few general statements that apply, if not universally, then at least broadly across the board. Here are some to consider:

First, few, if any, universities can escape the need to examine their programs and operations with a view to bringing aspirations and resources into balance. One president spoke of that inevitability in this way:

> I think the resource issue is the single most profound driving force that is going to shape the next ten or fifteen years. It may not be the present or the future that is so abnormal. It may be the immediate past that is extremely abnormal. We were living in a very abnormal period economically in the United States, [. . . which has] shaped our notion of reality during our professional lifetimes. As we look now at the present and on into the future, the great strength of American higher education is the diversity of its financial support. Our great strength has been the diversity of mechanisms that we can bring to bear to solve these problems. But as you look at all of these various mechanisms now, the indicators are either flat or pointing down. I can't think of a single indicator, at least available to [my university], where I think there is a great deal of upward potential. I think that the implications that are going to flow from this new prolonged period of fiscal reality are going to be profound, and they will touch, literally, every part of the university.

The failure to face the problem will lead to far worse results than any mistakes that might be made in the course of making the effort.

A second general truth is that very little can be done without the support, or at least the acquiescence, of faculty. The question is whether meaningful efforts to shape programs to available resources can win that support. That question does not arise because faculty are uniquely selfish or self-interested but because it is precisely the work of the faculty that is at issue in any attempt to plan under the expectation of limited resources.

The clearest example of the problem is also the most obvious one: proposals to close programs will predictably be met by protests from the faculty involved but also from other faculty who either disagree on the merits, fear that their programs may be next, or generally do not believe in the seriousness or duration of the problem. But that is far from the whole story as seen by one president:

> We can certainly cut costs in our administrative services in all sorts of ways. We've not done enough of that yet. We can also trim the fringes a

bit. But I think what we will need to do is to reallocate faculty time in the next decade, because one of the places in which costs have gone up is student ancillary services of all sorts. So, if you cut back on those, who is going to do them? It brings the faculty back into more contact with students, which is probably a good thing for the students and for the university. But the faculty won't see it that way immediately. But that's going to happen.

The hardy perennial of faculty teaching loads is also bound to be on the table. It is an issue on which generations of state legislators and newspaper editorialists have dined out, because it is only too easy to poke fun at what seems to be a six- or eight-hour-a-week work schedule. In fact, most university faculty in research universities work very hard. The combination of teaching, preparation for teaching, graduate student supervision, research, university service, and professional obligations off campus put them up with lawyers and doctors for sheer number of hours worked. Hard work is not the issue; how it is distributed is.

The typical presumption in setting a "standard" teaching load for research university faculty is that about half of the full-time responsibility is devoted to research. Like any arbitrary assumption, it does an injustice to some and more than justice to others. In many universities it is possible to be relieved of part of the teaching obligation by bringing in grant support or by negotiating a better deal. As a result, teaching loads tend to be smaller in the sciences, where outside research funding is the norm, than in the humanities and social sciences, where it is comparatively rare. But in this, as in most other aspects of university life, large discrepancies in conditions of work by field are hard to sustain, and so the humanists and social scientists have seen their undergraduate teaching loads reduced, as well. Indeed, smaller teaching loads are one of the currencies used in battles to recruit or retain faculty. Few, if any, institutions have provisions for moving in the other direction and adding courses for those who do less research. Yet, it is surprising how much difference small changes can make in this area. As the president of a private university reported, "I did a rough calculation as I was going out the door. If I can remember it correctly I think I figured that if every person in the arts and sciences faculty taught one extra course every three years, that was the equivalent of forty full-time faculty. And I don't think that is an unreasonable demand. So there is real potential there." Realizing the potential will be no easy matter until all available alternatives are seen to be worse.

Another hardy perennial: calls for increased productivity will be heard throughout the land. In the context of higher education, increased productivity means one or both of two things: higher teaching loads for faculty—

as we have seen, desirable in some cases but difficult to achieve—or the substitution of capital for labor. It is the latter of which much will be heard in the future, in part, at least, because it seems to offer the promise of avoiding the issue of teaching loads through the magic of technology. A recent report by two influential analysts of higher education, William F. Massy of Stanford and Robert Zemsky of the University of Pennsylvania, makes the case strongly. The authors conclude, as have many others, that, as yet, technology has enabled colleges to do more with more, but it has raised costs, not brought them down. But, they argue, that will not do in the future. "In an economy that is itself knowledge-based, the new information technologies offer an economical means of providing the continuous education the U.S. now requires, as well as a more readily accessible form of post-secondary education and credentialing. . . . If traditional colleges and universities do not exploit the new technologies, other non-traditional providers of education will be quick to do so." Moreover, they argue, "Using IT [information technologies] for more-with-less productivity enhancement requires that technology replace some activities now being performed by faculty, teaching assistants, and support personnel. With labor accounting for seventy percent or more of current operating cost, there is simply no other way." [14]

It is very difficult to know how to evaluate predictions about the effects of technology. The invention of the printing press certainly revolutionized both teaching and scholarship, but the invention of television has come nowhere close to having the revolutionary effect on education that its advocates predicted in the 1950s. New information technology is probably closer to the printing press than television in its potential for education, but it remains potential, not yet reality. Even assuming a major impact, it is far from clear that more-for-less can take the place of more-for-more. As one president put it: "We don't compete on price; we compete on quality, and we always have. Every time there is an advance or we find new sources of revenue, or new efficiencies, we use those new resources to increase the quality of what we do, measured in [either] increasing the things that faculty can use to create new knowledge, or increase [in] services for students, or increase [of] facilities, or what have you."

That is not exactly a socially irresponsible course to follow. Improvements in quality are, after all, highly desirable, and to admit that they are too expensive is profoundly unsettling. Zemsky was probably right when

14. The Massy and Zemsky paper, "Using Information Technology to Enhance Academic Productivity," was commissioned by Educom, a consortium of colleges and businesses whose purpose is to spread the use of technology in higher education. What follows is based on a report of the study and responses to it in the *Chronicle of Higher Education* (November 24, 1995).

he said in an interview following the publication of the paper, "This is a world in which you never want to bet against the technology. It may not be five or ten years from now, but it is coming."[15] Rapid development of new information technologies can be predicted with confidence; so, too, can the apparent paradox of the increased costs of applying them together with the decreased unit cost of work done with them. Whether that will all balance out to budget savings in the foreseeable future is highly problematic, but surely the more important question is what educational uses of new technology will produce genuine improvement in educational quality and what uses might actually degrade educational quality.

As always, though, the discussion of productivity enhancements generated by technology must come to terms with the software problem. The capacity for more efficient transmission of knowledge exists, but what is it that is to be transmitted more efficiently? One president put it this way: "On this productivity business, I agree that we haven't shown many improvements. . . . But I don't find the through-put analysis very helpful in a world in which the nature of intellectual activity is changing so dramatically that what we really ought to be thinking about is not how many or how much, but what."

For the media and the public, the drama is in the "how"—dazzling new capabilities like the Internet. However, without a better sense of the "what," it is not possible to talk sensibly about technology-induced trade-offs between quality and cost.

Turning Public into Private

A cloud can be seen forming over the nation's public universities, and what comes from it could reshape the landscape in important ways. For want of a better word, the development can be called "privatization." It is progressing rapidly as state funding for higher education sinks to smaller fractions of total institutional budgets. Here is the former president of a public university that went through a crash course on privatization.

> We had a taxpayer revolt, a property tax limitation measure, like Proposition 13, except that it made Proposition 13 look like a pussycat. In the three weeks after a call from the governor, I had to cut 25 percent of my state funding from the university budget. It wasn't that it would go next year—it had already been removed from the budget.
>
> We closed a college, closed all our teacher education programs, including the Ph.D. programs, and downsized or closed two dozen arts and sciences programs. We tried to change people's minds, but they would

15. "High-Tech Efficiency," *Chronicle of Higher Education* (November 24, 1995): A17.

rather see the university disappear and other state agencies disappear or be underfunded than pay taxes.

As a result, in 1990 we entered into a privatization of the university. And when I left last year, for all intents and purposes, that public university was private. It has less than 10 percent of its funding from the state. This is the same as Michigan and Virginia, and a number of other institutions. . . . When I left the university, the fact of the matter is that we succeeded in privatizing it. The university was in better financial shape than when I came, we had consolidated programs, morale was great, and the faculty were feeling very proud of themselves. . . .

It's a very healthy institution now, but it's a very different institution. And what it does, because of its high tuition, both in-state and out-of-state, is fail to serve the public purpose. The state has given up on it, and the university has accepted the fact that it is now a private institution. I'm not sure if that's good or bad, but it's surely different. And it certainly changes the class of people who have opportunities to go to that institution. And it changes the role of the institution in the state dramatically.

We were out in the forefront of these changes, but we are now seeing this in other major universities. Virginia is spinning off its schools one by one. And before it is finished, all that will be left is a small core of liberal arts and sciences that are supported by the state. Other than that, it will be a private university. Michigan is proceeding along the same lines, with great success. Public education is either going to change dramatically in this direction or be endangered.

Here is the response of the president of another large public university that has suffered through years of declining state support.

I believe that what has happened to your university is what is going to be happening around the country over the next few years, though hopefully with less speed and a less harsh final conclusion than in your case.

We are going to see a very different funding situation, and the way to success for most universities is going to be movement in the direction of privatization. If my university were an independent institution, it would have moved much further along that line than it has. And we have moved as far as we can within the constraints of our state system.

It is clear that funding from the state is going to decline for a much longer period as a percentage of the total resources available to the university. There is a substantial opportunity to provide additional resources to compensate for the decline in state resources, and the one that has been utilized least so far is tuition. The low-tuition–no-tuition concept is one in which the poor subsidize the rich. That makes no sense as public policy. I believe that a policy of high tuition and high financial aid can provide greater access to the poor than a low-tuition–low-aid policy.

When the public pays a mere 10 percent of the bills, it is worth contemplating just what it means to be a public university. What public, for example, is to be served? It is inevitable that tuition in public universities will begin to look more like that in private universities. No other source of income is so readily available as state appropriations fall further behind educational costs. Equally inevitable, in the face of such a development, is political resistance to higher tuitions. Although low tuitions are often justified as a benefit to the poor, they are in reality one of the largest state subsidies to middle- and upper-income groups, whose children are more likely to attend universities than are the children of the poor. This is the stuff of major political combat.

The privatization trend is, at least, a long-term recipe for greater institutional independence, which in itself will produce greater political strife. Faculties and administrations that must raise ever larger fractions of their keep are likely to grow restive under restraints imposed by central system offices and state legislatures. Nor is the phenomenon limited to a few institutions. To a greater or lesser degree, public universities are taking on some of the characteristics of their private counterparts. All are seeking funding outside of state appropriations, and many are moving to higher tuition. As they succeed, their independence from state authority will grow, and important questions about what such a public institution owes to the state inevitably will be forced onto the agenda.

Finally, university presidents will be tested as they have not been since the 1960s, though the test will be of a different kind. The presidents who came to grief in the 1960s did so largely because they failed to respond satisfactorily to episodes of campus disruption. The major causes of the disruptions were the Vietnam War and, following the murder of Martin Luther King, the demands that African Americans and then other minorities be included in the opportunities afforded by higher education. There was never great public support for the antiwar movement's attacks on universities, so the policy of firmness adopted by the "successor generation" of presidents eventually worked and was popular with the public and boards of trustees. The race-based problems were harder to deal with because there was no realistically attainable pace of progress that could satisfy the long-suppressed demand or mitigate the urgency with which it was expressed. In general, however, the impulses of faculty and administrations were sympathetic to the protests. There were far too few black students on college campuses and proportionally even fewer black faculty. Successful presidents and their administrations came to heed the wise injunction offered by Stanford's Herbert Packer after the first major black student protest at Stanford, to respond to the "the matter, not the manner of the protest."

The challenge faced by today's presidents is of a wholly different character. The university is no longer under assault by internal and external groups using coercive tactics to change its policies, as it was in the 1960s. Nor is it faced with urgent demands to do what most in the institution know should have been done long ago. There is no adversary to be defeated, yet much of what universities are now being pressed to do, for example, in their relations with industry, raises serious issues of institutional values. Leading an institution whose members have taken growth and prosperity as the natural order of things through what appears to be a prolonged period of slow or no growth will require political skills of a high order. An interesting and important question is whether the skills required are those of a leader of a democratic political system or of a corporate CEO. Here is the president of a large public system:

> Universities are becoming more and more like corporate entities. They have to disperse their activities and yet fight hard to preserve their core purposes and abilities. As we fight costs, as we fight the need to do much of our instruction and service off campus or on many different campuses, we need a matrix organization. We need to change from the typical departmental pyramids of a university to other forms of structure.
>
> I can give many examples of that in my own experience, where, instead of starting engineering departments or colleges all over the state, we purposely had just a couple that in turn broadcast their courses with interactive TV onto other campuses.
>
> When I arrived at one institution, we had five departments of biochemistry. And I said, "Hey, it's hard enough to have the best biochemistry department in the world. Let's merge it into one department, to serve not only multiple schools but multiple campuses and thereby get a stronger graduate program."
>
> We need [to build] a flexible organization, as corporations do all the time. They have basic core departments, but then they build task forces for every contract, in a matrix organization. I think that kind of flexibility is going to have to be built into universities in the future.

The president of a private university reflected on the course of his institution and also saw movement in the corporate direction:

> I can remember when our endowment was managed by a committee of trustees. If I go back to my student days, I remember when the security

force consisted of four night watchmen. I started the Government and
Community Relations Office in 1980—a little bit late, but I'll bet nobody
had one in 1960.

The whole range of management and information stuff didn't exist
when we began our academic careers. University administration has become more professional and more sophisticated. We have begun to look a
lot like corporations in our specialization and range of disciplines.

If university administrations are now being modeled on corporate
structures, can the rest of the university be far behind? The emphasis on
marketing, the search for institutional "image," and the pathetic concern
about where the institution stands in the latest *U.S. News and World Report*
rankings suggest that corporate styles are already embedded in the academic culture. Important questions remain to be addressed: Is it possible
to have in the same institution one major element that is driven by the
requirements of efficiency and whatever management theories prevail at
the moment and another—the part by whose labors the institution exists—marked by a strong preference for individual autonomy over any notion of efficiency? Can a university be part closed, the characteristic stance
of bureaucracies toward the use of information, and part open, the required stance for successful scholarship and teaching? Such conflicts are
inevitable. One president, for example, argued that in the future "we are
going to be taking a wholly different view about the nature of the facilities
we construct and how efficiently they will be used." It was not clear from
the context of the remark whether he included faculty in the "we," but it
is as certain as anything can be that the more efficient use of facilities will
require important shifts in faculty behavior and that those will not be
brought about by executive fiat.

It may be that successful presidents will be those who combine two
different sets of abilities, the management skills needed to run a major
business enterprise and the political skills required to lead a democratic
polity. Given the shortage of people who combine the two, it is likely that
boards of trustees, in their selection of new presidents, will look for individuals who have demonstrated one or the other and will hope that the
missing set of skills can be learned on the job.

It is the political skills of presidents that will be tested most in the years
ahead. Management responsibilities can be delegated to skilled subordinate
managers; the responsibility for political leadership rests squarely with the
president, and it cannot be delegated. Fortunately, the kind of leadership
that works best in a university is the kind that most people who become
university presidents should find congenial. It consists in articulating a
point of view about the nature of the institution's problems and opportu-

nities and leading discussion and debate through the institution's decision-making processes. Provosts and deans are critical to the orderly progress of the debate through their faculties, but only the president has the broad platform and the focus of attention to set the agenda for the debate.

Given the nature of the university, the key arena for the debate about the future must be the faculty. As we have seen, many presidents believe that most faculty are still in deep denial about the seriousness of the financial problems that lie ahead and are therefore resistant to seriously considering the painful choices that may be required. In one sense it is odd that this should be so; in another, it is only to be expected. Faculty are, after all, very smart people. They are capable of seeing what others see and of drawing the proper conclusions. However, faculty are also partisans in a struggle for resources, and they come to the battle armed with a strong sense of entitlement bred by many years of generous support and fortified by a strong sense of the value of the work they do. To hold both of those views simultaneously is a neat psychological trick.

The problem is compounded by what can only be called a failure of leadership. In universities, as in politics at large, education of the body politic is an essential part of the process. Until recently, at least, in most universities educating the faculty about the economic condition of the university was not a high-priority item for administrations or for faculty. I doubt that many faculty, for example, had any real sense of where indirect cost recovery fit into the economics of their university—what the basis for recovery was, how it was calculated, where the money actually went, and why they did not see it directly in their own operations. For many, if not most, it was a mystery, and a somewhat sinister one at that. When problems began to surface, a common faculty response was disbelief mixed with resentment, a devastating combination that could only make a bad problem worse.

That was a failure of leadership, and early responses to growing resource constraints, some of which have been described here, point to a larger and more pervasive failure of leadership. Ignorance of the circumstances in which they operate is a luxury that university faculties can no longer afford, and presidents who fail to take steps to end it will regret their failure when the time for difficult decisions can be delayed no longer.

Ending that condition is no easy task. It will not be accomplished by a few speeches and some financial data published in the campus newspaper, although those things will be needed. But what is essential is a process that forces individual faculty and their departments and schools to master the data on which decisions must be based and to confront the issues that emerge from the data. That is a long-term process, not a single event; it must be built into the fabric of the institution, not invented to meet a financial emergency. Since doing is still the best form of learning, it will undoubtedly require devolving more budgetary responsibility to lower levels of the organization. And since such a move might well accentuate institutional fragmentation and encourage the war of all against all, counterefforts will need to be made to build the sense of engagement in a common enterprise that is essential if university policy is to be something more than the sum of the most powerful present interests.

We are a long way from the age of the heroic president, but the presidents who can pull off the leadership tasks required in today's universities will have done a heroic job.

Chapter Seven

THE CHALLENGE
TO LEADERSHIP

E VEN THEIR STERNEST CRITICS believe that today's universities are valuable institutions. They may believe that universities have gone wrong, even badly wrong, but underlying their criticism is the conviction that these valuable, but betrayed, institutions would realize their full potential if only each critic's policy prescriptions were adopted.

Therein lies a problem. Whose prescriptions should prevail? What set of demands on the institution and its resources should carry the day? What kind of universities do we want, serving what constituencies, toward what ends? On those questions, consensus evaporates and all sorts of agendas—economic, ideological, social—lead in different directions.

Sometimes these questions devolve into a single, simpler one: Are today's universities providing what society wants and needs? The question is frequently asked by those who have already answered it in the negative, but when asked in all sincerity and with no underlying agenda, it is by no means a simple question to answer, for wants and needs are not in all respects identical and, indeed, are frequently in conflict. Most people prefer candy to cauliflower, even though cauliflower is a healthier food. In any case, determining what society needs is as much an exercise in values as in analysis, and consensus on values is hard to find these days.

Here, for example, is one person's—mine—short list of what society needs from its universities.

Rigorous academic standards. There is no large constituency clamoring to be made to work harder and be judged more rigorously. A policy of maintaining uniformly high and rigorous standards would be bound to produce more failures, at least in the short run, and to collide head on with the competing demands for occupational credentials and for broad access. Yet in many universities the declining level of academic preparation exhibited by incoming students has led to much greater emphasis on remedial work and, arguably, a broad easing of expectations and standards of performance. No society, certainly none in the modern world, can prosper under a regime of flabby standards for the higher education of its youth. Greater rigor is unpopular but necessary medicine.

It is important to be careful here, or else recognition of a problem can turn into an overly broad indictment. Deficiencies in preparation are not a serious problem in the most selective universities. Indeed, some would argue just the opposite. As the head of a prestigious public university put it, two things happened to the student body at his institution, and both were important. "First of all, it got a lot smarter, not just relatively, but any other way you want to look at it. The second thing, it got much more diverse with all the other kind of problems that are involved with that." A second public university president agreed. "It's true at our place, as well. Most of the alumni who are contributing over $100 million to [my university] wouldn't be admitted today, I would suspect." Private university presidents would probably agree with both of those observations, but not many public universities could claim that their students were either smarter or better prepared than in the past, and the evidence of declining SAT scores and increased remedial instruction certainly argues otherwise.

Engagement with the improvement of elementary and secondary education. Long-term improvement of academic standards in universities can only occur if the erosion of quality in the nation's lower schools is reversed. Many universities are working with schools in their areas, and some have mounted impressive efforts of broader scope. But the sum of it all adds up to considerably less than a response to an urgent need that is grounded in both self-interest and national interest.

Openly and honestly addressing the problems of racial and ethnic tension. This remains the American dilemma, and universities, as a major gatekeeper to the good life in America, have been thrust into the center of it. As a consequence, a variety of natural experiments have been taking place on campuses in every part of the country, and they go well beyond the now-routine affirmative action in admissions that is virtually universal. Some of these experiments impose some form of separatism—separate dormitories or social and cultural centers are the most common manifestations. Others have taken a more rigorously integrationist position. In few if any cases, however, have these experiments been seen as experiments. Rather, they have grown out of doctrine or political combat and have operated with largely unexamined consequences. There is no simple answer to America's racial and ethnic problems, but surely their resolution might be advanced by honest evaluation of and open debate about the consequences of the various approaches adopted on campus. Nowhere else in society will that evaluation and debate take place; it has not yet taken place in higher education, and its absence has constituted a failure of universities to provide for an urgent social need.

Avoidance of institutional partisanship on divisive social and political issues. American society needs universities to be active exemplars of the values that they have always professed, values like civility of discourse, respect for evidence and proper inference from it, and the insistence that today's truth may turn out to be tomorrow's folly, that dissent from conventional wisdom is an essential part of reaching for truth, and that dissenters are not only to be protected from sanction but listened to, because truth is often found in unlikely and unlovely places. Sustaining those values requires avoidance of institutional partisanship on divisive social and political issues. When institutions become partisans, none of those values is safe, and the loss to society is incalculable, for what is striking about this list of academic values is that all of them are central to a properly functioning democracy, and no other social institutions both profess and practice them. Universities are the natural teachers of democratic values because those values are embedded in their essential nature. If they fail to give society what it needs in this respect, then all of their other contributions, no matter how richly rewarding they may be, will be debased.

Any thoughtful observer of American society will develop a list that adds to or subtracts from this one. The differences will have as much to do with what each observer thinks about American society as the way he or she views universities. In contrast, it is much easier to find agreement about what society wants from universities. That question can be answered by market research, because determining what people want in commerce, politics, or education is the essence of the market system, and in this country, we are good at making markets work. So good, in fact, that the pressures to provide what society wants, and the rewards that come from doing so, have turned attention away from the more difficult question of what society needs. It is a condition that has contributed to disenchantment outside the academic gates and a measure of disquiet within.

There is one answer to the dilemma that has honorable roots in American educational thought, namely, that there is no dilemma at all. One president recalled the words of Robert Maynard Hutchins:

> "The university's highest obligation to society is to refuse to do what the society wants." And by that he meant that its job is understanding and criticism, that it is a center for independent thought. I believe firmly that there is no purpose in being an educational institution if all that you're trying to do is to contribute to the immediate problems of society. The purpose is, I think, to take a long-term view, to help train the human

capital that is going to be needed, and to act as a responsible citizen in the
ways that you can best act.

An educational institution is the last place left in the world to think
about the world and to prepare people to think usefully about it. And it's
essential to make that statement.

That is a powerfully attractive position, and in my view it is essential
that it continue to have eloquent adherents and visible exemplars. For most
universities in America, however, the dilemma is not so easily resolved. As
Martin Trow has pointed out, American higher education, alone among
educational systems in the world, grew up alongside a market-oriented
economic system and has always been imbued with the values of the market. As a consequence, American colleges and universities have been highly
responsive to what society wants of them, and where market forces have
clashed with what might be called the autonomous values of the university,
the former have almost always won out. The range of professional and
occupational programs found in any modern university is eloquent testimony to that fact. Adherents of the free market system will argue that
meeting wants at a price that consumers are willing to pay is the best way
of meeting needs. In this view, the distinction between wants and needs is
artificial, even elitist. Maybe yes, maybe no; my own view is that the process
of value setting for a society is far too complicated and important to be left
to a mechanism like the market, whose principle virtue is that its operations are arithmetic and, therefore, quantifiable. What is unambiguously
clear, however, is that in a market system, failure to supply what the public
wants will foreclose the opportunity to supply what it may need, as failure
of officeholders to win reelection will end their chances for further service
to the public.

Balancing responsiveness and self-direction has been and remains a
major task of educational leadership. It is a problem to which many presidents have necessarily devoted a good deal of thought. Whatever disagreement there may be about other roles for the university, on one point the
presidents whose words appear here are in substantial agreement: they
agree that what people value most is the teaching of their children. The
perceived failure to do that well has brought harsh criticism, and continued
failure to respond will have even worse consequences. That sense is especially strong among the leaders of public universities, who face state legislatures every year in budget negotiations, during which they hear about the
concerns of constituents. Here is the president of a public university:

> I spend a lot of time traveling the state and talking to people about what
> they want and expect from us. And I hear one thing over and over again:
> "We want you to teach the kids."

What does that mean? Well, "We want you to pay attention to them. We want you to teach them. And we want you to tell us that they'll have jobs when they graduate."

We talk to them about the research programs, about the stimulation of the economy, about the spin-offs from the research at our institution and the number of patents, and I get, "You know, out here we really don't care so much about that research. We just want you to teach the kids." It's just that simple.

Here is another public university president.

It is clear that if you look at the multipurpose mission of this university, the one that is of most concern to most people, and certainly to the legislature, is the university's commitment to educate all of the students who are eligible to attend.

The minute we break from that, the minute we break that part of the contract, our ability to get resources for other things will be dramatically reduced. I think we have to see to it that we make that our primary commitment.

It is easy to be cynical about such views, because they seem at odds with actual behavior. As another public university president put it,

It seems to me that at the research universities we are competing for the best people doing research and being creative. We are seeking research stars, no question about that. We don't go out and compete with one another with regard to people who are exemplary instructors and will put a lot of time in it. . . . I just remember the extent to which different institutions, in trying to bring great stars to the campuses, competed on the basis that you hardly had to teach at all.

I do not think cynicism is justified. It is true that there is a distance between professed values and actual behavior, but it is also true that, in contrast with a decade ago, the two are now actually in open conflict. There exists a real recognition of the value that the public places on teaching and a genuine desire to respond. Moreover, unlike some other demands on the institution, this one is wholly consistent with every university's basic mission. All changes take time, and few go as far as their advocates would like. Moreover, the demands of the moment, no matter how deeply felt they may be, can be excessive or short-sighted. Universities are not, after all, colleges devoted exclusively to the education of undergraduates; nor, at bottom, do we want them to be. There is an inevitable tension in them between the demands of teaching and research, and the complete victory of either function would fundamentally change their nature, at society's loss.

The fair criticism of universities is that they have moved too far in the direction of valuing research and devaluing teaching. What is required is a rebalancing, not a revolution. The move to meet the public demand for better teaching seems well established, in part out of a recognition of the imbalance and the need to correct it and in part because likely future research funding will not sustain the ambitions of all those who will compete for it. The pressures for regular faculty to spend more time in the classroom will grow; there will be resistance to those pressures, and out of that tension will come a new balance that is likely to place more emphasis on teaching.

There are other manifestations of the needs-wants dilemma on which there is considerably less agreement. This chapter looks at some of them—specifically, the role of universities in solving pressing social problems, the public leadership role of university presidents, and finally, why the public should continue to tolerate and sustain these odd, expensive, and often troublesome institutions even, perhaps especially, when they do not supply what is wanted but provide, instead, what may not be recognized as needed.

Universities and the Solution of Social Problems

It is certainly possible to be overwhelmed by the expectations that accompany success. In the years since World War II, American universities have been expected to contribute significantly to national defense, the treatment and cure of disease, economic growth at home and abroad, the education and training of the skilled workforce, an opening to society's benefits for previously excluded groups, and last, but maybe not least, the entertainment of the populace through competitively successful athletic programs. It is remarkable how well they have met all of those expectations. Along with success, however, comes disappointment, sometimes reaching the point of disillusionment, at the failure to deal with the problems that remain. Science and technology can strengthen the military, but the causes of conflicts that require military strength, and ways to mediate them short of force, are little better understood today than they ever were. Medical science has produced improved therapies, and in some cases even cures for disease, but there is still no answer to the question of how to assure that high-quality medical care is available to all who need it and at a cost that society is willing to pay. Notwithstanding the contribution of science and technology to higher living standards, poverty remains as intractable a problem as ever, and its correlates—poor health care, poor education, poor housing, and lack of opportunity—resist correction. Even athletic entertainment is not an unalloyed good; for some reason we are constantly surprised, even outraged, that universities are not able to attract students on the basis of their athletic abilities without compromising—even cheating on—their academic standards.

Such tests are, of course, unfair, even absurd. Designing new weapons or new therapies, dazzling as they might be, is nothing at all compared with the task of designing the political, social, and economic systems required to control the use of the one and maximize the use of the other. And designing the systems is the easiest part of reaching the agreement required to implement them. It is very hard for heirs of the Enlightenment to believe that difficult problems will resist the application of organized intelligence at its highest level. Since that is exactly what universities offer, and so successfully in so many cases, the urge to be "relevant" is irresistible. Is it realistic, though? And what are the costs of yielding to it?

The answer has many parts. Parts of the university, the professional schools, have been explicitly designed to be relevant. Business, law, medicine, education, engineering, and public health are closely connected to the professions for which they train students. The walls between faculty and profession are permeable, and the training of students almost always involves intern or apprentice training in the real-world institutions in which they will later be employed. Faculty research is often directed to contemporary problems and may have a profound impact on the practice of the profession. Some professional schools—medicine is the outstanding example—provide direct professional services to the public, often in competition with the professions they serve.

In general, American professional schools are much admired. To be sure, there are questions about whether medical schools are training too many specialists and too few general practitioners, whether law schools are sufficiently attentive to the ethical aspects of the legal profession, and whether education schools are sufficiently rigorous and substantive. But it is hard to argue that they are unengaged in society's business. To many, however, that is not enough. For them, the university is unengaged, failing in the full discharge of its social responsibility. One president reported on a study undertaken in preparation for a major fund-raising campaign:

> Over the last couple of years we have been moving toward another major campaign. As a part of that movement, we were engaged in a very extensive feasibility study. This involved interviews of about 350 people. These are not folks out there in the hinterland. They are people who have been our supporters in the past and will be our contributors in the future and are in positions of leadership of one kind or another. The singular response was, "What we want you to do is to help us solve the problems of society. We want what you do to have meaning, to have an impact, to help deal with the issues that are confronting us. We think that too much of

what you do is done on the basis that it is interesting. You've got to show us that what you're doing is something that is useful to the problems that we're facing on a regular basis."

That is a tall order, one that many presidents speak about in a tone of ambivalence, perhaps leaning toward skepticism, and about which some have doubts in principle. One private university president pointed to the organizational obstacles that stand in the way of effective approaches to social problems, both in research and in teaching. Another president spoke of "problems on which all kinds of disciplines converge."

> Whether it's environmental policy or nuclear proliferation policy, it's really at the intersection between the science and technology side and the social, economic, and public policy side. That is going to require really pretty severe fracturing of the departmental structures in order to organize the right sets of people.

> We haven't been as effective as we might be about finding rules of orthogonal gathering of intellectual forces so as to attack those problems. It's not just providing society with little formulas or recommendations about one thing or another. It's teaching about them.

That prompted the following response:

> We did, of course, begin as teaching institutions. That role will continue to be centrally important, [at both] the undergraduate and graduate levels. But then I want to fight the question a little bit. It overlooks the extraordinary things that have been happening in the area of the health sciences. I do believe that we're going to see almost magical things happen in the next twenty to thirty years, and they will happen in universities more than anywhere else.

> In the other realms, probably the single greatest contribution we could make over the next little while would be to have a healthy respect for our ignorance, which our colleagues sometimes forget. Our embarrassments in the social realm have often come from overexpectations, which we ourselves generate. So a little humility, I think, is in order.

A considerably more upbeat view of the matter was expressed by a president whose own career had spanned the academic and public policy arenas.

> I remember talking to a federal judge who said that, as a judge, the cases he found it the most difficult to deal with were those that had scientific and technological implications. Legislators, too, have to make judgments based on whatever knowledge they have access to—already a problem.

Alternative policy options, allocations of scarce resources—and then what kind of delivery systems if you're talking about delivering some sort of service? And values come into this importantly because you have to make judgments about how to allocate resources.

So it seems to me there is a constellation of factors here which universities are better equipped to deal with than a host of other institutions in society, because we ought to be able to bring together the relevant scholars and researchers and teachers from the various disciplines in new ways to deal with these problems.

A third president spoke of the troubling problem of the inability of single disciplines—the basic structure of the university—to address social problems that stubbornly insist on crossing over disciplinary lines. Because of the risk of too intense a preoccupation with the immediate, he saw the need for structures that made such a focus possible by mitigating the risk.

I worry very much about having a university that has as its principle of organization gaining solutions to practical problems. Those problems and the world are going to change rapidly year to year. And you can't be stuck with a whole university organized in order to attack one problem or another.

So, crosscutting mechanisms—institutes, programs, whatever you want to call them—allow students and faculty to come together outside their home schools and departments. They need to have some kind of authority that gives them some wallop; they need to have incentives that they can provide to bring people into their mix. But they also ought to be thought of as things that come and go, which can be easily created and easily dispensed with when their usefulness has passed.

I do think that universities need to be much more involved in the real world in all sorts of ways and much more visibly involved in providing benefits to society in the near term. But I think those ought to be collateral activities and not the major organizing principles of the universities.

A public university president looked at the capacities of those institutions.

The extent to which we should try to harness university resources in direct allocation to major contemporary issues will be, for public universities, an increasingly hard question. I'm not talking about training students or about the work of individual faculty, I mean actually trying to harness the resources of the universities and apply them in a socially relevant way.

The temptation is very real, because, just as we like to say that what we do generates economic growth and generates wealth, it would be nice on a second front to demonstrate that we are also very valuable.

I, personally, come at it with some skepticism as to whether we're well suited to doing that, going beyond locating our medical clinics in the community and having legal services clinics in the community. Those are the easy questions. The hard [one is]: Can we really array our intellectual, academic, and research resources in direct contribution to defined social problems?

We're not well organized for that. The nature of our institutions, the things we celebrate in them, the things that are at the core of our role, make it unlikely that on a sustained basis we could do this better than public policy institutes or other kinds of organizations. So I worry about making a claim of the sort of next-stage social relevance, because I'm not sure we'll deliver on it very well over time.

It's easy to set up the institute. It's easy to raise the money initially. It's very hard to sustain the effort over time, given the appropriate independence of mind of the people. A university is not a consulting company. It's not a public policy research institute where people can be hired on contracts, then leave when they change their minds about directions.

Another president, perhaps with tongue in cheek, was more direct: "What I was tempted to say, and will say, is over the next fifty years, we will not refrain from contributing to the solution of those social problems, we'll just get it wrong."

While there is ambivalence about the possibility of directing the university's research efforts toward social problems, there is none about the advisability of organizing at least part of the curriculum around interdisciplinary programs in areas of policy relevance.

One of the things that worked very well at my university was putting together an extraordinary energy and resources group. It has a core faculty of about four people: a physicist, an economist, a geologist, and one other, and about thirty faculty who really are interested in those kinds of problems. They have put together a graduate curriculum, but they are now teaching an undergraduate curriculum that goes along with it. You could do this in food and nutrition and in a variety of environmental areas.

Maybe we're all doing things of this sort. I think if we all look around, the number of undergraduates majoring in something like this, rather than in the traditional disciplines, has been rising steadily. And I find that a good thing.

If the undergraduate curriculum is to respond to pressures for greater relevance to current social problems, where are the models to be found on which the new programs will be based? It is not surprising, given their success, that the professional school model seems mightily attractive and the arts and sciences, the traditional heart of the undergraduate curriculum, less so. Said one president:

> I have sometimes wondered whether the patterns of teaching, research, and indeed of professional service in our professional schools, particularly our law schools, might not bear broader replication, perhaps even in arts and sciences. It strikes me that a good law school provides an enormously effective education for doing and thinking about just about anything. There are clinical aspects to that education. It is very closely tied to the reality of the law and the reality of social issues. Is that something, that spirit and style, that we could spread further to our benefit?

That question prompted the following response:

> I think there are a lot of things that people in the arts and sciences can and should learn from the sort of enduring core of a combination of both primary research and application that you see clearly in the health sciences, clearly still I think in engineering, and to some extent in American law schools.
>
> American law schools never went over fully to the arts and sciences mode. But I really think that the old values of the professional schools can be tapped to help the arts and sciences.
>
> At my place, I'm trying to figure out ways to get our arts and sciences faculty to create professional programs of their own that would do a lot of things that I think would be important. For example, I think our place could develop a professional program in government service, in public administration, out of the arts and sciences, and do it with the help of maybe the law school, and do a terrific job.

In interesting ways, the professional school model seems to some to answer both the search for relevance and the perceived loss of confidence in a necessary core of learning that has marked the arts and sciences. That was captured in this observation:

> If you want to find at my school the best organized single year of any curriculum, it's the first year of law school, hands down. By comparison, the first year of medical school is chaotic. There's a very clear reason for it—that law school faculty has a deep sense of collective responsibility for the outcome of the first year of law school. And it's fierce.
>
> That, it seems to me, is the tradition that we really need to import from the law school into arts and sciences, where now a very smart but naive sophomore can come to a science course that's trying to teach about in-

quiry and falsifiable hypotheses and how you find things out. And then over in the English department an hour later, an equally credentialed person argues that there's no such thing as objective reality.

What's a person supposed to make out of that?

The major reservations to the idealization of the professional school come from presidents with professional school backgrounds. One president, for example, actually saw the influences moving in the other direction—into the law school from the arts and sciences—and the result, in his view, was not a happy one.

> The most chastening experience I had after a six-year absence was to come back to the law school and start teaching. I was absolutely astounded. I think there's still cohesion in the first year, but thereafter it departs rapidly. The incursion of the social sciences into the law curriculum is really extraordinary. I don't think there is anything wrong with it, but it has lost its relevance to what I thought the law school curriculum was about.

Still, one version or another of professional education seemed alluring. This president found his model for undergraduate education in the MBA programs of the business schools.

> First of all, they teach in modules. There is no reason to believe that nature is cut at the joints of the academic disciplines, nor is it cut in ten- or fifteen-week segments. The reason why we have quarters and semesters is for the convenience of the registrar. I believe we've gotten more sophisticated than that in terms of our computerization, and that we can develop modules, over time, of the entire undergraduate curriculum as they do in the MBA program.
>
> Second, there is team teaching in the best MBA programs; people from different disciplines come and teach as teams. The interaction, when it works, is fantastic and, again, a model that we can emulate at the undergraduate level.
>
> The third interesting feature of the MBA program is that the students go in cohorts. Remember what happens? The students sit there and the faculty change. What that develops among the students is a sense of community for sixty, eighty, sometimes a hundred students, who go through at least a year together.

The arts and sciences have long been understood to constitute the core of undergraduate education in America. Professional education is generally reserved to the postbaccalaureate years, and where that has not been the case—in business and education, for example—the undergraduate versions of those curricula are often thought to be of lower quality. Notwithstanding that fact, Business Administration is the most popular undergraduate major, nationally, a circumstance that says something important about what has happened to the arts and sciences. For many reasons, some having to do with outside pressures for greater relevance and occupational utility in the baccalaureate degree and some having to do with intellectual styles in some areas of the humanities and social sciences, the place of the arts and sciences in undergraduate education has been moved somewhat off center. At the end of the daylong symposium of past and present presidents, from which much of this section is derived, one of those present made the following observation about the discussion:

> I wanted to make a point that is so obvious that perhaps everyone thought it didn't need to be made. But if that's not the case, it is remarkable that no one has made the traditional arts and sciences claim about the essentiality of the university as a repository of [the] best thinking and knowledge of the culture, not only in the humanities and the arts but in the sciences and the social sciences. That is really remarkable in a group of present and former presidents, and I think it says a lot about the changes in the role of the presidents of universities.
>
> It's not, I think, an accident that silence is coupled with a kind of yearning look at the professional school models of teaching, with their focus and internal morale, and so on. The reason for that is that law schools and medical schools still are prepared to defend the conception of an essential education that everybody going through the schools should have. That gives the curriculum a focus and cohesion that makes all the difference. That's with all due account to the ferment going on in the law and medical schools. With all recognition of that, there is still a claim about a core of knowledge and ability and critical thinking.
>
> I put it to you that the faculty of arts and sciences has by and large lost its willingness, or its capacity through its governance processes, to defend such a proposition. In most undergraduate institutions and research universities the undergraduates are thrown into the smorgasbord of courses, many of which have graduate education characteristics in the degree of their tight focus on the faculty's research interests.
>
> I have scars all over me from trying to introduce, as a purely voluntary component in the curriculum, something that would reflect the idea that, for at least some people, the systematic study of Western civilization might be a core from which to go on and do other things.
>
> The politics of our universities has made it very difficult to try to defend a conception of coherence at the heart of the liberal arts and sciences. And yet, historically, that would be the area where most of us would agree the universities have an essential contribution to make. University presidents

ought to be prepared to fight for that conception. I know that many of you have. But the times have made it a challenging proposition within our universities, and I think it is a self-inflicted wound.

Self-inflicted the wound may be. But wherever one chooses to lay the blame, the shift away from the traditional liberal arts as the defining core of the education of undergraduates is real and probably irreversible. America's commitment to mass higher education makes the kind of consensus on values that underlies curricular coherence, and whose loss is so widely lamented, difficult to retrieve, if indeed it ever really existed. The attraction of the professional school model seems to promise a return to that consensus, but it is illusory. In the professional schools, to the extent that such consensus does exist, it is based on substantial agreement among students, faculty, and the outside profession about the purpose of the education. Nothing could be further from the reality of undergraduate education in the arts and sciences today.

More promising as a way to rejuvenate the undergraduate curriculum and to make it more rigorous are the initiatives, several of which have been referred to here, to organize multidisciplinary programs whose focus is on areas of society, or a set of social issues, that cannot be satisfactorily addressed by a single discipline. Such programs can be both engaging of student interests and rigorous, two major requirements for a successful educational experience. The proliferation of such programs, a likely eventuality, hardly foreshadows the death of the liberal arts. If there is further weakening of those fields, especially the humanities, it will occur from within, not from without. It will be the result of the failure of humanists to find a compelling contemporary setting for their work. That is a battle that will be won or lost by the practitioners themselves.

The Public Leadership Role of University Presidents

One of the things that the public is often said to want from universities is some kind of public leadership from their presidents. It is an odd, though perhaps understandable, wish. It is odd because there is no particular reason to expect university presidents to possess any special wisdom beyond the field of higher education or their own academic specialties. It is understandable because wise public leadership from its traditional sources seems to be in especially short supply. Certainly, few people these days look to political leaders for guidance, even on political issues. The only religious leader with any substantial visibility and influence is the pope, and he is Polish, lives in Italy, and his views on many matters are widely discounted in America, even by Catholics.

With few exceptions, the presidents in this study are reluctant to see themselves in public leadership roles beyond the borders of their own institutions. They are already hard pressed to keep up with the demands of their daily calendars. Few are heavily staffed in the manner of corporate CEOs or prominent politicians, and few have much protection, or would want it, from problems coming up through the organization. But there is a reluctance beyond these practical constraints. One president spoke plainly about it:

> The reason I don't speak out [on social issues] is not that I'm too busy trying to raise money. It's actually that I don't know enough. It's a reflection of maybe some uncharacteristic modesty to not go around taking positions on issues which I don't have time to think hard about, read [about], and study. It's also a respect for my colleagues on the faculty who are better at it. It's actually with some reluctance that I speak, except in areas of my own academic expertise or higher education itself. Otherwise, I generally decline to speak out or put my name on something.

Another president, from a very different background, recalled with approval the words of the speaker at his own inauguration: "I remember what Dan Boorstin said when he came to my installation, that he thought the country needed more secular archbishops, and university presidents ought to be engaged in that line of work."

That is, I think it fair to say, a minority view among presidents. Presidents like John Brademas and John Silber, both active in public life outside their universities, are the exception, while the rule is closer to "Shoemaker, stick to your last." Nor is that a cowardly or unprincipled stance. Quite the contrary, the principled case for refraining from engaging in noneducational public dispute rests on the conception of the university as a place for the full and free debate of public issues of all kinds. To the extent that the university itself is a partisan, the effect may well be to chill debate on campus out of fear of being thought disloyal or, in the extreme, fear of retribution. The president cannot separate his or her personal position from the institutional role, so the president's position may be seen as the institution's position, with all the potential adverse consequences.

One of the virtues of nonengagement, held to rigorously, is that it protects the president against the inevitable demands from students and others to become a partisan in their causes. Yet, it is a vaguely unsatisfying position. University presidents occupy positions of high visibility and, still, considerable prestige. And the line between what is an educational issue and what is not is a vanishingly fine one. Thus, when the future of affirmative action programs became a hot issue in California in 1995, Stanford's president, Gerhard Casper, an articulate advocate of the noninterventionist position, decided to offer his views on the subject, even though Stanford would have been untouched by any of the proposals then circulating to end State of California–sponsored affirmative action. His statement to the Faculty Senate, offered "in the hope that it will facilitate further examination and discussion," was well crafted to do just that. It was precisely the kind of thoughtful, measured examination of the issue that was so badly needed in a highly charged and emotional political climate, and one that would have been unlikely to come from an active combatant on the issue. Clearly, the issue of affirmative action affected Stanford. As Casper acknowledged at the outset, "With increasing frequency, students, faculty, trustees, alumni, and others have asked where Stanford should be on affirmative action." But clearly, too, thoughtful advocacy supported by careful analysis, especially when rooted in local concerns, can make a useful contribution to broader debate.

That is a goal to which many university presidents can realistically aspire. Such national issues as health care policy, educational reform, and tax policy, to mention only three, affect universities and can be treated with concern for the broader context in which they exist. Indeed, it can be argued that their implications for universities cannot be dealt with outside their broader context. These are issues on which some presidents will have professional competence or experience and on which many more will have institutional concerns and a cadre of specialists on which to call. At the very least, presidents can use their public roles to demonstrate the value of informed deliberation, drawing on the best available scholarship and conducted with respect for those holding other views.

No course of action is entirely risk free, and this one carries the risk of engaging the institution and the president in controversy from which both may suffer. However, so long as there is a plausible link between the university and the issue in question, neither universities nor presidential tenures are so fragile that they are likely to suffer serious damage. It may even be that a greater risk lies in universities being recognized as having important effects on the society while their presidents are seen as being remote from the issues that are of greatest public concern. Presidents should do what they sign on to do, namely, run their universities as well as they can. It just may be, however, that the definition of what that requires is broader than is generally recognized by them.

The Value of Universities: Why Should We Care?

If it were put to a vote, the result would probably be that most of the public wants universities to devote more attention to teaching, especially of undergraduates, and less to research. At a minimum, that would mean more faculty and fewer graduate students and various kinds of "parafaculty" in the classroom. A vote among university faculty would surely produce a different result. The two positions represent divergent views of the university and its role in society. The complete triumph of either, something that will not happen, would produce universities as different from today's as today's universities are from those of a century ago. More to the point, significant movement along that continuum in either direction would have profound consequences, as the postwar shift in the direction of research demonstrates. The conflict between teaching and research is one of several important points of tension that arise out of the conflict between what society wants from its universities and what it needs but may not recognize.

When all is said and done, decisions about what functions universities should take on must rest on some notion of comparative advantage. What is it that universities do that is of great value to society and that would be done less well if universities were to stop doing it or, more realistically, do it less well because they are burdened with other functions? The problem here is not unlike the one that plagued industry during the great wave of conglomerate formation in the 1970s and 1980s. It turned out, for example, that having the skill and knowledge to run a successful airline did not guarantee the ability also to run a rental car company and a hotel chain. Worse yet, the energies and resources devoted to the latter badly undermined the ability to do the former well. It is an example that was repeated many times in many industries.

In so diverse a society, encompassing so wide a variety of interests and served by so diverse a set of institutions, it is not surprising that there should also be a diversity of views about what universities do that is of distinctive value and what is not. That natural and healthy condition of American life is compounded by the rapid development of the capacity to store, manipulate, and transmit great quantities of information, producing considerable uncertainty about what information-based institutions like universities will look like in the near future.

In a speech titled "Come the Millennium, Where the University?" Gerhard Casper addressed these issues. In it he quotes the late sociologist, Edward Shils, on the enduring attachment of societies to their universities:

> Universities cost immense sums of money, their achievements cannot be measured in any clear and reliable way, many persons fail in them, and they certainly do not accomplish the solution of economic and social problems which some expect of them. Nevertheless, these societies cling to them. The universities do not survive simply because professors have a vested interest in their survival. . . . That would never be enough. These societies cling to them because, in the last analysis, they are their best hope for a transfigured existence. . . .

Much of the criticism of the self-indulgence of the universities is an act of hypocrisy by their beneficiaries. . . . It is too late . . . to decide whether modern societies can get along without universities. For good reasons and bad, they must have them—much as they have been.[1]

Others look to a quite different future, one in which technology will challenge some the major traditional functions of the university. It is already possible to provide lectures and interactive classes to students at a distance from the campus, and many universities are now doing that for employed students, who can take their courses without leaving their places of work. It has long been argued that the lecture, still the most common method of teaching in universities, is outmoded and can be replaced at lower cost and no loss in educational quality. Libraries are undergoing major transformations, and while the existence of the great collections in the major universities may not be in doubt, the ways in which they can be used and future collecting policies are very much in doubt. Scholarly journals, the traditional network through which scholarship is evaluated and transmitted, face an uncertain future as on-line journals come into existence, providing faster publication times and, building on capital investments made for other purposes, at less cost. Information technology makes possible forms of collaboration in research and teaching never before possible.

A major transformation of the ways in which knowledge is acquired, stored, and transmitted is in progress, and all knowledge-based institutions, of which the university is the most important, will be transformed also. Though universities are the creators of much of the technology that is the instrument of their change, they are not better than most other institutions at understanding and dealing with the changes that they themselves face. Change happens in universities; it is rarely the product of organized self-analysis, still less, for reasons we have examined here, of systematic planning for change.

I suspect that in many, perhaps most, universities, the words "the best hope for a transfigured existence" would have a strange ring. The explanations of their value that faculty and presidents are accustomed to making are of a more practical character. On many occasions over ten years in Washington, I heard one proposal or another for funding justified as contributing to a tangible improvement in the quality of life; I never once heard anyone speak about a transfigured existence. Yet, in the end, that may be what really counts.

1. Gerhard Casper, "Come the Millenium, Where the University," keynote address, American Educational Research Association annual meeting, San Francisco, April 18, 1995).

When all the technologically induced changes have been incorporated into institutional practice and the predictions of the futurists about the transformation of American life have been proved right or wrong, there will still remain the question of whether society needs what only the university as a "physical space," as Casper calls it, can provide. In asking the question, he provides an important opening to a necessary debate about the future of the university. He suggests nine traditional functions of the university. Some, such as education and professional training and credentialing, may meet stiff competition from the "virtual university." It would be harder to find acceptable substitutes for others, such as social integration, knowledge creation and assessment, the selection of academic elites, and peer review. But it is not obvious, unless one is led to think about it, that those are essential, or even highly desirable, for a healthy society. Can that case be made? Or, to put it somewhat differently, is there a case for the university against more efficient providers that is different from and larger than the defense of its separate activities?

The answer to that question depends in large measure on whether the senior leaders of universities—presidents, faculty, and trustees—have a conception of what society needs from them and can convey that conception in a compelling way. The evidence is mixed. While it is unfair, as I have suggested, to fault university presidents for failing to play the role of all-purpose wise men, it is not unfair to ask whether they have been effective in arguing the case for their own kind of institution, as opposed to their own institution. There have been notable exceptions in recent years, among them some of the participants in this study, but more commonly, presidents have become so preoccupied with the demands and stresses of managing their own institutions that larger issues tend to be left for ceremonial occasions when bromides are the expected order of the day.

One president spoke about the presidential role in this way:

It is the amount of time that's now required raising money, particularly, but also in terms of community relations, and the sheer task of presiding in some fashion over the administration of a billion-dollar-or-more annual budget—it's really reached a point in which university presidents simply have too little time to attend to either contributing to the national debate or in some cases contributing in a really intensive way to the intellectual problems of their own campuses. And I don't think that's an indictment of university presidents. They have a structure in which they are the key people in raising money and in making administrative decisions, and you have a set of needs there that has grown so great that unless you figure out a way of changing the structure you're bound to run into this problem. Nobody has ever accused university presidents of being lazy. They're working harder than they ever have, but the problem is that they can't raise the hundred and fifty million dollars plus that they're supposed to every year and tend to these vast administrative things and so forth, and then still sit down and write really elegant responses to questions of this kind.

As the university's principal public person, the president carries the burden of explaining to the public what it needs from the university and how that may be different from what it thinks it wants. But the most artic- ulate and persuasive advocate in the end is no better than the facts of his or her case, and in recent years the facts have tended to undermine what should be a strong case. Modern universities, after all, have proved them- selves to be the most effective knowledge-creating institutions in history. In the process of creating knowledge, and because the process is closely linked with the training of future scholars, they also provide society with its next generation of knowledge producers and transmitters, and they do so at a level of quality that attracts students from all over the world. The values that sustain the university—openness, respect for dissent, commit- ment to evidence and the proper inference from evidence as the best in- strument for settling disputes, integrity, intellectual honesty—are the val- ues that also sustain a free society. Moreover, universities are their principal, and in some cases their only, exemplars and practitioners. To change the university fundamentally is to risk the loss of a great deal, in- deed.

But it is also true that years of prosperity and preferred treatment have bred elements of carelessness, self-indulgence, a sense of entitlement, and not a little arrogance. Carelessness about faculty misconduct, inatten- tiveness to the educational needs of undergraduates, disingenuousness about the ability of university research to produce economic benefits, the willingness to accept restrictive conditions in exchange for research funds from industry, the use of political tactics like the pork barrel that under- mine the image of universities as something more than another self-inter- ested supper at the public trough—while none of these fairly describes all institutions, all are real, and the cumulative effect has produced a level of cynicism about universities that can only be destructive and that, if nothing else, distracts attention from efforts to make the case that is so badly needed.

If those flaws are treated as problems of image best dealt with by image makers, then the future is bleak. If, however, they are seen as real problems to be addressed by real solutions, then there are grounds for optimism. Indeed, there is no alternative to optimism. The virtual university, like the virtual everything else, is by definition a false university. It may do some things that are now done in universities, but it cannot replace them. Values are given life by institutions. Political theory without political institutions to give it life is mere rhetoric; educational values without educational institutions to live them are mere platitudes. In the end, the health of individual universities, no matter how well managed they may be, will depend on the health of the institution of the university. To attend to the former without attending to the latter is ultimately a failing strategy. That is the challenge modern university presidents face.

We should all pray for their success.

INDEX

AAAS (American Association for the Advancement of Science), 25, 70; Colloquium on R&D Policy (1986), 143
AAU (Association of American Universities). *See* Association of American Universities (AAU)
AAUP (American Association of University Professors), 46
"Academic Earmarks," 64n
academic president. *See* president
academic standards, 173–75
administrator, 118
affirmative action program: at Stanford University, 187–88; at University of California, 126–27
Albino, Judith, xiin. 2
American Association for the Advancement of Science (AAAS), 25, 70; Colloquium on R&D Policy (1986) of, 143
American Association of State Colleges and Universities, 46
American Association of University Professors (AAUP), 46
American Council on Education, 50, 104
American Council of Learned Societies, 118
"American Research University, The: Continuity and Change," xii
American university, xiv, xvi–xvii, 1–3; post–World War II, 1–3; and scientific revolution, 2. *See also* research university; university
anti-university wave, 41
anti-Vietnam War movement, 4, 7–8, 9; at Stanford University, 113–16
appropriation: and budget, 31–36; earmarked, 37–39, 54–65; merger with law, 31–32
Asilomar Conference, 29
Aslin, Richard, 162
"Assault on David Baltimore, The," 89n. 8

Association of American Universities (AAU), xii, 9; and CAIT, 50; change of focus, 20–21; and clearinghouse, 31, 35, 36; and congressional budget, 31; creation of policy guidelines in dealing with research misconduct, 87–88; in debate regarding unrelated business income tax, 47–48; and earmarked appropriation, 38–39; establishment of Pings Committee, 75; and facilities program bill, 53; framework for managing institutional conflict of interest, 98; history and purpose of, 20–21; as lobby group in Washington, 44; policy statement on integrity in research, 37; as political group, 20–26; president for, 21; relationship with William Bennett, 42; role in school reform, 26–27; and Subcommittee on Oversight and Investigation, 42–43
Atkinson, Richard, 25
Atomic Energy Commisssion, 4

Baltimore, David, 89, 89n. 8
Bartlett, Thomas, as president of the AAU, 21
Basic Research Tax Credit, 51, 52
Bayh-Dole Act (1980), 13
Beckman, Arnold, 29
Bell, Terrell, 25, 41
Bennett, William, 16, 41–42
Bentley, Arthur, 45
bill, for facilities program, 52–53
biomedical research, 4
biotechnology industry, birth of, 12–13
Birnbaum, Jeffrey H., 68n
Bloch, Eric, 95, 144
board of trustees, 110, 112, 123–27; and president, 124; at private universities, 124–25; at public universities, 125–26; role of, 124
Bok, Derek, xi, 106, 110

Library of Congress Cataloging-in-Publication Data

Rosenzweig, Robert M.
   The political university : policy, politics, and presidential leadership
in the American research university / Robert M. Rosenzweig.
      p.   cm.
   Includes bibliographical references and index.
   ISBN 0-8018-5721-X (alk. paper)
   1. Higher education and state—United States.   2. Universities and
colleges—Political aspects—United States.   3. Federal aid to higher
education—United States.   4. Federal aid to research—United
States.   5. Research—Political aspects—United States.   6. College
presidents—United States—Interviews.   I. Title.
LC173.R67 1998
379.1'214'0973—DC21   97-25109 CIP